THE MIRROR OF CONRAD

Books by E. H. Visiak

Verse

BUCCANEER BALLADS (1910)

FLINTS AND FLASHES (1911)

THE PHANTOM SHIP and other poems (1912)

THE BATTLE FIENDS (1916)

BRIEF POEMS (1919)

Fiction

THE HAUNTED ISLAND (1910)

THE WAR OF THE SCHOOLS (1912)

MEDUSA (1929)

Biography

MILTON AGONISTES (1923)

MILTON'S LAMENT FOR DAMON, and his other Latin Poems—Introduction and prefaces to, (Oxford University Press, 1935)

MEMORIES OF W. H. HELM—Biographical Introduction to, (Richards, 1937)

Edited

MILTON — Compendious Edition (Nonesuch Press, 1938)

THE MASK OF COMUS — Introduction, etc., compiled with critical apparatus, (for Nonesuch Press, 1938)

Joseph Conrad—a pencil sketch

THE MIRROR OF
CONRAD

by

E. H. VISIAK

HUMANITIES PRESS

New York 1968

Printed in U.S.A. by
NOBLE OFFSET PRINTERS, INC.
NEW YORK 3, N. Y.

To
KENNETH HOPKINS
*in token of esteem as
friend and author*

That quality of sadness which is the natural constituent and admixture of genius, was reinforced, for him, by the Sea's mystical communications, not in storm alone, but in 'such a tide as moving seems asleep, too full for sound and foam'. It is the breath that breathes on the face of the waters: it is more even than that, the motive essence of the heart and core of things.

F. C. OWLETT

CONTENTS

A facsimile letter from Joseph Conrad to the author is between pages 224 and 225

ILLUSTRATIONS

PREFACE

THE popularity of a great writer during his lifetime does not, as a rule, last after him, but declines rapidly. At length it returns, slowly; in a modified form. Such a phenomenon is evident in the case of Joseph Conrad—the most remarkable, if not the very greatest, of those great writers who lived and died and were forgotten in recent times—and the cycle is near completion.

At least, it would appear so 'by all concurrence of signs'; second-hand bookshops are being ransacked for copies of Conrad's works; his novels are being rendered on the radio and the screen; his name comes up in the press with increasing frequency.

I was hopeful enough to attempt the present work. I little thought, although it should have been obvious, that Conrad required 'sea-room'; a single volume was not enough. It then transpired (in this appropriately marine way of regarding the matter) that there were such contrivances as 'water-tight' compartments; there could be two volumes—each 'water-tight', entire, adjacent, and interdependent.

This was a capital idea, since Conrad's own life was actually divided in that way, and almost *amidships*, as it were: half on the sea, half on the land; half as a sailor, half as a writer, and (what was especially convenient) these periods were both complete in themselves and complemental. Best of all, these divisions in entirety, and entireties in division, were requisite to, and yet, at the same time, independent of each other, since Conrad's earlier life was alone adequate to a biography, while his

11

later, literary life could provide the content of an interesting record even if he had not, as he had, derived and produced the materials of his books from his former experiences; even if he had conjured them, as it were, out of his head—or (in plain truth) conceived and pictured them as reflected in an illusive, instead of a mnemonic, glass.

I shall trust, therefore, that my expedient cable holds, and hope, if all goes well, to proceed with the second volume.

Meanwhile, my acknowledgments are due, with sincere thanks, to Messrs J. M. Dent and Messrs William Heinemann, for kindly permitting me to include passages from, respectively, *The Collected Edition of the Works of Joseph Conrad* and G. Jean-Aubry's *Joseph Conrad: Life and Letters.*

Especial commendation is also due to Mr R. L. Mégroz's *Joseph Conrad's Mind and Method* (Faber and Faber), as a work of brilliant critical exposition.

I am deeply indebted to my old friend, Mr John G. Wilson, for the loan of multifarious Conradian material; much of it otherwise unobtainable; chiefly serviceable and valuable for my projected further volume.

The necessity of using these works, in the main, as I have done, is patent. Messrs Dent's edition, needless to say, is unrivalled; while Jean-Aubry's great, official biography is invaluable (even apart from its qualities of competence and its exhaustive nature) in virtue of its unique documentation and photogravures; indispensable to the library of every Conradian student.

I have been greatly helped in the actual work by Mrs Gwenol Heneker, whose remarkable critical insight has been an unfailing corrective throughout.

There is safety in numbers, especially in a factual literary endeavour, and I gladly thank, also, Mrs D. L. Hobman, Mrs Frances Rosser, Mr F. C. Owlett (who has compiled the Index), and, last but assuredly not least, Mr Arthur Vesselo; their assistance has been invaluable.

E . H . VISIAK

CONRAD AT LOWESTOFT
(A Prefatorial Sketch)

IN the year 1878, in the old seaport of Lowestoft, a certain stockily-built, black-bearded young sailor might have been seen (in the period phrase) moving about on the quay and fish market of the always active harbour.

He was on the look-out to make himself as useful and agreeable as possible, lending a hand, on occasion, as with the mooring of a fishing smack.

At the same time, he exercised tact. Being a gentleman born and trained and an able seaman, he was adept in these endeavours; his only difficulty, which was also the reason for his activities, was—he did not know more than about a dozen words of the English language. He was attempting to add to his vocabulary. If, then, his dexterous handling of a rope's end—or whatever it might be— induced an expression of thanks, he received it with intent appreciation, extracting as much as possible the sense from the verbal sounds, developing the conversation with interest. If, by ill chance, the fisherman's response was in contrary terms, he still received what was intelligible into his retentive memory.

From such small beginnings there was produced the wonderful writer in English, Joseph Conrad.

It was the first time he had set foot in England, the country in which he was to be re-born; for nothing less than such a transformation eventually occurred.

The wonder is not in Conrad's capacity for writing in impeccable English. His English, in fact, was not impeccable; it was faulty, inferior to that of other foreign novelists writing in English—but he *imagined* in English.

13

In English he expressed the deepest, the most vital, most subtle impressions left upon his mind, as naturally as if it were his native language.

And the language of a country is integral with the life of those who think in it, and speak it, thus naturally and spontaneously. It is, in general, an index of their spiritual state, as Plato has implied.

In Conrad, imagination and memory were virtually united; they worked together metabolically: he *saw*, he *remembered*, he *imagined*. There is a comparable case— one only. Milton mnemonically absorbed, selectively converted, and poetically transmuted what he had read; he invented nothing.

Conrad's mnemonic material was produced by the experiences of his earlier and middle life; experiences which he used as a mirror, the mirror of his imagination; hence the title of the present work which records them. He looked into that mirror and wrote. The present work treats of the content of the mirror.

In physical mirrors, the mercurial background is dark, and the substratum of Conrad's *Mirror of the Sea*—the sea regarded as a mirror—is dark as the oceanic depths; so the nativity and childhood of Conrad himself were tragically as dark as night.

So also, the fundamental quality of Conrad's genius is tragic in the Athenian sense of the word; that is to say, it is reactive and dynamic; its effect is invigorating and not, as bad writers in that genre are, depressing. It is this quality that renders his stories so graphic and so enthralling.

IN RUSSIA AND POLAND

(1857-74)

. . . one of the many plain hints in Conrad's stories that they are fragments of his spiritual biography, in tracing out which one may look at a mirror not of the sea but of the creative soul of an artist

R. L. MEGROZ

IN RUSSIA AND POLAND

(1857-74)

i

JOSEPH CONRAD was born on 3rd December 1857 at
Berdicev, in the Polish province of Podolia. His real
name was Teodor Josef Konrad Nalecz Korzeniowski.
Although a Pole by birth, he was a Russian national.
The reason of this anomaly was that Poland, in those days,
was partitioned between Russia, Austria, and Prussia, and
Conrad's birthplace was under Russian rule. That rule was
oppressive, and was shortly to be exacerbated into abso-
lute tyranny in consequence of an insurrection of the
Poles.

These were tragic circumstances but, what cast the
darkest shadow over Conrad's young life, the leader of the
insurrection was his own father, Apollo Nalecz
Korzeniowski.

This patriot was a character. A member of the Polish
landed gentry, he represented politically their extremist
faction, which was composed mainly of young men who
wanted direct action against Russia, being too impatient
to abide the gradual mitigation of Czarist oppression
brought about by the slow, compromising policy of Count
Wielopolski.

The extremists, with their followers—servants and
peasants of their estates and villages—fervently united
around Apollo. He himself in nationalistic zeal excelled.

'He had no other thoughts', writes Conrad's contemporary and compatriot, Mr J. H. Retinger, 'but those for his
country; no life but the life of a patriot. He was like a
sentimental miser, living for self-sacrifice, saving every

17

breath, every atom of personal happiness for his mother-
land.'[1]

Apollo, however, was not only a politician; he was also
a journalist; a journalist in patriotic action: an active
volcano in both capacities. In common with other
animated spirits among the Poles, his patriotic fervour
was cultural as well as political and, possessing a great love
for English and French authors, he desired to make them
better known among his fellow countrymen. With this
object in view, he translated into Polish Shakespeare (*The
Two Gentlemen of Verona, Othello*, and *As You Like It*),
Victor Hugo, Fenimore Cooper, Marryat, and the poems
of De Vigny and Heine.

Moreover, he was himself a poet; he seems, indeed to
have been a visionary,[2] for the following verses (Dr Morf's
translation) are strangely prophetic of his famous son:

> . . . *Your eager boat, with eagle's wings,*
> *Will make a rapid passage,*
> *And, steered by reason, governed with strength,*
> *Will reach the shores of fame!*
> *But, resting from your journey,*
> *In the golden land of fortune,*
> *Remember, O remember with a sigh,*
> *Those who perished in the tempest!*

Conrad describes his father as a 'man of great sensibilities; of exalted and dreamy temperament; with a terrible
gift of irony and gloomy disposition. . . . His aspect was distinguished; his conversation fascinating, but his face in
repose sombre, lighted all over when he smiled.'[3]

His mother, Evelina, Conrad reveals to us only in
glimpses, such as the one relating to the year 1862, when
he was five or six years old. He recollected seeing her
standing dressed in black among persons with grave faces

---

[1] J. H. Retinger, *Conrad and his Contemporaries*. (Minerva
Publishing Co.)

[2] In keeping with the family characteristics, as will appear in
due course.

[3] There is a detailed account of Apollo in a letter from Conrad to
Edward Garnett, dated 20th January 1900.

who came and went. His memories of her were sacrosanct; too intimately intense to be subjected to realistic description.

The family to which she belonged—the Bobrowskis—was noble, and she, indeed, was a noble personality; one possessed of an eager and cultivated mind, deeply in sympathy with her husband's ideals. Ford Madox Hueffer, who collaborated with Conrad in *Romance*, describes her as a 'woman of great beauty of physique and character. Her face was oval, her black hair braided round it, her eyes intent, her manner quiet but spirited,'[4] and he impresses us by asserting that, although it pained Conrad to think that his father had been a revolutionary, he spoke of his mother's revolutionary activities with enthusiasm. It was as a revolutionary, indeed, that Conrad in that early memory had seen her; the black dress of his recollection was a symbol of national mourning forbidden by the Russian Government; the scene was his parents' house in Warsaw, and the occasion was one of the first meetings of the secret Polish National Committee, which Apollo, Conrad's father, was then organising.

But the Russian authorities had espied these clandestine meetings, and Apollo, caught red-handed before his plans were completed, was arrested and removed to the citadel. Four months afterwards (February 1863) he was deported to Vologda in North Russia.[5] His wife, with their infant son, went with him into exile; Evelina's action was the more heroic because she was weak in health and because permission to accompany her husband had been given only on the condition that she endured the same hardships as he did.

Her health broke down on the way and she had to be

---

[4] *Joseph Conrad.* (Duckworth and Co.)

[5] Conrad remembered being in a prison-yard on the road: 'The Kossacks of the escort' (these are Conrad's exact words repeated over and over again) 'were riding slowly up and down under the snowflakes that fell on women in furs and women in rags. The Russians had put the men into barracks, the windows of which were tallowed. They fed them on red herrings and gave them no water to drink. My father was among them.'—Ford Madox Hueffer, *Joseph Conrad.* (Duckworth and Co.)

carried by the escort. She was permitted to rest for some days at an inn; a relief afforded by the intervention of a Russian officer who, happening to be riding by and witnessing the brutality of the guards, galloped away to report them to the police. The child also had been ailing, and was tended by a friendly doctor, similarly through intervention.

The Governor of Vologda was a humane man, and alleviated the hardships suffered by the Polish *déportées* as much as he possibly could, but the climate was very cold, and Evelina's strength continued to decline. On this score, the Nalecz Korzeniowskis were eventually permitted to remove farther south, to Tchernikow, where they lived in a small house on the outskirts of the town.

Nevertheless, the health of the invalid became worse rather than better; an integral cause of the declension being that she was homesick.

'Homesickness, like a rust' (Apollo wrote to a friend), 'has slowly eaten away my poor wife's strength. A year and a half ago she attributed her condition to nerves. In my anxiety—I could never have done it for myself—I begged and prayed that we might be moved from this place. My petition having been repeatedly refused, I have lost all hope. Since many months she has been suffering from fever, tuberculosis and an internal tumour, the result of bad circulation, which calls for an operation. . . . Her mind alone remains unshaken. I ask myself, is this courage or does she not know how ill she really is? Who could read the answer in her eyes, if I, to whom they have ever been an open book, cannot see what is written there? And yet, I cannot read her eyes. Only, sometimes, a stronger pressure of her hand in mine, or in little Konrad's, betrays her courage. We are wretched and unhappy indeed, but we thank God that we have been allowed at least to bear it all together.'

At Tchernikow Evelina was joined by her mother, who helped to look after the child, and later by her favourite

brother, Pan Tadeusz, who brought a doctor with him.
But her condition was hopeless. She was dying. Before the
end came, however, she had the sunset happiness of
visiting her brother, at Nowofastow. The official permit,
which was for three months' leave from exile, was obtained through the 'Highest Grace'; that is to say, through
influence exerted in virtue of the memory of her eldest
brother, who had served in the Guards and left many
powerful friends in the great world of St. Petersburg.

This gracious leave was granted in 1864 when Conrad
was six years old, and the visit enshrines a childhood
recollection that he thus relates in A *Personal Record*:

'This is also the year in which I first begin to remember my mother with more distinctness than a mere
loving, wide-browed, silent, protecting presence, whose
eyes had a sort of commanding sweetness; and I also
remember the great gathering of all the relations from
near and far, and the grey heads of the family friends
paying her the homage of respect and love. . . . I did
not understand the tragic significance of it all at the
time, though I remember that doctors also came. There
were no signs of invalidism about her—but I think that
already they had pronounced her doom. . . . For me it
seems the very happiest period of my existence. There
was my cousin, a delightful quick-tempered little girl,
some months younger than myself, whose life, lovingly
watched over, as if she were a royal princess, came to
an end with her fifteenth year. There were other
children, too. . . .'[6] (The company of other children
being an unwonted experience to him.)

A fortnight before the expiration of her leave of absence,
Evelina became critically ill. Her brother petitioned for
an extension of the term, but was refused by the Governor-
General of Kiev, who seems to have been as brutal as the
Governor of Vologda was humane. Both Conrad and Jean-

---

[6] *A Personal Record*, 1912. (First published as *Some Reminiscences*.) All further quotations, unless otherwise specified, refer to
that autobiographical work.

Aubry put his name on record as a testimony against him. The name was Bezak. The name of the humane Governor of Vologda was Treminski.

In another place in Conrad's rambling reminiscences, he describes their departure back to exile:

'The elongated, bizarre, shabby travelling-carriage with four post-horses, standing before the long front of the house, with its eight columns, four on each side of the broad flight of stairs. On the steps, groups of servants, a few relations, one or two friends from the nearest neighbourhood, a perfect silence, on all the faces an air of sober concentration; my grandmother all in black, gazing stoically, my uncle giving his arm to my mother down to the carriage in which I had been placed already. . . .'

Evelina died on the 6th April 1865. She was thirty-six years of age.

Apollo was now alone with his little son. Broken, ailing, disillusioned, he was indeed a figure of tragedy. Upon his bereavement he suffered extreme grief; 'sacred days of agony,' as he describes it in a letter to a friend:

'I have kept my eyes fixed on the Cross and by that means fortified my fainting soul and reeling brain. . . . When my bitterness chokes me, I read your second dear letter and the pride of despair changes into divine sadness. My tears flow, but their fount is reason. Then, my composure recovered, I take up my life again, which is entirely centred upon my little Konrad. I teach him what I know, but that, unfortunately, is little. I shield him from the atmosphere of this place, and he grows up as though in a monastic cell.'[7]

---

[7] Conrad usually referred to him as 'my poor father'. The earliest of such references, written on the back of a photograph of himself at the age of five, reads: 'To my dear grandmother who helped me to send cakes to my poor father in prison—Pole, Catholic, gentleman, Konrad. 6th July, 1863.'

It is odd, in this connection, that Conrad, referring to one of his fellow owners of the *Tremolino* in *The Mirror of the Sea*, writes, 'Poor J.M.K.B., *Americain, Catholique, et gentilhomme*, as he was disposed to describe himself. . . .'

In another letter he laments :

'The poor child does not know what it is to have a companion of his own age. He sees the sadness of my old age' (he was fifty years old), 'and who knows? perhaps that sight may freeze and wither his own young heart; that is one of the chief reasons which make me wish to send him away from me.'

Alas for Apollo, with his mind's eye dimmed; he had lost the power to descry, as once he had been able to do, the 'eager boat with eagle's wings' speeding to the 'shores of fame'. His little son's mind was not really in danger of being frozen or withered by the sight of his father's misery. A child is not influenced by appearances that it does not understand or only imperfectly understands. Thus, Conrad at the age of six had not 'understood the significance' of the tragic environment at Nowofastow when his mother was dying.

On the other hand, a child may readily be influenced by close and continuous association with a kindred personality. In Scriptural language, it is not that which goes into a child by observation, but that which comes out of him—i.e. by sympathetic response—that influences him. Conrad not only inherited certain qualities from Apollo, but these qualities were brought out into deeper characterisation by the segregated conditions under which they lived; these influences, being constitutionally in affinity with the child's essential nature, tended to develop that nature in accordance with the needs of his potential genius.

The eventual resemblances between father and son are impressive. Thus, to compare Conrad's description of Apollo (as already quoted) with his own characteristics :

'*A man of great sensibilities.*'

Great sensibilities are patent in Conrad's life and work.

Of '*exalted and dreamy temperament*'.

Such, too, was Conrad's, as is manifest in his works. Of such a book, for example, as *The Rescue*, it may truly be said, adapting Milton's words, 'This is no mere amatorious novel, but one of the highest arcs that human contemplation circling upwards can make from the globy sea whereon she stands.'

A *'terrible gift of irony'*.

Witness the jibe in Conrad's *Nostromo*:

'Time itself has got to wait on the greatest country in the whole of God's universe', etc.[8]

'Gloomy disposition.'

The biographer himself received two successive letters from Conrad in both of which he referred to his 'grave'.

His 'aspect was distinguished'.

Conrad's photographs speak for themselves.

His 'conversation fascinating'.

'Fascination', according to John Galsworthy, was Conrad's distinguishing feature.

His 'face in repose sombre, lighted all over when he smiled'.

'His' (Conrad's) 'expression was one of such enduring sadness that no exposure could be made' ('Conrad's Dislike of the Camera', *Graphic*, 1st November 1924).

And his face certainly 'lighted all over when he smiled'.

Conrad's description of his father was, in Poe's words, a 'portrait painted after death'; it represented the impression formed in his mind during his early childhood as developed later on in his imagination. Then, indeed, he saw Apollo in his tragic light; but this, instead of having a withering or freezing effect, implanted in his mind the seed of a philosophy that vitalises and inspires his greatest novels.

ii

There is a resource for a man stricken with a great grief; there is a blessed haven; the haven of creative endeavour: Apollo, after the death of Evelina, plunged into literary work.

He was then translating Victor Hugo's *Les Travailleurs de la Mer*. The proofs arrived, as it happened, at a time when he was indisposed and, lying on his bed, he told his little son to read them to him. Conrad, who was then about

---

[8] *Collected Edition*, p. 77. (Dent.)

nine years old, had learnt to read under his father's
tuition, and he performed the task to 'complete satisfaction', although Apollo was the 'most exacting of masters'.
That the boy read them thus intelligibly would imply that
he read them intelligently, taking in what he was reading;
and, at his early age, this would involve his subconscious
mind, springing his young imagination.

As a potent novel with an intense atmospheric sea-
setting, *Les Travailleurs de la Mer* could scarcely have
failed to influence Conrad—not only in starting the train
of imagination that led to his becoming a sailor; it might
also in an instinctive way have aroused his native ideality.
The effect would be the greater because the quality of
romantic tragedy in Victor Hugo's work was essentially
in tune with Conrad's own genius. Tragedy as presented
by classic authors consisted of sublimity manifested in
humane feeling; in modern writers, the compound has
been contracted and coloured into romanticism; so in
Hugo and Conrad.

Conrad's late novel, *The Rover*—written at a time when,
according to his wife, his imagination had a 'homing
tendency'—expresses a variety of the same theme as *Les
Travailleurs*. In both works, the chief character immolates
himself in order to enable the woman he loves to marry
the man of her own adoration and, to compass this, em-
ploys means of subterfuge.

The passion of love that leads to the *dénouement* is in
both cases pure, although Peyrol, the hero-martyr of *The
Rover*, is an old, tough, indurated privateer.

Gilliat, the seaman recluse of *Les Travailleurs*, on the
other hand, is an innocent; innocent in heart and mind.
He lives alone with his mother in Guernsey and is friend-
less except for the sea-birds whose nests he protects from
marauding boys. His capacity for love, intensified by the
simple ascetic life that he leads, is awakened by a girl's
irresponsible action of tracing his name in the snow. (In
The Rover, the woman character traces her beloved's
initials in the dust on a table.)

The passion Gilliat conceives for the girl—Deruchette—

is so matutinal in quality as to be comparable to those intimations of romantic love that arise in childhood itself, and this makes the book more likely to have taken due effect upon a boy of Conrad's emotional nature. Déruchette, moreover, belongs to the order of merely charming Miranda-like femininity—all sweetness and softness—which Conrad suggests so well in his women characters in an aspect of romantic sensuality, exquisitely refined.

Another parallel between *Les Travailleurs* and a work of Conrad occurs in his *Freya of the Seven Isles*. In *Les Travailleurs*, Mess Lethierry, the father of Déruchette, has two loves, his daughter and his steam-boat. In *Freya*, Jasper Allen loves Freya in conjunction with his brig. In *Les Travailleurs*, Clubin, a malignant character, deliberately wrecks Lethierry's steam-boat on rocks. In *Freya*, Heemskirk, with fiendish jealousy, deliberately wrecks Jasper Allen's brig on a rock.

There is a parallel, also, between *Les Travailleurs* and Conrad's great book, *The Rescue*; a parallel, not so much in the matter of circumstance as in quality of feeling. There is a correspondence in the suggestion of the unearthly—of tragedy in the classical superhuman sense—in the climax and close of both works. Thus there is absolute desolation in the soul alike of Gilliat and Lingard. Both have given up all for a woman.

It is true that Conrad read *Les Travailleurs* in early childhood. At the same time he was precocious. 'Since the age of five', he writes in *A Personal Record*, 'I have been a great reader. . . . At ten years of age I had read much of Victor Hugo and other romantics. I had read, in Polish and in French, history, voyages, novels. I knew *Gil Blas* and *Don Quixote* in abridged editions. I had read in early boyhood Polish poets and some French poets.'

He makes no further reference in *A Personal Record* to *Les Travailleurs de la Mer*. In fact, he writes in his *Notes on Life and Letters* that it was Captain Marryat and Fenimore Cooper who together 'shaped' his life; the 'youthful glamour, the headlong vitality of the one and the profound sympathy, the artistic insight of the other'.

This, however, does not invalidate the probable influence of *Les Travailleurs* in inspiring within him an imaginative love of the sea. I quote a nautical passage:

'Mountains on the right, mountains on the left, penguins and stormy petrels all about. A terrible place. Ah! by Jove, what a howling and what cracks you get there! The hurricane wants no help. That's the place for holding on to the sheer-rails; for reefing topsails. That's where you take in the main-sail, and fly the jib-sail; or take in the jib-sail and try the storm-jib. Gusts upon gusts! and then, sometimes four, five, or six days of scudding under bare poles. Often only a rag of canvas left. What a dance! Squalls enough to make a three-master skip like a flea. I once saw a cabin-boy hanging on the jib-boom of an English brig, the *True Blue*, knocked, jib-boom and all, to ten thousand nothings. Fellows are swept into the air there like butterflies. I saw the second mate of the *Revenue*, a pretty schooner, knocked from under the fore-cross-tree, and killed dead. I have had my sheer-rails smashed, and come out with all my sails in ribbons. Frigates of fifty guns make water like wicker baskets.'[9]

iii

The interest Conrad took in his father's literary activities doubtless developed his imaginative mind; on the other hand, in the general conditions of Tchernikow his health declined.

Apollo, therefore, as soon as he could brace himself for the parting, sent his son for a change of air to Nowofastow, where, as related, he had stayed with his dying mother.

He remained there for four months and then returned to his father; but his health declined again—apparently he suffered from some sort of stomach ailment—and he was taken by his grandmother to Kiev for medical treat-

---

[9] 'She leaked fully . . . like a basket.'—*The Mirror of the Sea.*

ment. After this he went again to Nowofastow. There he met Prince Roman Sanguszko, an old comrade-in-arms of his Korzeniowski grandfather during the insurrection of 1831.

Persecuted nations produce martyrs and saints, and this Prince was one of them. He was venerated among the Poles, and naturally so. Exalted in heart and mind through the shock of bereavement from a beloved wife, he had transmuted his sorrow into the spirit of service for his persecuted countrymen, resigned his commission in the Guards, and thrown in his lot with the insurrectionists under the guise of a peasant. He was captured in an ambush and exiled to Siberia; whence, after fourteen years in the salt mines and subsequent service as a common soldier in the Caucasus, he had returned to devote his life —what was left of it—to assisting other returned exiles. Conrad gives in *Prince Roman* an enthralling account of his interview with the old man, infirm and stone deaf, gentle and courtly.

At Nowofastow, Conrad suffered from homesickness; although nobody could have been kinder to him than were his grandmother and uncle. He hankered after his father and his old environment; to which, like a prisoner long immured, he had become attached. Apollo writes with affectionate irony:

'Konrad has gone to his uncle in the country. We are both of us unhappy. The child is silly enough to be troubled by my solitude and to regret a life in which my gloomy face and his lessons have been his only distractions. He pines for me in spite of the country and games with a cousin of his own age. Even under the wing of his grandmother's tender care and in spite of the indulgence of his uncle, who spoils him and has transferred to him all the love he had for his mother, the boy pines for me. As his uncle always thought the unforgotten dead a wonderful human being, he lavishes on the little boy a sort of tender respect. He languishes because he is a little fool. I am afraid he will always be one. He has grown, his face has changed; he begins to resemble his mother. May God bless him, for I, alas, cannot and never shall be able to do anything for him.'

After spending the spring and summer at Nowofastow, and the autumn with his grandmother at Jitomar, Conrad rejoined his father—but not at Tchernikow; for in December of that year (1867) Apollo, who had become too debilitated to be accounted a danger any longer by the Russian authorities, had been liberated from exile and was living at Lemberg, Galicia.

Conrad was now eleven years old, and he was sent to the Polish High School; but his father was very dissatisfied with the educational system at the school and particularly with the debased way in which Polish was taught there, wretchedly mispronounced; for he was as exacting on the subject of pronunciation as a Platonic philosopher or a Miltonic scholar.

To such a man a bad accent or enunciation is as offensive as a bad smell. Apollo could not endure that his own son should speak in the way that he condemns again and again in his letters as the 'Galician language'.

At the beginning of the next term, Conrad was unwell, suffering from 'painful cramps in the stomach'; and Apollo determined to carry on his education himself. He felt the more able to do so because his own health had improved. He had been cheered by the political outlook. The Austrians, as a result of losing the battle of Sadova, were willing to conciliate the Poles under their rule, and they no longer forbade them to speak and write in their own language. To Apollo, this was a great concession; it gave him a new zest in life. He writes in high spirits :

'I am absorbed in looking after my own health and also Konrad's; I am deep in the mountains at Topolnica and my time is so taken up with drinking sheep's milk that when the Imperial and Royal police came to ask how I spent my time in Galicia, I was able conscientiously to answer "drinking sheep's milk".'

Besides drinking sheep's milk, he meant to resume his

old pre-exile occupation of journalism; but the improve-
ment in his health was only temporary—a sort of physio-
logical St. Martin's summer—and as the winter came on
his new-found strength relapsed. At last, he was confined
to his room, and unable to teach Conrad any longer. 'I
only watch to see', he writes, 'that during his lessons Polish
is not changed into the Galician language'.

In February 1869 father and son went to live in
Cracow, and Conrad was sent to a preparatory school.

It was a great advantage to him at this time that he
lived in an environment such as afforded him ready access
to excellent books. He read with avidity authors that
nowadays are regarded, and neglected, as 'classics'. In those
days, in the 'eighties, editions of Captain Marryat's novels
abounded. One especially remembers, in this country,
picture paper-cover illustrations of *Poor Jack*, with his
bare legs and his oar, and of *The Phantom Ship* stared at
by terrified mariners. No less familiar was *The Toilers of
the Sea* in lurid shilling 'yellow-backs' depicting Gilliat
fighting in the toils of the giant octopus.

And books were really *read* in those thorough-going
times, especially by schoolboys, undiverted by the 'pictures', radio, television, and American comics.

But besides his natural love of reading, Conrad had also
the stimulus of repression. As the winter drew on, his
father's condition became worse. In the afternoons, the
boy would return from school to the great old house in
which Apollo lay prostrated in his last illness. There in
the evenings he worked at his preparation and afterwards
read in a 'large drawing-room, panelled and bare, with
heavy cornices and a lofty ceiling'. His table, lit with two
candles in the environing gloom, 'faced a tall, white door,
which was kept closed; now and then it would come ajar
and a nun in a white coif would squeeze herself through
the crack, glide across the room, and disappear. There
were two of these noiseless nursing nuns. Their voices were
seldom heard. . . . When they did speak to me it was with
their lips hardly moving, in a claustral, clear whisper. . . .
The air around me was all piety, resignation, and silence.

'I don't know what would have become of me if I had
not been a reading boy. My prep. finished, I would have
had nothing to do but sit and watch the awful stillness
of the sick room flow out through the closed door and
coldly enfold my scared heart. . . . There were many
books about, lying on consoles, on tables, and even on
the floor. . . . I read! What did I not read! Sometimes
the elder nun, gliding up and casting a mistrustful look
on the open pages, would lay her hand lightly on my
head, and suggest in a doubtful whisper, "Perhaps it is
not very good for you to read these books." I would
raise my eyes to her face mutely, and with a vague
gesture of giving up she would glide away.

'Later in the evening, but not always, I would be
permitted to tiptoe into the sick-room to say good-night
to the figure prone on the bed, which often could not
acknowledge my presence but by a slow movement of
the eyes, put my lips dutifully to the nerveless hand
lying on the coverlet, and tiptoe out again. Then I
would go to bed, in a room at the end of the corridor,
and often, not always, cry myself into a good sound
sleep.'

iv

Apollo knew that he was dying. He had followed his
patriotic lure, just as Milton in his 'patriotic piety' had
been captivated by the 'sweet sound'. His own 'patriotic
piety', or pious patriotism (for they are interchangeable),
had left him in thick darkness, the irremovable curtain
behind which his son had conceived the anarchic linea-
ments of Inexorable Fate.

He, Apollo himself, had been an anarch, in his own
fashion, the leader of a revolt, having put his trust in the
god of force, the Miltonic 'Almighty'; as if the 'stars in their
courses' would fight against Nicholas.

No doubt, he died, as he had lived, in the same state of
obfuscation; whereas Milton, blind and resigned, attained
to disillusion when the idealised abstraction crashed.

Only, Apollo destroyed his *Memoirs*, the records of his

heroic life. Conrad, at the open door, observed the heca-tomb. His father, propped up in his arm-chair, supervised the operation as batch after batch of MSS (which it is a wonder he had been allowed to retain) was placed on the blaze, poked about, consumed, incinerated; a demonstration in ashes to ashes that burnt papers tell no tales, implicate no accomplices, incriminate no friends.

Apollo had left this final act late; it probably cost him a considerable effort. His *Memoirs* were the creation and literary companion of his exile, more companionable, in that way, than an intimate diary. They were also his *apologia pro vita sua,* the kind of possession that he would willingly have left behind him with something of the prospective egotism of a Milton.

He was, in fact, characteristically Miltonic; as the following description of him in Tadeusz Bobrowski's *Memoirs* will testify :

'Exceptionally harsh and uncompromising in his writing, he was often too indulgent to those around him. In his judgment of the powerful he was severe, and towards the weak he was very benevolent. He selected as victims of his mockery either those who had personally offended him or struck him as unduly proud of their social position. He called himself an ardent democrat and he was sometimes taken for a Socialist, but, as I told him many times, his carriage and behaviour were much more aristocratic than mine and no one attributed to me democratic sentiments.'

On 23rd May 1869, fifteen days after burning his manuscripts, Apollo died.

Conrad's reactions to the event were remarkable.

'I looked forward to what was coming', he writes in *Poland Revisited,* 'with an incredulous terror. I turned my eyes from it sometimes with success, and yet all the time I had an awful sensation of the inevitable. I had also moments of revolt which stripped off me some of my simple trust in the government of the universe. But

1 Joseph Conrad at the age of 26

2 Apollo Nalecz Korzeniowski, Joseph Conrad's father (1862)

when the inevitable entered the sick-room and the white door was thrown open, I don't think I found a single tear to shed.

'The day of the funeral came in due course. . . . There was nothing in my aching head but a few words, some such stupid sentences as, "It's done", "It's accomplished" (in Polish it is much shorter), or something of the sort, repeating itself endlessly.'

'It's done—it's accomplished!'

These words are the utterance of Conrad's conception of fatality, inevitability (the Miltonic 'necessity'), the cardinal motif of his novels. Apollo's patriotic fanaticism implied mental instability and, in that sense, defective self-control; and these related conditions seemed to prepare the way, in his case, for the approach of death, slow, steady, and as if stealthy.

The impressions, although obscure, inspired in Conrad's mind an 'awful sensation of the inevitable', an 'appalling feeling of inexorable fate, tangible, palpable'. The complex of ideas—fanaticism, mental instability, and failure of self-control—connected up with the concept of violence, and this became associated in his mind with the disastrous insurrection of 1863, which his father had organised. It had been disastrous indeed. It had driven his father and mother into exile. One of his uncles had died fighting in it; another uncle had been exiled, like his father, and this to a worse place, Siberia. The aftermath among the Poles was hopelessness, listlessness, and abandonment to drunkenness and lechery. Had Conrad already read Hamlet, and been able to put two and two together, in that way, he might well have reflected on that striking illustration of obsession combined with mental instability producing inevitable disaster.

This adumbrated conception of inexorable fate caused him to become eventually a tragical writer in the old, classic signification rather than, what he is usually styled, a romantic realist; his protagonists are heroes, doomed, overcome but unyielding.

The funeral of Apollo was an impressive one. Conrad describes the procession; in which, in a space kept clear behind the hearse, he walked alone: the 'enormous following', the 'clumsy swaying of the tall black machine', the 'chanting of the surpliced clergy at the head', the 'flames of tapers' showing up as they passed under the low archway of the Florian Gate, the 'rows of bared heads on the pavements with fixed, serious eyes'.

'They had not come', he continues, 'to honour a great achievement, or even some splendid failure. The dead and they were victims alike of an unrelenting destiny which cut them off from every path of merit and glory. They had come only to render homage to the ardent fidelity of the man whose life had been a fearless confession in word and deed of a creed which the simplest heart in that crowd could feel and understand.'

Yet the procession—attended by half the population of Cracow, the 'Youth of the School, the grave Senate of the University, the delegations of the Trade-guilds'—was also a means of propaganda and protest. It was virtually the only form of protest remaining to the nation under the shadow of the Russian Empire; a protest cloaked and protected beneath the ægis of the conventional religion (in Poland, Roman Catholicism) with which the Czarist autocracy was obliged to compound.

V

Conrad has written very little about his father: besides the fatalistic impressions he felt at his death, the panegyric concerning his funeral, his compendious description of Apollo's personal characteristics, virtually nothing. The relative he wrote most about, going on and on, or round about on the subject, in his rambling, ambling *Personal Record*—page after garrulous page—was his grand-uncle, Mr Nicholas B. Mr. Nicholas B., 'Sub-lieutenant of 1813 in the French Army, and for a short time *Officier d'Ordonnance* of Marshal Marmont; afterwards Captain

in the 2nd Regiment of Mounted Rifles in the Polish Army'
—who had once eaten roast dog.

The fact, related to Conrad in his childhood, affected
his mind with compassion and horror. It strikingly resembles the motif of his story, *Falk*; the story of a sailor
who had eaten human flesh. Mr Nicholas B., along with
two fellow officers of Napoleon's army, had eaten dog on
an occasion when, having strayed from the *Grande
Armée* during the retreat from Moscow, they were lost and
famished in snowy wastes; Falk ate human flesh, along
with other survivors of the famished crew of a steamer
which, uncontrollable through the breaking down of her
steering-gear, had drifted among Antarctic ice-floes.

Falk suffers such a feeling of horror and shame at his
unnatural repast, that he cannot look a woman in the eyes.
A psychologist would probably attribute this idea to
Conrad's juvenile obsession, especially as 'sex' (the
Freudian obsession) is involved; Ford Madox Hueffer tells
us, on the other hand, that the original of Falk was a
master mariner who was 'reputed to have become a can-
nibal after the screw dropped off his vessel in the
Antarctic, drifting helpless for months', while Mrs Conrad
tells us that the fantasy was 'culled from a short paragraph
in a newspaper'.[10]

The story of the roast dog was the first realistic story
that Conrad had ever heard, and it was the more affecting
by reason of the peculiar quality of its realism. Conrad
possessed an exceptional power of visualisation and, as
he says himself:

'Of course I know what our village dogs look like. . . .
It was not thin . . . on the contrary, it was unhealthily
obese; its skin showed bare patches of an unpleasant
character. However, they had not killed that dog for the
sake of the pelt. He was large. . . . He was eaten. . . . The
rest is silence. . . .

'A silence in which a small boy shudders and says
firmly:

' "I could not have eaten that dog".'

---

[10] *Joseph Conrad as I knew Him.* (Heinemann.)

"And his grandmother remarks, with a smile:
" Perhaps you don't know what it is to be hungry".'

But this modifying remark was not enough to dispel the horror in Conrad's mind, any more than it is enough —or of the slightest effect on a juvenile spectator of a gangster film—to attach a retributive moral. In such cases, 'all's' not 'well that *ends well*'. The horrible roast persisted in the child's imagination; while Mr Nicholas B., *Chevalier de la Légion d'Honneur* etc. appears and disappears through *A Personal Record* like an illustrious equivocal ghost. As Conrad himself tells us:

'From my early boyhood to this day, if I try to call up his image, a sort of mist rises before my eyes, a mist in which I perceive vaguely only a neatly-brushed head of white hair, and a thin, curved, dignified nose.'

With this dual aspect, the story assumes the kind of interest that is inspired by a Grimm's fairy tale, although the paradoxical quality of its fascination consists in a nauseous, rather than a gruesome, appeal. Also, like a child's favourite fairy tale, it had to be told on repeated occasions. It is here expanded with elaborate iteration.

'It was during the memorable retreat from Moscow—'

With these words Conrad is fairly launched into what he wishes to do.

But why would he thus disclose to a 'cold and fastidious world', as he expresses it, 'that awful episode in the family history'? It is not as if the story were particularly interesting of itself. Mr Nicholas B. was not the only unfortunate who, like Antony in the play, had 'eaten strange meats'. Can it be that Conrad, who romanticised himself, imagined that the recital of the exploits, promotions, decorations, etc., of Mr Nicholas B. might perhaps shed more lustre upon the escutcheon of the B. family than the repellent roast-dog episode could sully?

The truth is, he was as proud of his kinship with the illustrious Bobrowski family as he was sensible of his Polish nationality; this, in the special circumstances, was natural.

Poland, arrested in its growth by conquest and sub-jugation, retained in a sluggish, hopeless atmosphere its old feudal traditions which the external bonds had tended to intensify, producing close communal relations between the gentry and the peasantry. One Polish gentleman, for example, addressing another, upon a cordial occasion, would adopt the peasant's familiar word for 'brother'.

Conrad's patriotic feeling was thus involved in his pride of family; a state of feeling which his uncle, Tadeusz Bobrowski, who became as influential to him as a beloved parent, constantly promoted.

This Polish feudal family feeling between high and low, rich and poor, had largely been compacted by the fellow-ship of discipline and hardship undergone by the Polish legions under Napoleon; in which military service, inci-dentally, Mr Nicholas B. might be thought by people of bellicose mind to have washed out his gastronomical sin in the blood of his country's foes.

Conrad himself, perhaps, would have thought so, although he deprecated war itself, and described Napoleon not as an eagle, as it was the fashion to do, but 'more like a sort of vulture, preying upon the body of a corpse-like Europe'. It may be that he took it both ways, just as Milton, after protesting that he was 'not sedulous by nature to indite wars', indited them with tedious elabora-tion.

vi

Conrad is less ingenuous in regard to the paternal side of his family.

The Nalecz Korzeniowkis,[11] according to Tadeusz Bobrowski, who wrote his *Memoirs*, were very different in character and temperament from his own kindred. As Mr

---

[11] The Nalecz Korzeniowskis are to be distinguished from other Korzeniowskis unrelated to them. Their arms were a handkerchief having two of its corners tied together, as shown inside the covers of Conrad's *Collected Works*. (Dent.) This symbol was probably a visual pun on the linking of the two families (of Nalecz and Korzeniowski) and the name Nalecz, which itself means 'tied together'.

Mégroz puts it succinctly, the 'Bobrowskis were practical and "level-headed", and generally "well-off"; the Nalecz Korzeniowskis . . . were brilliant and visionary, and often ruined themselves by fantastic schemes'.[12]

A typical Nalecz Korzeniowski was Conrad's paternal grandfather, Teodor. Conrad tells us that he was a comrade-in-arms of Mr Nicholas B. during Napoleon's Moscow campaign, and later on a fellow officer in the Polish Army. He characterised him, with most un-Conradian brevity, as belonging to that type of Polish squire whose only ideal of patriotic action was to 'get into the saddle and drive them out'.

Teodor Nalecz Korzeniowski was headstrong, rough-and-ready, and autocratic. He was also a visionary, a 'Utopian', and he formed impracticable ideas about estate-management which he tried out on his own estate—a small hereditary property that he had retired to when, in 1830, the Polish Army was disbanded. The result of these experiments was disastrous and, together with hazardous speculations and the gambling debts of his eldest son, Robert, brought him to ruin. Robert—as already stated—died fighting in the insurrection of 1863; while his brother, Hilary, who was also a speculator and a 'Utopian', was exiled to Siberia.

All this is duly set forth by Tadeusz Bobrowski, in his *Memoirs*. He shows also that the autocratic Teodor was a braggart story-teller who romanticised his soldierly past. As Dr Morf puts it, 'he was a teller of stories of that particular kind which first lie to themselves, get to believe firmly their own lies, and then pass them on to others and quarrel with those that will not believe them'.[13]

Mr Mégroz suggests that there is in this story-telling propensity an 'inkling of the gift which was employed more creatively by the old martinet's grandson'. This is probable, since it often appears as if (to adapt the adage) the grandfather were 'child' to the grandson.

---

[12] *Joseph Conrad's Mind and Method.* (Faber & Faber.)
[13] Gustaf Morf, *The Polish Heritage of Joseph Conrad.* (Sampson Low.)

The most important factor, according to the true standard of values, in Conrad's constitution, however, was the influence of his mother; that ennobling influence of sensibility which, as Anatole France explained, is the 'very secret of genius'. It implanted in his mind an ideal conception of women, such as he expresses, for example, in the characters of Mrs Gould and Antonia in *Nostromo*. Indeed, the subtly impressive words he used in describing his mother in *A Personal Record*, the 'awe of her mysterious gravity', might be precisely applied to Antonia.

In general, just as in the character of his father the wild tendencies of the Nalecz Korzeniowskis were concentrated, the stable qualities of the Bobrowskis were transmuted in his mother into a steadfast flame.

Thus, the two sides of Conrad's family, the practical and the visionary, operated as complemental opposites, centripetal and centrifugal forces, in his psychological system.

vii

After the funeral of Apollo, Conrad, who was now eleven years old, was cared for by Stefan Buszcynski, apparently the father of one of his schoolfellows; of whom Mr Retinger writes :

> 'At the time he had few friends, with the exception of Konstanty Buszcynski, also a son of a Polish patriot and a minor poet himself. Buszcynski later in his life became well known as an agriculturalist. Conrad did not meet him after their schooldays until I brought him back to Poland in 1914.'

According to Jean-Aubry, Conrad was placed, in conformity with his father's wish, *en pension* with M. Georgeon at Cracow, and he attended classes at the St Anne's High School'.

Mr Retinger writes, however, that he was 'boarded in a house kept by the Georgeon ladies. They were described to me often, not only by Conrad but—rare coincidence— also by relatives of my first wife, to whom they were distantly related.

'There were three of them: Madame Georgeon, an old Polish lady, who had married a descendant of French *émigrés* settled in Poland, and her two spinster daughters, who at that time were past middle age. I believe the last one died only a few years before the War. They took care of boys of good family at school in Cracow.

'Refined and perfumed, prim and snobbish, for many years they made livings out of this *pension* in which the fatherless Conrad, as a boy, spent, according to himself, the saddest hours of his life, notwithstanding the evident care of the Georgeon females.'

It was a period for Conrad of sadness and loneliness, the sorrow of his bereavement being in unison with his environment; the environment of Cracow, that sombre city.

His school life was sufficiently discouraging of itself. The curriculum conformed with the period scholastic system in which chief importance was attached to the memorising of Latin and Greek verses. Conrad had no aptitude for classics. He was good at French, which had been taught him by a governess during his stay with his mother at Nowofastow; but he was bad at German, as well as at Latin. As for grammar, he abominated the subject, as he told Mr Mégroz in the important interview narrated in his work, *Joseph Conrad's Mind and Method*:

'Oh, what a grind I had when (later) I tried to get hold of English grammar! As I had always been a reading boy I remained a reader after going to sea, and reading is the best way to pick up any language. But I still absolutely refused to learn grammar. . . . After all, grammar is so arbitrary, why bother about it? And my boys have inherited that inability, distaste, and horror of grammar.' In a letter to a literary correspondent, dated 23rd January 1911, he writes, 'I have never opened an English grammar in my life.'

With such an antipathetic disability in his nature, Conrad might well have been bad at Latin. Nor, not 'bothering about' grammar, could he have mastered English. He admits, himself, in the above letter, that he had not 'mastered it'. But he has 'acquired' it, he says; and he told Mr Mégroz that, whereas he 'corrected one or two faults of grammar' in the collected editions of his works, his faults were 'not faults that a foreigner would make but faults that a very careless man using English as a native language would make'. Perhaps it is pedantic to trap Conrad in the very words he uses in formulating his claim; but 'faults' are not 'made' even by a very careless English writer.

In such a writer as Conrad, syntactical faults may be overlooked, and, indeed, the confusions in his works between 'shall' and 'will', 'should' and 'would' are such as, at any rate, a Scotsman (even a careful Scotsman), using English as his native language, might 'make'; nevertheless, in such a matter as the sequence of tenses, Conrad makes mistakes such as no educated Englishman, however careless, would make; for example :

'This constitution will be promulgated immediately after the three Powers had settled the frontiers.'— *A Note on the Polish Problem*, 1916.
'This friend of ours has abandoned his enquiries when he heard of the police getting hold of the letters.'— *Under Western Eyes.*

If Conrad had learnt grammar, how easily he would have detected such irregularities in verbal time!

In regard to Latin, also, there would have been advantages if he had taken the subject seriously. For instance, it would have moderated the vexation of which he complained to Mr Mégroz, 'Always he gets the right word at once,' he said (of another author), 'while I have to ransack all round my poor head.' He would have been able to act on the rhymed principle :

> *If the right word be far to seek,*
> *Think of the Latin or the Greek.*

Conrad was 'good at mathematics'; a circumstance very

advantageous later on, when he had to learn navigation. At composition, he was good; at history, only 'fairly good'. This is strange, considering the great knowledge of the subject he eagerly acquired in his later life. In such books as *The Rover* and his unfinished *Suspense*, the historical background is presented as if he had lived in the actual times.

He was good at geography—but very discontented with the way in which it was taught at the High School.

'Unfortunately,' he writes in *Last Essays*, 'the marks awarded for the subject were almost as few as the hours apportioned to it in the school curriculum by persons of no romantic sense for the real, ignorant of the great possibilities of active life; with no desire for struggle, no notion of the wide spaces of the world—mere bored professors, in fact, who were not only middle-aged but looked to me as if they had never been young. And their geography was very much like themselves, a bloodless thing with a dry skin covering a repulsive armature of uninteresting bones.

All this time at school, however, Conrad was working assiduously to make up his arrears.

During the year 1870, his position in family matters was arranged by a deed which placed him under the joint guardianship of his grandmother, Mme. Bobrowska, and Count Ladislas Mniszek. His grandmother, who took him to Wartenberg, Bohemia, for the summer holidays, decided to remove to Cracow before the new term began. It was also arranged that a Mr Pulman, a young student of the University of Cracow, should supervise his studies.

Mr Pulman was a success. Conrad got on well with him, in both senses of the word. Nevertheless, he found the discipline and routine of his studies very irksome. There passed an uneventful, tedious time.

In December 1872, when the remembrance of his father's death had sunk, wreck-like, in his young mind, the heavy consciousness was brought to the surface again. In honour of the revered patriot the Municipal Council of

Cracow bestowed upon his son the freedom of the city.

'This favour', Jean-Aubry observes, 'should have entailed his being naturalised as an Austrian subject, and proceedings to that end were begun.' But, for political reasons, apparently, the right was refused and, 'since he could not be legally what he was in fact, a Pole, anything was better than being a Russian'. It was decided, therefore, that he 'should continue to remain at Cracow without once setting foot on Russian territory'.

viii

At about this time, Conrad divulged his desire—his heart's desire, for it was nothing less—to become a sailor: he had been keeping it secret for over two years, afraid, with a boy's diffidence, to divulge it. Descended from Polish patriots, son of an ultra-patriotic martyr, patriotism in the very air that he breathed, he felt that going to sea would be tantamount to deserting his country. He had never seen the sea; he had never seen an Englishman; yet he wanted, not only to be a sailor, but to be a sailor in an English ship —like one of Captain Marryat's sailors. At the same time, he knew perfectly well that for a Pole—let alone a Polish gentleman—to become a sailor was something unheard of. Agriculture was and had been for generations the main business in Poland. There were minor occupations—those permitted by the Russians—for example, the law (a necessary concomitant to land-owning), or journalism. But, as for anything connected with the sea, nineteenth-century Poland might well have been the desired destination of that mythical sailor who, sick of the sea, walked inland carrying an oar, until he should come to a region where no man could tell what sort of thing it was that he carried.

Conrad's disclosure, received with amazement and consternation, eventually spread itself 'over several provinces', stirring up a 'mass of remonstrance, indignation, pitying wonder, bitter irony, and derisive chaff'.

'I don't mean to say', Conrad continues, 'that a whole country has been convulsed by my desire to go to sea. But for a boy between fifteen and sixteen, sensitive enough in all conscience, the commotion of his little world had seemed a very considerable thing indeed. So considerable that, absurdly enough, the echoes of it linger to this day. I catch myself in hours of solitude and retrospect meeting arguments and charges made thirty-five years ago by voices now for ever still; finding things to say that an assailed boy could not have found, simply because of the mysteriousness of his impulses to himself. I understood no more than the people who called upon me to explain myself.'

Not only in the foregoing passage, but very elaborately on other pages of A *Personal Record,* he treats of this desire that so fluttered his Volscians in Corioli.

The continual commotion of criticism and argumentation would seem to have produced in the distracted boy an obsession comparable with that occasioned by the story of Mr Nicholas B. and the roasted dog. In fact, in A *Personal Record* he actually links them together. Thus Mr Nicholas B. had eaten dog not merely to appease hunger. No. *'Pro patria!'* he had eaten it for the sake of his country. Conrad himself, on the other hand, was proposing to eat 'salt junk and hard tack' for what? 'Alas!' he exclaims, 'I have the conviction that there are men of unstained rectitude who are ready to murmur scornfully the word "desertion".'

It is remarkable, in this connection, that the theme of conscientious or shame-faced contrition comes up repeatedly in Conrad's works, even to the point of morbidity; especially in *Lord Jim, Nostromo, The Shadow Line,* and *Falk.*

'Thus,' Conrad proceeds philosophically, 'the taste of innocent adventure may be made bitter to the palate. The part of the inexplicable should be allowed for in appraising the conduct of men in a world where no explanation is final. No charge of faithlessness ought to be lightly uttered. The appearances of this perishable life are deceptive like everything that falls under the judgment of our imperfect senses. The inner voice may remain true enough in its secret counsel. . . . It would take too long to explain the intimate alliance of contradictions in human nature which makes love itself wear at times the desperate shape of betrayal. And perhaps there is no possible explanation. Indulgence—as somebody said—is the most intelligent of all the virtues. I venture to think that it is one of the least common, if not the most uncommon of all.'

Conrad's desire to become a sailor, therefore, was inspired by a form of love, an ideal. The sea, for him, was the symbol of freedom, the means of release after repression, the gateway to adventure and discovery. In going to sea he was satisfying an instinct, aroused and stimulated by his romantic and geographical reading, to visit the 'wide spaces of the earth'. This instinct was adumbrated in an experience of his childhood. 'It was in 1868, when nine years old, or thereabouts,' he writes in *A Personal Record*, 'that while looking at a map of Africa of the time and putting my finger on the blank space then representing the unsolved mystery of that continent, I said to myself with absolute assurance and an amazing audacity which are no longer in my character now:

'"When I grow up I shall go *there*".'

He thought no more about the incident until, twenty-five years afterwards, he actually did 'go there'—to the region that, in the meantime, had been named the Stanley Falls, or Belgian Congo.

ix

A great influence in the life of Conrad was that of his uncle, Pan Tadeusz Bobrowski; who was to him, as it were, a 'second father' and, after the death of Apollo, became his virtual guardian. Tadeusz was devoted to Conrad in a peculiar way. His sensitive, delicate, and intensely imaginative nephew intimately represented to him his beloved sister, Evelina, Conrad's mother, and to this deep affection the boy instinctively responded.

Ford Madox Hueffer tells us:

'Conrad was inordinately proud and fond of his uncle and fully four-fifths of his conversation when it referred to his Polish days concerned itself with this relative': while J. H. Retinger writes:

'Conrad was extremely devoted to this uncle of his and, although rather reticent about others of his kin, never tired of talking about this old companion of his father's.'

But Tadeusz was very different in temperament and outlook from Apollo.

Tadeusz, as if he had two eyes in his mind (and these eyes on either side like a whale's), was balanced and shrewdly matter-of-fact by nature, being thus able to see both sides of a matter. Apollo, on the other hand, saw straight before him, blankly. Thus, Tadeusz was opposed to the insurrection of 1863; Apollo rushed into it.

As if in illustration of this, Hueffer describes Tadeusz (from his talks with Conrad) as having a 'longish, as if squared face, a long nose, meditative hands that were always pausing in some action, and long brownish hair that fell rather Germanly on to the collar of a velvet coat'.

He writes also:

'This uncle stood well with the Russians. Before that abortive revolution he had been a close friend of one of the Grand Dukes, and had had a part in drafting the constitution that the Tsar had proposed to grant to Poland. In the revolution he had taken no part, not because he was indifferent to the interests of Poland but because he knew it must prove abortive and cause much suffering and persecution to the Russian Poles. Besides, it brought about the rescinding of the constitution. After the revolution he busied himself with alleviating the suffering of his compatriots; he fed legions of the starving dispossessed; he secured the return of their patrimonies to the children of the exiled.

Amongst these last was Conrad: his uncle secured the return to him of half the great confiscated estate of his father and got him permission to reside in Russian Poland, in his own great house. The emissary of Palmerston had, by the by, been sent away with a flea in his ear.'

This 'emissary of Palmerston', Hueffer had related, had come to Tadeusz, one night, driven in a sledge without bells, and 'cloaked and muffled to the hat rim . . . and was closeted for long' with him. He then 'drove away over the snow. Conrad said he could imagine that he heard the voice of *l'or de la perfide Albion,* jingling in great bags as the sledge went away.' In fact, the departing emissary was sowing gold (in Tadeusz's case on unprofitable ground) all over Poland so that the Polish revolutionary spirit might be kept alive and Russa embarrassed in her encroachments on Pera or Afghanistan.

Mr Retinger says of Tadeusz that he 'made a religion out of patriotism and democracy' and that he, 'having the right to a title, dropped it in obedience to his principles, which were disgustingly democratic'.

X

When Tadeusz first heard of his nephew's extraordinary longing to become a sailor, he was astonished and bewildered, like everybody else who came to hear about it.

However, he reflected, like the equable and deliberate Bobrowski that he was. This mad, preposterous notion, he thought, was the effect in Conrad of the wild Korzeniowski strain—it would not last.

But he could not be sure that it would not last. He could not be sure of anything in connection with such a character. It was incumbent on him, he considered, to go thoroughly into the matter, and he journeyed all the way from the Ukraine to get to the bottom of it. He never did do so, however; which is no wonder, for, on Conrad's own showing, it was incomprehensible.

Yet his long, tedious journey from the Ukraine was not

profitless. It gave Conrad a 'glimpse', as he himself describes it, of an 'inexhaustible and noble treasure of clear thought and warm feeling, which through life was to be mine to draw upon with a never-deceived love and confidence. Practically, after several exhaustive conversations, he concluded that he would not later on have me reproach him for having spoiled my life by an unconditional opposition. But I must take time for serious reflection. And I must not only think of myself but of others; weigh the claims of affection and conscience against my own sincerity of purpose. "Think well what it all means in the larger issues, my boy," he exhorted me finally with special friendliness. "And meantime try to get the best place you can in the yearly examination".'

At the end of the school term Conrad took a good place in the yearly examinations—'which for me (for certain reasons)', he says obscurely, 'happened to be a more difficult task than for other boys'.

In consequence, probably, of the special efforts that he made to attain such a position, his health broke down, and in the following year, May 1873, he was sent, upon medical advice, on a tour through Germany and Switzerland. This tour had a double purpose; a mental as well as a physical object. Mr Pulman, Conrad's young tutor, accompanied him; he had already been asked to dissuade the boy, if he could, from his crazy design, as it was accounted, of becoming a sailor, and it was hoped that, amid new surroundings, cities, lakes, mountains, his influence and arguments would have the more effect.

Mr Pulman performed his duty conscientiously; he argued *en route* to such an extent that Conrad, as he protests, 'began to feel crushed' before they 'reached Zürich!' 'He argued in railway trains, in lake steamboats, he argued away from me the obligatory sunrise on the Right, by Jove!'

At last, after they had made their way through the Valley of the Reuss, the indefatigable tutor 'started to argue on the top of the Furca Pass:

'What reward could I expect from such a life at the end

3 Evelina Korzeniowska, *née* Bobrowska
Joseph Conrad's Mother (1862)

4 *Loch Etive*

5 *Palestine*

of my years, either in ambition, honour or conscience?'

Conrad would now, after listening to him in 'despairing silence', have abandoned the desire; but, at that moment, an Englishman, the first one he had ever seen, happened to pass by. He wore a knickerbocker suit, short socks, laced boots. His 'calves exposed . . . dazzled the beholder by the splendour of their marble-like condition and their rich tone of young ivory. . . . The light of a headlong, exalted satisfaction with the world of men and the scenery of mountains illumined his clean-cut, very red face, his short silver-white whiskers, his innocently eager and triumphant eyes. In passing he cast a glance of kindly curiosity and a friendly gleam of big, sound, shiny teeth towards the man and the boy sitting like dusty tramps by the roadside, with a modest knapsack lying at their feet.'

The effect of the experience was as that of a vision: the Englishman illustrated in realistic guise—all the more visionary, on that account—Conrad's intuition of the freedom and abounding vigour of the sea.

Conrad 'felt no longer crushed', and his eyes met those of his tutor with a look in them which as much as expressed the inexpressible, explained the inexplicable—his incomprehensible longing to become a sailor.

Mr Pulman 'picked up the knapsack suddenly and got to his feet.

' "You are an incorrigible, hopeless, Don Quixote. That's what you are." . . .

'I walked behind him for full five minutes; then without looking back he stopped. The shadows of the distant peaks were lengthening over the Furca Pass. When I came up to him he turned to me and in full view of the Finster-Aarhorn, with his band of giant brothers rearing their monstrous heads against a brilliant sky, put his hand on my shoulder affectionately.

' "Well! That's enough. We will have no more of it".'

The tour was originally intended to be for six weeks, but on account of a cholera epidemic in Cracow, it was extended to nearly three months. This prolongation gave Conrad and his tutor the opportunity of proceeding to Milan and Venice, and there, from the Lido, Conrad had the enthralling experience of his first sight of the sea.

xi

The travellers returned to Cracow at the end of July 1874, and Mr Pulman made his report to the family. Uncle Tadeusz agreed with him that the sea-struck youth was incorrigible. He decided to let him have his heart's desire, and proceeded to take the means necessary to such an end.

Like most of the Polish gentlefolk of those days, he had connections in France, and he wrote to an influential friend in Marseilles, a Polish aristocrat named Peter Schodszko, who was in the marine service. Schodszko cordially consented to assist the would-be mariner. Other arrangements having been effected, Uncle Tadeusz decided that Conrad should leave for the port in October.

In the meantime, he was sent to stay with his cousin, Antoine Léon Syroczynski,[14] at Lemberg. At about that time he had his first experience of romantic love, a subject of which he was to write so realistically. In fact, he had two such experiences, and he describes them himself, although in the third person: the first, in an Author's Note to *Nostromo*; the second, in a cancelled passage in a manuscript stated by Jean-Aubry to be then 'in the collection of Mr T. J. Wise'. Jean-Aubry, in quoting them, gives it as his opinion that these 'disappointments of first love' were another incitement to Conrad to leave Poland.

The first description (from *Nostromo*) is as follows:

'If anything could induce me to revisit Sulaco (I should hate to see all these changes) it would be Antonia and the true reason for that—why not be frank about it?—the true reason is that I have modelled her on my first love. How we, a band of tallish schoolboys, the

---

[14] Léon Syroczynski told Angela Zagorska, another cousin of Conrad's, that Conrad, at eleven or twelve years old, used to write comedies and act them with the Syroczynski girls.

chums of her two brothers, how we used to look up to that girl just out of the schoolroom herself, as the standard-bearer of a faith to which we were all born, but which she alone knew how to hold aloft, with an unflinching hope! She had perhaps more glow and less serenity in her soul than Antonia, but she was an uncompromising Puritan of patriotism, with no taint of the slightest worldliness in her thoughts. I was not the only one in love with her; but it was I who had to hear oftenest her scathing criticism of my levities—very much like poor Decoud—or stand the brunt of her austere, unanswerable invective. She did not quite understand —but never mind. That afternoon when I came in, a shrinking yet defiant sinner, to say the final good-bye, I received a hand-squeeze that made my heart leap and saw a tear that took my breath away. She was softened at the last as though she had suddenly perceived (we were such children still!) that I was really going away for good, going very far away—even as far as Sulaco, lying unknown, hidden from our eyes, in the darkness of the Placid Gulf.'[15]

The second description reads:

'. . . He was in love with her. But he never betrayed this sentiment to her to anybody. He rather affected resistance to her influence. He even tried to cheat his own self in that respect.

'The secret of this resistance is that she was not his first love. That experience had come to him the year before in the late summer of his last school holiday. . . . From the nature of things first love can never be a wholly happy experience. But this man seems to have been exceptionally unlucky. His conviction is that, in colloquial phrase, he had struck something particularly wicked and even devilish. He holds that belief after thirty-five years, and positively shudders at the mere recollection. If she was really devilish, then she may

---

[15] Reproduced in the preface to *Nostromo* in Dent's collected edition.

count it for an amazing success. My opinion, however, is that the girl was simply very ordinarily stupid. Stupid people are very prone to turn a genuine display of sentiment into ridicule—and, women, of course, have special opportunities in this way. I imagine that at first he amused her, then he bored her (perhaps was in the way of some more serious flirtation), and, discovering that she could make him suffer, she let herself go to her heart's content. She amused herself again by tormenting him privately and publicly with great zest and method and finally "executed" him in circumstances of peculiar atrocity—which don't matter here.

'Perhaps he was unduly sensitive. At any rate, he came out of it seamed, scarred, almost flayed and with a complete mistrust of himself, an abiding fear. He still thought her a superior being, but not yet a devil. That opinion came later. But he said to himself : if that's it, then never, never again.

'In common parlance : once bit—twice shy. But there was something more there. He had been bitten all over as it were, enough to make him shy of expressing himself for ever.'

In October, Uncle Tadeusz, with Mme. Bobrowska, took Conrad from Lemberg to Cracow; where they saw him off, with 'tears and blessings', for Marseilles. Besides ordinary luggage, they had provided him with a few family relics, old papers, faded photographs, and a copy of Adam Mickiewicz's *Pan Tadeusz*.

IN FRANCE

(1874-78)

IN FRANCE

(1874-78)

i

By far tho most popular foreign country among the
Polish educated classes in Conrad's early days was
France. It was the adopted land of tens of thousands
of Polish *émigrés*, and they had been so well received there
after the insurrection against the Russians that they were
scarcely conscious of being foreigners at all. During the
Napoleonic wars against Austria and Russia, in which the
Poles joined heartily, France was the Land of Hope and,
it the Empire had lasted, it might perhaps have seemed
also the Land of Glory. At any rate, it became for a time,
after the return of the Royalist *émigrés*, the land of
Aristocracy. The Polish gentry, nobility, *literati*, in France,
made friends with the Royalists, supporting them during
the period of political transition, and were in return
received by them into princely, if on occasion somewhat
dilapidated, habitations.

Paris, the seat of social amenity and of cultivated inter-
nationalism (an enlargement of the Polish blend of
feudalism and democratic feeling) was, as Jean-Aubry
describes it, the 'real capital of Poland', while to the Poles
French was almost a native tongue owing to the outlawed
state of their own language. Their children prattled in
French, taught by French governesses.

Conrad himself learnt French in this way, as has already
been stated, during the three months when he was staying
with his mother at Nowofastow. Next to Polish, it became
his most intimate language, and it shows through his writings in English idiomatically as in a palimpsest.

Therefore, when Conrad left Poland for Marseilles, he was not, in any repellent sense, departing for a foreign country; he was not, for example, like R. L. Stevenson in the American emigrant train. He was not even like an English boy going out to a British colony.

In wanting to go to sea he had no thought of becoming a naval man. Thus, he rejected the chance offered him of a career in the Austrian Navy, which he could fitly have accepted, since the feeling in Poland against the Austrians was not so strong as it was against the Russians. He wanted to become simply a sailor, and to get out of Poland.

Schodszko, to whom Uncle Tadeusz had written, was away from Marseilles when Conrad arrived there, which was on 17th October 1874, but he had put his protégé's sea business under excellent management. His deputy was a young man named Baptistin Solary, and the name fitted him well, for his nature was sunny. 'Very good-looking, with a fine black, short beard, a fresh complexion, and soft, merry black eyes', as Conrad describes him, he was 'hail-fellow-well-met' (or the Gallic equivalent of the term) among the shipping community of Marseilles. He was also connected with this community by family ties.

'One of his uncles', writes Conrad, 'was a ship-broker of good standing with a large connection amongst English ships; other relatives of his dealt in ships' stores, owned sail-lofts, sold chains and anchors, were master-stevedores, caulkers, shipwrights.'

Solary had been a sailor himself; but he possessed too keen a sense of humour to discourage Conrad from going in for the *métier de chien,* as he called it—acting on Blake's principle that if a fool should go on in his folly he would become wise.

He introduced himself by bursting into the room where, in a 'modest hotel near the quays', Conrad was sleeping off the fatigues of his journey from Cracow. He flung open the shutters to let in the sun. With boisterous chidings for lying abed, he startled and enchanted the boy, who was scarcely awake, with 'noisy objurgations to be up and off instantly for a "three years' campaign in the South Seas".'

'O magic words!' exclaims Conrad at the recollection, 'Une campagne de trois ans dans les mers du sud—that is the French for a three years' deep-water voyage.'

It took some considerable time, however, for the 'magic words' to be effected; for Solary, too humorously optimistic, as Conrad discovered, 'did not enter upon the quest for a ship for me in a very solemn spirit'.

However, what he actually did for Conrad was excellent: he introduced him to the Corporation of Pilots, who gave him the freedom of their boats—large, half-decked boats, one-masted, with lug-sail rig. This meant that, instead of plunging directly into the arduous conditions of a deep-sea voyage, Conrad was initiated into a seafaring life gradually and delightfully, brought in contact with hardy, honest, and kindly men. They took to him at once in their instinctive way, calling him le petit ami de Baptistin, and were pleased to see him in their homes as well as in their boats.

'I have been invited', he writes, 'to sit in more than one tall, dark house of the old town at their hospitable board, had the bouillabaisse ladled out into thick plates by their high-voiced, broad-browed wives, talked to their daughters—thick-set girls, with pure profiles, glorious masses of black hair arranged with complicated art, dark eyes, and dazzlingly white teeth.'

The Pilots' Corporation was a really communal body of men. It was divided into five companies, or boatfuls. The men expressed in their nautical fashion the famous slogan, Liberté, Egalité, Fraternité. The slogan was sound and fury among the old revolutionaries but, with these simple, plain seamen, the practice of such sentiments was obligatory. The severe, inexorable conditions of their calling produced the liberté, egalité, fraternité, of being metaphorically 'all in the same boat'.

Besides le petit ami de Baptistin, they took out with them a superannuated old pilot who had been pensioned off years before, but who invariably joined them on the quay. He did so, apparently, from 'force of habit'. As the patron of the boat's company once confided to Conrad in a whisper, 'the old chap did no harm. He was not in the way.' He had to be helped to get on board and, of course, he could not do any work, 'except, perhaps, to cast off some rope when hailed, "*Hé, l'ancien,* let go the halyards there, at your hand"—or some such request of an easy kind.'

The aged Charon appears in Conrad's account of the last time that he went in one of the boats. The writing is nostalgic and, like the ramble about Mr Nicholas B., it goes on page after page. The descriptions are as vivid as the moonlight effects they include, and as lively as the pilot crew who, at first sleepy, suddenly become, when there is work to do, as hilarious as high-spirited schoolboys.

ii

'The *patron* of the Third Company . . . is the brother-in-law of my friend Solary (Baptistin), a broad-shouldered, deep-chested man of forty, with a keen, frank glance which always seeks your eyes. He greets me by a low, hearty, "*Hé, l'ami, Comment va?*" '

It was midnight, and Conrad had joined the pilots on the quay for the last night he was to spend with them. The *patron,* standing at the tiller, 'pulls out his watch from under a thick jacket and bends his head over it in the light cast into the boat. Time's up. His pleasant voice commands in a quiet undertone "*Larguez*". A suddenly projected arm snatches the lantern off the quay—and, warped along by a line at first, then with the regular tug of four heavy sweeps in the bow, the big, half-decked boat full of men glides out of the black, breathless shadow of the port. The open water of the *avant-port* glitters under the moon as if sewn over with millions of sequins, and the long white breakwater shines like a thick bar of solid silver. With a quick rattle of blocks and one single, silky swish, the sail is filled by a little breeze keen enough to have come straight down from the frozen moon, and the boat, after the clatter of the hauled-in sweeps, seems to stand at rest.'

'. . . for hours I suppose no word was spoken in that boat. The pilots seated in two rows facing each other dozed with their arms folded and their chins resting upon their breasts. They displayed a great variety of caps: cloth, wool, leather, peaks, earflaps, tassels, with a picturesque round beret or two pulled down over the brows; and one grandfather' (the superannuated pilot) 'with a shaved, bony face and a great beak of a nose, had a cloak with a hood which made him look in our midst like a cowled monk.

'My fingers itched for the tiller and in due course my friend, the *patron,* surrendered it to me in the same spirit in which the family coachman lets a boy hold the reins on an easy bit of road. . . . "Keep her in the furrow of the moon," the *patron* directed me in a quiet murmur, sitting down ponderously in the stern-sheets and reaching for his pipe. . . . The pilot station in weather like this was only a mile or two to the westward of the islets; and presently, as we approached the spot, the boat we were going to relieve swam into our view suddenly, on her way home, cutting black and sinister into the wake of the moon under a sable wing, while to them our sail must have been a vision of white and dazzling radiance. Without altering the course a hair's-breadth we slipped by each other within an oar's-length. A drawling sardonic hail came out of her. Instantly, as if by magic, our dozing pilots got on their feet in a body. An incredible babble of bantering shouts burst out, a jocular, passionate, voluble chatter, which lasted till the boats were stern to stern, theirs all bright now and with a shining sail to our eyes, we turned all black to their vision, and drawing away from them under a sable wing. That extraordinary uproar died away almost as suddenly as it had begun; first one had enough of it and sat down, then another, then three or four together, and when all had left off with mutters and growling half-laughs the sound of hearty chuckling became audible, persistent, unnoticed. The cowled grandfather was very much entertained somewhere within his hood.'

The chuckling, as Conrad tells us, continued for a long time until it had exhausted itself. No one, apparently, took any notice of it. It was as if the old pilot were no more than a shade on board, his voice as inappreciable as his person, while the effective pilots addressed a word or two to him now and then out of consideration for his feelings. They were conscious that he himself was sensible of his equivocal state—in part an automaton moved by 'force of habit'; in part, a shade.

He did, in fact, feel the disadvantages of his position, and made an effort now and then to assert himself. At the time when the two extremes in the matter of years— *le petit ami de Baptistin* and the aged grandfather—had first met, the elder hastened to assert, 'mumbling tremulously with his toothless jaws', that he had once seen the Emperor Napoleon. He described the appearance of the Great Man with a vividness of detail worthy of Joseph Conrad himself.

On the present occasion, the chuckling being spent, he made a 'professional remark' in a self-assertive if quavering voice:

' "Can't expect much work on a night like this".'

And, as it happened, there was no work; not another ship appeared that night, and there was nothing for the pilots to do but sail gliding to and fro on the calm sea within their appointed bearings.

A little before sunrise, they landed on a small islet to 'break a crust and take a pull at the wine bottle'.

'It was literally no more than that,' Conrad adds appreciatively.

After their frugal repast, the pilots behaved very much as the spirit moved them. Conrad reanimates the scene. Some wander about, stamping their feet and blowing on their nipped fingers; some 'sit apart perched on boulders like man-like sea-fowl of solitary habits'; others gather in gesticulating knots, while one after another distributively manipulates a great telescope, which is 'everlastingly changing hands with brandishing and levelling movements'.

At length, came the moment for which they had been waiting. Through the long brass tube of the telescope, a speck had appeared like an 'insect posed on the hard edge of the offing'.

The speck was the smoke of an incoming steamer. The pilots embarked and made towards her. She proved to be a big, period cargo-steamer, 'black hull, with low, white superstructures, powerfully rigged with three masts and a lot of yards on the fore'.

She was an English ship, the first English ship that Conrad had ever seen—the *James Westoll*; for he never forgot the name. The 'very grouping of the letters was alive with the romantic feeling of her reality'. Impetuously he volunteered to pull bow in the dinghy that shoved off to put the pilot on board. The dinghy was soon alongside, and then, on the deck above—where there was no bulwark to obstruct the view, only a rail and stanchions— there appeared a 'big, fat fellow . . . in a blue woollen shirt and roomy breeches pulled up very high, even to the level of his breast-bone, by a pair of braces quite exposed to public view'.

It was a figure, the like of which, Conrad declares, he never saw again, except in illustrations to stories by W. W. Jacobs.

The ungainly apparition growled down to him, 'Look out there.'

They were the first words he had ever heard spoken in English—the 'speech', as he writes, 'of my secret choice, of my future . . . of my very dreams'.

iii

'Look out there!' The words of the corpulent, braced-up man on the deck of the English steamer were nothing out of the common. They merely preceded the throwing down of a rope; but to Conrad, who correlated all things, they might well have betokened something more. They might have suggested other warning words—words spoken to him by a lady, and this not many hours before he had set out to join the pilots. She had said to him, '*Il faut, cependant, faire attention à ne pas gâter sa vie.*'

This lady was a Madame Delestang, an imperious, handsome personage in a statuesque style; she belonged to 'one of the old aristocratic families in the South'; while her husband 'belonged to the *Haute Bourgoisie* only'. M. Delestang was a banker, and Uncle Tadeusz had opened an account for Conrad at his bank. He was also a shipowner. His firm, Delestang et Fils, owned two ships; one old, the other new—the *Mont-Blanc,* a three-master (whether a full-rigged ship or a barque), built in 1853 and a schooner, the *Saint-Antoine,* built in 1870.

The Delestangs were Royalists. M. Delestang was most ardent for the cause; Mme. Delestang no less so, presumably, despite her languid, *négligé* air—and he, a man of money; she, a woman of family; both had the *entrée* to the most elegant circles of the Conservative or Legitimist society of Marseilles. Madame—'*la belle Mme. Delestang*', as she was called—gave afternoon receptions at which, over cakes and tea-cups, the talk about legitimist chances waxed optimistic. These chances all came to nothing, but the Republican rule in France was not so surely established at that time as to render its overturning unfeasible.

M. Delestang himself was especially optimistic. He was, in Conrad's words, 'such an ardent—no, he was such a frozen-up, mummified Royalist that he used in current conversation terms of speech contemporary with the good Henry IV; and when talking of money matters reckoned not in francs, like the common, godless herd of post-revolutionary Frenchmen, but in obsolete and forgotten *écus*. . . . As though Louis Quatorze were still promenading in royal splendour the garden of Versailles, and M. de Colbert busy with the direction of maritime affairs.'

The Delestangs took a kindly interest in Conrad, and Madame Delestang occasionally invited him to one of her receptions; a privilege that, apparently, he failed to appreciate at its face value. At any rate, he does not refer to these socio-political amenities in *A Personal Record.*

Besides asking Conrad to her receptions, Mme.

Delestang would sometimes invite him to drive with her
and her husband in their carriage. Upon catching sight
of him, she would beckon him towards her, and would
suggest, 'with an air of amused nonchalance, "*Venez donc
faire un tour avec nous*", to which her husband would add
"*C'est ça. Allons, montez, jeune homme*".'

It was at the end of one of these drives, when Conrad,
standing at the door of the carriage, was taking his leave,
that Mme. Delestang pronounced those words:

'*Il faut, cependant, faire attention à ne pas gâter sa vie.*'

Conrad was naturally taken aback by the startling
admonition. He understood it as being directed against
his intention of becoming a sailor, signifying that in
persisting in this intention he was in danger of spoiling his
life. Mme. Delestang's words, as it seemed to him, were
one more expostulation, one more warning added to all
the other expostulations and warnings he had received
against going to sea; they were a last shot at his heart's
desire. But that last shot was not the less disturbing be
cause it was delayed and, in *la belle Madame Delestang's*
insouciant tones, it came languidly, listlessly, as if spent.

It was so sudden, so unexpected. The aristocratic lady
had spoken to him very little; had never really talked to
him in the sense of expressing any opinions. Just a word,
or phrase, here and there, had proceeded desultorily from
her lips, and fallen as the dew from an exclusive heaven.
She had never previously breathed a word against his
ambition; neither had she shown the least sign of dis-
approval when he had talked about his cruises with the
pilots: on the contrary, she had seemed to be 'entertained
—as far as that ineffable woman could be entertained'. Her
innuendo murmured out at the last moment seemed
preposterous. Yet her head was very near his as
she leaned over from the carriage, and she had 'detained
his hand with a slight pressure'. She meant kindly, as he
himself acknowledges, and so did her husband, the 'frozen-
up, mummified Royalist', who while she spoke 'sat motionless, and looking straight before him'.

She 'made his heart beat' and started him thinking

tumultuously; still, he thought her warning '*bizarre*' and at the same time 'commonplace'.

'Can the transports of first love', he exclaims, 'be calmed, checked, turned to a cold suspicion of the future by a grave quotation from a work on Political Economy? I ask—Is it conceivable? Is it possible? Would it be right? With my feet on the very shores of the sea and about to embrace my blue-eyed dream, what could a good-natured warning as to spoiling one's life mean to my youthful passion?'

He 'tried to understand and tried in vain'. He brooded and worried all the evening until the time came for him to join the pilots. It was the last time that he was to go out with them—the occasion was the one that he has described in *The Mirror of the Sea*, from which I have quoted.

The fact—that it was the last time—taken in conjunction with his statement that he was about to 'embrace his blue-eyed dream' would signify, although he does not say so, that he was on the eve of his first sea voyage. Also it was on this account, no doubt, that he had jumped to the conclusion that Madame Delestang's warning referred to his going to sea. And so it obviously did—but not in the way that he took it. It referred, rather, as I conjecture, to the voyage itself. Madame Delestang, as the wife of a shipowner, was aware of the temptations and dangers that beset a young apprentice visiting tropical islands, and was solicitous that Conrad should beware that they did not spoil his life.

Her warning was cryptic, but likely, on that account, to leave the greater impression.

iv

Conrad, with the negligence in respect of dates that was characteristic of him, stated merely that his last cruise with the pilots was on a December night. Even that fragment of information, however, is enlightening; for, if the inference I have drawn from, conjointly, Mme. Delestang's warning, Conrad's metaphoric 'blue-eyed dream', and the termination of his cruises with the pilots, be valid—if, that is to say, these circumstances together denote that Conrad had his first sea voyage in the month of December, they lighten an obscurity of his Marseilles period. Jean-Aubry's researches divulge no record of Conrad's going to sea before his voyage in the *Mont-Blanc* on 25th June 1875, whereas there is a passage in *The Mirror of the Sea* in which Conrad states that he was on a ship in the Gulf of Lyons on Christmas night, and that he had had hardly two glimpses of salt water until then.

According to Jean-Aubry, Conrad cannot be referring to the *Mont-Blanc's* previous (1874) voyage, because that ship 'left Marseilles for Martinique on 11th December 1874 and could not have arrived at the Gulf of Lyons by Christmas'. (The inference surely would be rather that the ship would have passed through the Gulf of Lyons long before Christmas night.) Jean-Aubry concludes that, if the date of departure was as stated, Conrad had either confused the date or was alluding to another ship. Conrad may indeed have been alluding to another ship; one provided, perhaps, through the agency of Solary. On the other hand, the ship in question could well have been the *Mont-Blanc* on her 1874 voyage, but, in that case, would have left Marseilles later than the date recorded.

The obscure passage in *The Mirror of the Sea* is as follows:

'The very first Christmas night I ever spent away from land was employed in running before a Gulf of Lyons gale, which made the old ship groan in every timber as she skipped before it over the short seas until we brought her to, battered and out of breath, under the lee of Majorca, where the smooth water was torn by fierce cat's-paws under a very stormy sky. We—or rather, they, for I had hardly had two glimpses of salt water in my life till then—kept her standing off and on all day, while I listened for the first time with the curiosity of my tender years to the song of the wind in the ship's rigging. . . . The thing (I will not call her a ship twice in the same half-hour) leaked. She leaked fully, generously, overflowingly, all over—like a basket. I took an enthusiastic part in the excitement caused by that last infirmity of noble ships, without concerning myself much as to the why and wherefore.'

That the leaky craft was on her way to the West Indies (the destination of *Mont-Blanc*) is clear from passages that follow. For example:

'The West Indies awaited my coming. I had to go there. . . . the ridiculous and ancient *galère*, the old, weary, disenchanted sugar-waggon, seemed extremely disposed to open out and swallow up as much salt water as she could hold. . . . But no catastrophe occurred. I lived to watch on a strange shore a black and youthful Nausicaa, with a joyous train of attendant maidens, carrying baskets of linen to a clear stream overhung by the heads of slender palm trees. The vivid colours of their draped raiment and the gold of their earrings invested with a barbaric and regal magnificence their figures, stepping out freely in a shower of broken sunshine. The whiteness of their teeth was still more dazzling than the splendour of jewels at their ears. The shaded side of the ravine gleamed with their smiles. . . . The resonant, laughing voices of these gorgeous maidens scared away the multitude of humming-birds, whose delicate wings wreathed with the mist of their vibration the tops of flowering bushes. . . . I withdrew unseen. . . .'

In the 1875 voyage of the *Mont-Blanc*, Conrad shipped as an apprentice or, in Messrs Delestang's designation, a 'midshipman'. The ship left Marseilles on 25th June, bound for St. Pierre, Martinique. She arrived there on 31st July and, after remaining at that island for two months, proceeded to Cap-Haitien, Haiti, touching at St. Thomas on the way. The cargo of logwood that she took up at Cap-Haitien was destined for Le Havre; where she arrived on Christmas Eve. But the last month had been stormy, and the old craft was so battered that she was unable to proceed to her home port and had to be laid up for repairs.

Conrad went on to Marseilles by train, but he broke his journey for a few days in Paris. The city was especially esteemed by the Poles; no doubt, Conrad had a particular inducement to alight there. He had undergone ordeals, both physical and mental, and was in need of recreation.

Probably the most severe of these ordeals, considering his proud, sensitive nature, was the endurance of what in the French Marine (as in any other national service) is known as 'discipline'; a discipline very different in kind from that exercised by the pilot *patrons* of Marseilles. A younker aboard ship had need of a 'thick skin'. He had need also of a strong stomach. What Conrad's state of health may have been at this period, and whether he was free from the stomach ailment incident to his childhood, does not transpire. He had probably outgrown it; but even so, it would have left him the less able to sustain the crude ship's fare; the 'hard tack and salt junk'. Solary, who had retired from *la vie de chien*, would have said it was only fit for a dog, and certainly the 'hard tack' resembled dog-biscuit.

In this voyage, also, Conrad experienced the alarms and labours of a storm at sea; an ordeal that his own people had hoped would have succeeded where their arguments had failed in disenchanting him with his passion for a sea-faring life. Perhaps they had had in mind how cogently a storm at sea had brought home to the young Robinson Crusoe his father's wise, admonishing arguments. Robinson was terribly frightened; Conrad, no doubt, was impressed. The storm, in his case, seems to have been a raging tempest, judging by the battered condition in which it left the *Mont-Blanc*. Such a tempest as is described, for instance, in *The Nigger of the Narcissus*. But Conrad was not disenchanted; neither was he discouraged by any other experience on board; for his passion for the sea was 'of imagination all compact', exerting the triple power of desire, will, and courage.

He was not deterred from going on in the path that he had chosen; yet there is but little doubt that his life as an apprentice at sea was a severe probation. He never liked to talk of these early experiences in his after life; with the exception of the passage I have cited, there is no reference to them in *The Mirror of the Sea* or in his other autobiographical writings.

The thought of the West Indies had been fascinating to him in his boyhood, and he had formed the impression that they *awaited his coming.* 'It was a sort of mystic conviction', he writes in *The Mirror of the Sea,* '—something in the nature of a call.' The West Indies, however, are not represented in his novels as are the East Indies. The East Indies formed the *mise en scène* of *Almayer's Folly, The Outcast of the Islands, Lord Jim, The Shadow Line, Victory,* and *The Rescue,* as well as some of his long short-stories such as *The End of the Tether.*

The main reason for Conrad's preference for the East Indies, in this respect, is obviously that he had become the more conversant with them during his travels. It is probable also that they appealed to him in a temperamental way. The East Indies and the West Indies are, of course, very different in their atmospheric qualities. The West Indies are more limpid, soft, and lush, in their radiant splendour. The East Indies, on the other hand, have a harder though not less radiant quality, which may well have accorded more temperamentally with Conrad's imaginative vision. In fact, he seems even to exploit it by vivid intensification. Thus, he describes natural effects of the tropics in terms of hardness : the sea as a 'wall of polished steel', an 'iron plate', a 'sheet of ice', etc., the forest vegetation as 'steel', a pool as 'glass', the young moon as a 'slender shaving thrown up from a bar of gold', or—a more subtle instance—'Decoud had often felt his familiar habit of ironic thought fall shattered against Antonia's gravity'—or, at the summit of such examples : (of a lighthouse), 'The whole refracting apparatus . . . glittered and sparkled like a dome-shaped shrine of diamonds.'

This idiosyncrasy for hard aspects applies also to his descriptions of human beings. He especially emphasises their teeth. Thus, the Englishman whose appearance fascinated him so much on the top of the Furca Pass, gave him a 'gleam of big, sound, shiny teeth'. The pilots' daughters in the passage quoted from *A Personal Record* possessed 'dazzlingly white teeth'. Doña Rita, in *The Arrow of Gold*, is a 'woman of granite', and her teeth are spectacularly 'solid' (as 'solid as Mr Blunt's'). Ford Madox Hueffer had some trouble, in collaborating with Conrad, in this matter. 'It was only with difficulty', he writes, 'that he was restrained from adding good teeth to the catalogue' (of a woman character's charm). 'Why not good teeth?' (asks Conrad) 'Good teeth in a woman are a part of her charm. Think of when she laughs. You would not have her *not* have good teeth? They are a sign of health. Your damn woman has to be healthy, doesn't she?'

Conrad's women characters, in general, are dentally superb; they might well be, in this respect, so many film stars, or fashionable brides, showing their teeth in the pages of popular illustrated weeklies.

Nevertheless, Conrad's first sight of the West Indies must have had a deep effect on his mind; a mind conditioned by heritage and early experience of Polish gloom. The contrast between the radiant tropics and the austere land of his birth may even have had the effect of releasing his creative genius; for genius is dependent upon a kind of antinomy in conditions, the coming together of what philosophers describe as 'complemental opposites'. Such, indeed, was the fit union in this sense of Conrad's own parentage; the dichotomy in his nature of the Nalecz Korzeniowski and Bobrowski strains, observed earlier in these pages.

v

While the battered *Mont-Blanc* lay docked at Le Havre, the schooner, *Saint-Antoine,* her sister-ship, was away in the West Indies; whence she would not return until the end of May—not to sail again until July.

When, therefore, Conrad arrived in Marseilles in January, he was without a ship. Whether Solary could have found him one at that time is unknown, but there is no record that he was asked to do so. Conrad was in no hurry. He had 'decided' to wait for the *Saint-Antoine*.

His spell of relaxation in Paris was to be followed by over six months of reaction in Marseilles.

Of his manner of life there, Mr Retinger, whom it is always a pleasure to quote, says that he 'never liked to talk much about it,' but adds, 'one could gather from his reluctant words that his was the typical life of the *jeunesse dorée* with good connections. One can imagine him easily; a stocky, healthy, good-looking young fellow, with plenty of loose coin in his pockets, playing at being a sailor in the smart uniform of a naval *élève*, with one thought only in his mind—how best to enjoy himself, tasting life. The *Cannebière* and the *Hôtel de Noailles* must have seen a lot of him, for ever afterwards . . . the *Cannebière,* the noisy, and elegant thoroughfare, had a particular sentimental appeal for him, and he always remembered it as the most adventurous, most enticing, most glamorous avenue of world cities. I do not think that girls even then played a great rôle in his life. As is usual for very manly men, they were necessary for him to form a background for the scenery of his life . . . they never, however, became the central figures of any important episode in his career . . . he lived from episode to episode, like a healthy animal, carefree, enjoying every moment, and trying to cram into the shortest space of time the utmost adventure.'

Among these adventures, according to Ford Madox Hueffer, was the hiring of an 'unpainted four-in-hand', the driving of it, 'buried in actresses and the opera chorus, to the races'. 'Conrad would relate the instance of the unvarnished coach with great energy and power and then, dropping his hands with mock senility, exclaim: *"Alas! tel que vous me voyez, . . .* Now I am an extinct volcano".'

He also, according to these lively ebullitions, 'painted red the port of Marseilles and intrigued for Napoleon III, in company with some "Macmahonists"' — whose acquaintance he had probably made at Mme. Delestang's receptions.

Jean-Aubry writes in his serious style:

'It is probable that the beginning of the year 1876 is the date of an adventure which may be found "arranged" in the form of a story called "Ashes" in *From the Four Winds* by John Sinjohn, the first book by John Galsworthy. This is a story of an evening spent at Monte Carlo in the company of some cleaned-out gamblers, who, being unable to pay for their dinner, sent young Conrad, who had never gambled in his life, to stake their last five francs. He brought back, it appears, more than enough money to pay the bill.'

At about the same time, Uncle Tadeusz writes to Conrad:

'In 1876 a letter dated 5th April from Mr Victor Schodszko informed me that after having drawn out the whole of your allowance for eight months (1,200 fcs.) you lent this money (or perhaps you lost it) and that you found yourself in great embarrassment. Later in May you wrote to me and apologised without giving any explanation. On 21st May you wired asking me to send you 700 fcs. which I did, and on 2nd July, on receipt of another telegram, I despatched another 400 fcs. On your departure from Marseilles you asked me to pay 165 fcs. to M. Bonnard, a friend who lent you this sum. This I also did. Therefore, in three months you spent 1,265 fcs. Since each of us should pay for his own follies, and especially for those which affect his own pocket, and as I have no superfluous money to meet the superfluous expenses of my nephew, I met the demand by making use of 500 florins which belonged to you.'

'Uncle Tadeusz probably concluded', comments Jean-Aubry, 'that his nephew was indulging in the wildest excesses. . . . In any case, it is clear that Conrad had what is called a "good time".'

More expressively, perhaps, he was 'letting himself

go', 'having his fling', 'flinging the shutters open to the sun of Provence', as his jovial friend, Solary, had done on the morning after his arrival in Marseilles. He was 'sowing his wild oats' after the Polish winter of his discontent.

But although he had thus let himself go in Marseilles, it was in no ignoble manner. His nature was noble and, as Ishmael in Herman Melville's *Moby Dick* observes, the eagle, however much it descends, is still on a higher level than the crow. At any rate, he much enjoyed thus sowing his wild oats, and he reaped in his later years a golden harvest; the very word 'Marseilles' would conjure in his thoughts delightful recollections.

His favourite haunts during this period were the various cafés of the *Cannebière*, the rendezvous of the *jeunesse dorée*, as Mr Retinger has intimated, where the *habitués* discussed politics like the youthful doctrinaires in Turgenev's novels, or any other subject from *philosophie, science, et beaux-arts* to Woman and the Races, the only forms of 'sport' in those times to detract from the interest of other topics. Conrad especially affected a café in the rue Saint-Ferréol, as well as the Café Bodoul, which he mentions in *The Arrow of Gold*, in the passage:

'I was the one to speak first, proposing that my companions should sup with me, not across the way, which would be riotous with more than one "infernal supper", but in another much more select establishment in a side street away from the *Cannebière*. It flattered my vanity a little to be able to say that I had a corner always reserved in the *Salon des Palmiers*, otherwise *Salon Blanc*, where the atmosphere was legitimist and extremely decorous.'

Ibid:

'For lunch I had the choice of two places, one Bohemian, the other select, even aristocratic, where I had still my reserved table in the *petit salon* up the white staircase.'

vi

On 10th June 1876 Conrad embarked in the *Saint-Antoine*. He was now rated in the firm's books as "Lieutenant"; on the crew list, 'steward' ('monthly wages 35 fcs.'). The ship's complement consisted of four officers and thirteen men. She was commanded by Captain Escarras. The name suggests romantic adventure; and this is fitting, for the voyage had its romantic aspect. Although it was a voyage to the West Indies similar to the former one of the *Mont-Blanc*, it was extended, unofficially, to the transporting of arms and munitions to a Central American Republic; the identity of which is unknown. Conrad himself treats the matter with what seems almost studied vagueness as if, even after the lapse of so many years, the secret must still be kept. However, he discloses in a footnote on the miscreant Ricardo in *Victory*:

'It so happened that the very same year Ricardo—the physical Ricardo—was a fellow passenger of mine on board an extremely small and extremely dirty little schooner, during a four days' passage between two places in the Gulf of Mexico whose names don't matter.'

Also in a letter:

'Puerto Cabello where I was ashore about twelve hours. In La Guayra[1] as I went up the hill and had a distant view of Caracas, I must have been two and a half to three days. It's such a long time ago! And there were a few hours in a few other places on that dreary coast of Venezuela.'

The contraband part of the voyage was an adventure after Conrad's own heart and, looking back on it in *The Arrow of Gold*, he acknowledges for the first time the tropical splendour of the West Indies. His eyes after his return were 'full of it'; while his 'experiences, lawful and unlawful', had 'their charm and their thrill; for they had startled me a little and had amused me considerably'.

Besides the pleasurable excitement he experienced from

---

[1] Immortalised in the fictional world in *Westward Ho!*

the dangerously illicit traffic of the voyage, Conrad gathered during his three or four days in Venezuela the material for two of his novels—*Romance* and *Nostromo.*

Romance, a romantic adventure story, charged with melodrama, was written in collaboration with Ford Madox Hueffer. *Nostromo* is a prodigy of imagination working on rapidly registered impressions, probably developed by reading up the subject. In it the Hispano-American atmosphere of an imaginary South American Republic becomes a torrid glare, illuminating in lurid detail seaboard, town, islands, mountains, railway, silver mine, Hispano aristocrats, and half-breed desperadoes.

The other circumstance of the voyage destined to prove of major importance to Conrad in his literary career was the presence on board, as one of the ship's officers, of Dominic Cervoni. A great imposing figure of a man, he was to exercise over the impressionable youth a peculiar fascination, to become his mentor in sea-training and his ideal of a romantic hero. In this capacity, Dominic became the prototype of Nostromo (the megalomaniac hero of the book), the model of Peyrol (the retired privateer of *The Rover*), and of Attilio (the pro-Napoleon smuggler agent of *Suspense*). In *The Arrow of Gold* he appears in his own person.

Dominic Cervoni was a Corsican. A man of middle-age, he had followed the sea—partly in the Navy, partly in the Mercantile Marine—for twenty-five years. In his literary days Conrad had, hanging in the air, as it were, in front of his desk, a nostalgic portrait of Dominic, as described in *The Mirror of the Sea*:

'His thick black moustaches, curled every morning with hot tongs by a barber at the corner of the quay, seemed to hide a perpetual smile. But nobody, I believe, had ever seen the true shape of his lips. From the slow, imperturbable gravity of that broad-chested man you would think he had never smiled in his life. In his eyes lurked a look of perfectly remorseless irony, as though he had been provided with an extremely experienced soul; and the slightest distension of his nostrils would give to his bronzed face a look of extraordinary boldness. This was the only play of feature of which he seemed capable, being a Southerner of a concentrated deliberate type. His ebony hair curled slightly on the temples. . . . On board the *Tremolino,* wrapped up in a black *caban,* the picturesque cloak of Mediterranean seamen, with those massive moustaches and his remorseless eyes set off by the shadow of the deep hood, he looked piratical and monkish and darkly initiated into the most awful mysteries of the sea.'

Characters in novels have often been formed on single or composite models; but Dominic was surely unique in being thus, like a painter's model, the prototype of many characters, as if he represented a Platonic pattern.

On board the *Saint-Antoine* there was also another who was to have an influence on Conrad's future life; a very eventful influence, as it transpired. This was one of the three apprentices in the ship; his name was Cesar Cervoni, and he was a nephew of Dominic.

In the course of the voyage so full of adventurous experiences, the following letter arrived from Uncle Tadeusz:

'You are always restive and careless. You remind me more of the Korzeniowskis than of my dear sister, your mother. I note you have lost your trunk and your belongings. Do you need a nurse or suppose that I am one? Now you inform me that you have lost your family photographs and your Polish books and you want me to send you others. . . .'

However, Uncle Tadeusz sent the photographs and arranged about the Polish books. He was fussy, but reasonable and kindly; providentially so in regard to his nephew's genius in its nonage. A parallel instance is that of Milton's indulgent father. He, however, was wisely indulgent, being cognizant of his great son's character and genius; Uncle Tadeusz, unaware of Conrad's genius, made allowances for the character of his prodigal nephew; he blamed its Korzeniowski strain; with a certain sense of family Bobrowski self-righteousness.

Milton quarrelled with his tutor; Conrad with his banker. On the latter occasion, Tadeusz wrote simply: 'You have probably forgotten the old Polish proverb: "He who is humble benefits in both ways", otherwise you would not have had this quarrel with Monsieur Delestang.'

The awkward affair took place soon after Conrad's return from the Gulf of Mexico, at a time when, after 'letting himself go', during his former period in Marseilles, he was 'going the pace'—at least, he had begun to accelerate in that way. He had not re-embarked in the *Saint-Antoine*, but her gun-running excursion that he had found so amusing had excited in him a desire for more of such dare-devil adventure, and an opportunity for the very thing, as it happened, was near at hand.

It was to occur in consequence of the Carlist rising in Spain, which engaged the sympathies of the Legitimists in Marseilles. Conrad, before leaving for the West Indies, had heard sympathetic talk among these people about the 'king', *Rey netto*, Don Carlos de Bourbon, the Pretender to the Spanish throne. At the time of his return to Marseilles, the Carlist rebellion was far spent, but there was still time for what he wanted, gun-running.

Conrad's chance of engaging in gun-running did not arise at once, however, and—in a pet of money and other difficulties, as Jean-Aubry suggests—he wrote to his uncle, saying that he was going to join the Carlist forces. His uncle responded by threatening to stop his allowance.

Meanwhile, the impetuous youth—he was now about nineteen years old—mixed much in Legitimist society; more, no doubt, in the cafés than in the *salons*. The mental atmosphere in the *salons* tended to the sentimental— towards the *eikon* of the princely, manly-bearded Don Carlos; in the cafés it would be more robust. And in a café, one day, Conrad met (as usual when something was going to happen to him) an Englishman.

This was a very different sort of Englishman from the

two he had met previously on momentous occasions. He was 'narrow-chested, tall, and short-sighted'; and was seen most characteristically when out walking in the streets and lanes, with his 'long feet projecting far in advance of his body, and his white nose and gingery moustache buried in an open book'. That he was both a poet and a gun-runner is not so strange, since poetry appeals to adventurous hearts. The old Norse pirates had a great liking for it.

The name of the Englishman is on record merely as Henry C—: Henry C—, having broken loose from his family in a 'well-to-do London suburb, introduced himself meekly to strangers as a "black sheep".' He was regarded in Legitimist circles, however, as a 'lion'.

The function of poetry, as has often been asserted, is purely to give pleasure, and Henry C— took part in gun-running, as he read poetry, for the 'thing-in-itself'; for the pleasure he derived from it; the pleasure of dangerous, unlawful adventure; the lure of gambling for high stakes —life or limb, or the horrors of a Spanish prison.

He was not disappointed. His case is a conspicuous disproof, in fact, of Conrad's erroneous assertion that 'no adventure ever came to one for the asking'. Fortune favours the brave, and Henry C— had had to swim for his life; he had had to scuttle ashore from his gun-runner craft in the Gulf of Gascony while she was being blown to pieces by a Spanish gunboat.

It was for this gallant escape that he had been lionized in the *salons*, and, as it was of recent occurrence and the repute of it had accompanied him hot-foot from Gascony, the meek and self-depreciatory way in which he introduced himself to strangers was the more fascinating. Conrad was chiefly attracted, when they met, by the adventurous gun-runner's quiet composure.

THE TRAGEDY OF CONRAD

THE TRAGEDY OF CONRAD

i

THE meeting between Conrad and Henry C— was
not a fortuitous one; as Conrad himself tells us, in
Tho Arrow of Gold, where Henry C— is 'Mills'.

'At the time of the meeting in the café, Mills had
already gathered in various quarters a definite view of
the eager youth who had been introduced to him in
that ultra-Legitimist *salon*. What Mills had learned
represented him as a young gentleman who had arrived
furnished with proper credentials and who apparently
was doing his best to waste his life in an eccentric
fashion with a bohemian set . . . making friends with
the people of the Old Town, pilots, coasters, sailors,
workers of all sorts. He pretended rather absurdly to be
a seaman himself and was already credited with an ill-
defined and vaguely illegal enterprise in the Gulf of
Mexico. At once it occurred to Mills that this eccentric
youngster was the very person for what the Legitimist
sympathisers had very much at heart just then, to
organise a supply by sea of arms and ammunition to
the Carlist detachments in the South. It was precisely
to confer on that matter with Doña Rita that Captain
Blunt had been despatched from Headquarters.

'Mills got in touch with Blunt at once, and put the
suggestion before him. The Captain thought this the
very thing.' (Conrad observes that they 'did not give a
single thought to his flesh and blood.')

This extraordinary business, the selection of a youth
not out of his 'teens for such an enterprise, proved, in
effect, the starting-point of Conrad's adventurous career,
of which his voyages to the West Indies were preliminary;

81

while, in his literary course, it produced the delightful narrative of what ensued, the story of the gun-running *Tremolino*, a great factual short-story related in *The Mirror of the Sea*; as also, its elaborated sequel, *The Arrow of Gold*.

The *Tremolino* was a 'balancelle' (a Mediterranean craft akin to the picturesque felucca) 'of 60 tons with two short masts raking forward and two curved yards each as long as her hull, a true child of the Latin lake, with a spread of two enormous sails resembling the pointed wings on a sea-bird's slender body, and herself, indeed, like a bird, skimming rather than sailing the seas'. She was purchased by a syndicate composed of Henry C—, J. M. K. Blunt, Roger P. de la S— and Conrad himself. They used to meet, when the enterprise was set going, in a tavern on the quays to plan the successive voyages.

Henry C— introduced himself, as I have said, meekly as a 'black sheep'; but J. M. K. Blunt, of North Carolina, described himself as *Américain, Catholique, et Gentilhomme*.[1]

Blunt was, in truth, all three; that is to say, in the restricted sense which he himself attached to the words. He further declared, 'I live by my sword' (he eventually died by it, as Conrad tells us). In short, he was an 'adventurer'; an 'adventurer' as distinguished from a lover of adventure like Conrad and Henry C—. Conrad describes him as 'keen of face and elegantly slight of body, a distinguished aspect, with a fascinating drawing-room manner and with a dark, fatal glance'. The American *gentilhomme* was closely allied in his capacity of adventurer with his mother; virtually united, in fact, in a predatory combination of self-seeking and self-assured pretentiousness. Mother and son, as described in *The Arrow of Gold*, leave the same kind of impression of coldly ruthless pride as is left after reading about Mark Twain's *gentilshommes américains* in *Huckleberry Finn*.

The fourth member of the syndicate, Roger P. de la S—,

---

[1] Similar terms to those in which Conrad described himself at the age of five. See p. 22.

was a Provençal squire, descended from Vikings and looking like one; 'authoritative, incisive, wittily scornful', with a taste for writing comedies. He was hopelessly in love with his 'beautiful cousin, married to a hide and tallow merchant'. She had a Carlist *salon*, where a 'possibility' of raising Catalonia in the interest of the *Rey netto* was much discussed, and the gun-running syndicate was probably promoted.

ii

All four 'owners' of the *Tremolino* appear to have been more or less impecunious, and Conrad admits that a banking-house was 'concerned' (presumably in subsidising them)—a 'very respectable banking-house'. Also financially helpful to the cause were the ladies of the *salons*.

The most important of these, the wealthiest, and the one who exercised the greatest emotional influence on the syndicate, was the original of Doña Rita, the heroine of *The Arrow of Gold*. She is there described as having an 'indefinable quality of charm beyond all analysis' (which) 'made you think of remote races, of strange generations, of the faces of women sculptured on immemorial monuments and of those lying unsung in their tombs'. In fact, she inspired the feeling that there was in her 'something of the women of all time'.

On the occasion, however, when Conrad—who was just going to be introduced to the bewitching Rita—was thinking of her in such visionary and idealistic terms, she, as if to discourage such illusions, 'treated us to an exhibition of teeth as dazzling as Mr Blunt's and looking even stronger'.

In *The Mirror of the Sea* she is described as having 'something of a lioness in the expression of her courageous face (especially when she let her hair down), and with the volatile little soul of a sparrow dressed in Parisian feathers. . . .'

Rita, the beautiful daughter of a Basque peasant, had attracted the notice of a magnificent and exceedingly wealthy recluse—Henry Allègre. He was an artist and connoisseur as well as a Crœsus and a solitary, and he had annexed her for his collection of *objets d'art*. He had taken her over, it was said—probably at vast expense—from no less a personage than Don Carlos himself. Conrad fell passionately in love with her. J. M. K. Blunt wished to marry her, and his mother[2] took an occasion to impress upon Conrad the great advantage, socially, it would be to Doña Rita (who was not received in the *salons*) to ally herself with so aristocratic a family as the Blunts. The American gentlewoman was dressed exquisitely in mourning, which she wore because her husband—whom she stated to have been one of the Presidents of the United States[3]—was 'still dead'. She talked to Conrad for a long time, appealing to him, on the strength of the great love he had for Doña Rita, to withdraw from the contest. She had heard that he had been to the West Indies, and she suggested that he should go there again.

Mme. Blunt, as the self-styled wife of a President of the United States of America, naturally took a practical view of life. Her son, J. M. K. Blunt, had no money; her desiderated daughter-in-law, Doña Rita, had no aristocracy; it ought, therefore, to be obvious to Conrad, she implied, that it was his duty to stand aside and not obstruct their union in matrimony.

But Mme. Blunt, although she put an edge on her words, was really obtuse; she did not know whom she was talking about. Doña Rita was not prevented from marrying Blunt by the suit of Conrad or by any other lover. Also, she did not care about social standing, and did not want to attend the *salons*. She was virtually outside all the artificial and conventional circles of life, the codes and institutions of mundane society. Rita remained natural, spontaneous, unsophisticated; it was as if Henry Allègre, in adding her to his collection, had preserved her unspoilt, unsullied—as if she had been kept in some psychological cabinet. Inevitably seductive, she yet betrayed an aversion to erotic sentiment; an aversion perhaps promoted by the pertina-

---

[2] Jean-Aubry traces her to the *Souvenirs* of Judith Gautier.
[3] Repudiated by Judith Gautier in *Le Second Rang du Collier*.

cious advances in her girlhood of her cousin, an uncouth, repugnant boy.

The way in which she reacted to sexual advances is illustrated in the following passage:

Conrad—or Monsieur George, as he calls himself in the book—is about to embark in the *Tremolino,* and Rita, in taking leave of him, implies that she will not see him again.

' "But it is true that you will go. You will surely. Not because of those people but because of me. You will go away because you feel you must."

'With every word urging me to get away, her clasp tightened, she hugged my head close to her breast. I submitted, knowing well that I could free myself by one more effort which it was in my power to make. But before I made it, in a sort of desperation, I pressed a long kiss into the hollow of her throat. And lo—there was no need for any effort. With a stifled cry of surprise her arms fell off me as if she had been shot. I must have been giddy, and perhaps we both were giddy, but the next thing I knew there was a good foot of space between us in the peaceful glow of the ground-glass globes. . . .'

It was in keeping with this asexual state that she was capable of becoming, in the old-fashioned term, a 'tom-boy', as on the occasion related in *The Mirror of the Sea*:

'. . . one evening, entering incautiously the *salon* of the little house just after the news of a considerable Carlist success had reached the faithful, I was seized round the waist and whirled recklessly three times round the room, to the crash of upsetting furniture and the humming of a waltz tune in a warm contralto voice.

'When released from the dizzy embrace, I sat down on the carpet—suddenly, without affectation.'

Another aspect of Doña Rita is indicated in the same work, in the words:

'She was always taking little houses for somebody's good, for the sick or the sorry, for broken-down artists,

cleaned-out gamblers, temporarily unlucky speculators
—*vieux amis*—old friends, as she used to explain
apologetically, with a shrug of her fine shoulders.'

To Conrad, Doña Rita's main characteristic, subtly
united with the child-like quality he felt in her, was that
which first impressed him—that she was a universal; a
'woman of all time'. Here is another expression of this
feeling:

'She listened to me unreadable, unmoved, narrowed
eyes, closed lips, slightly flushed face, as if carved six
thousand years ago in order to fix for ever that something secret and obscure which is in all women. Not
the gross immobility of a sphinx proposing roadside
riddles but the finer immobility, almost sacred, of a fate-
ful figure seated at the very source of the passions that
have moved men from the dawn of ages.'

With all this, the patroness of the *Tremolino* venture
possessed powers of intelligence well suited to superintend,
no less than to inspire, the Carlist enterprise.

iii

In due course, the ship itself was put into efficient service.
The *padrone* was Dominic Cervoni, and Conrad—the only
sea-going member of the syndicate—acted and, at the
same time, went on acquiring seamanship, under his
direction.

The craft was, officially, a 'fruit and corkwood trader',
and her usual destination was a concerted landing-place in
the Baie de Rosas. There, at certain times, Conrad had
to deliver to Aragonese muleteers 'humbly affectionate
messages' from Doña Rita to her uncle, a zealous Carlist
parish priest. The success of the syndicate's plans depended largely, in fact, upon these messages from the
Royalist beauty to the Aragonese priest. They, together
with the contraband guns, were secretly transported
inland. Other information needful for success and com-
parative security (but still permitting of adventurous
risks) was obtained from Custom-house officials, suborned

with great expenditure of gold, and also from key-persons on a higher level. The most important part of this information related to the positions and movements of patrol craft.

Included among the ship's complement was Cesar Cervoni, Dominic's degenerate nephew. Dominic sincerely apologised for bringing that young man aboard. Cesar was, in fact, a miscreant:

' "Some cursed witch must have stolen my brother's child from the cradle and put that spawn of a starved devil in its place," Dominic would say to me. "Look at him! Just look at him!"

'To look at Cesar was not pleasant. His parchment skin, showing dead white on his cranium through the thin wisps of dirty brown hair, seemed to be glued directly and tightly upon his big bones. Without being in any way deformed, he was the nearest approach which I have ever seen or could imagine to what is commonly understood by the word "monster" . An utterly, hopelessly, depraved nature was expressed in physical terms. . . . You imagined him clammily cold to the touch, like a snake. The slightest reproof, the most mild and justifiable remonstrance, would be met by a resentful glare and an evil shrinking of his thin dry upper lip, a snarl of hate to which he generally added the agreeable sound of grinding teeth.

'It was for this venomous performance rather than for his lies, impudence, and laziness that his uncle used to knock him down. It must not be imagined that it was anything in the nature of a brutal assault. Dominic's brawny arm would be seen describing deliberately an ample horizontal gesture, a dignified sweep, and Cesar would go over suddenly like a ninepin. . . . But, once down, he would writhe on the deck, gnashing his teeth in impotent rage . . . which was pretty horrible to behold. And it also happened more than once that he would disappear completely—which was startling to observe. This is the exact truth. Before some of those majestic cuffs Cesar would go down and vanish. He would vanish heels over head into open hatchways, into scuttles, behind up-ended casks, according to the place where he happened to come into contact with his uncle's mighty arm.'

But this incessant knocking-down at length aroused the devil in Cesar—the inveterate devil of the Cervoni family. It had formerly come up in his father when he shot a man, one day. Cesar's father had had no personal cause of ill-will against the man, but there was a vendetta—a very old vendetta—between their respective families and, going home with his gun on his shoulder, he was irritated by the placid, contented way in which the man was enjoying his evening meal as he sat by the wall of his house. His ancestral dead cried out to him.

He crouched down behind a wall of stones, and just gave the man notice by shouting out before taking deadly aim, that a bullet was coming his way. And 'as the other looked up innocently he took aim at the forehead and squared the old vendetta account so neatly that', according to Dominic, the dead man 'continued to sit with the bowl of broth on his knees and the piece of bread in his hand'.

Dominic's view of the incident was that his brother had heard and unquestioningly obeyed ancestral voices : 'All our dead cried out to him,' he explained. His view of what Cesar did in response to the devil he had raised up in him will transpire in due course and, as best expressed, in his own words.

His treatment of his nephew is explicable; not justifiable. He was proud of his family, the Cervoni's of Corsica, and Cesar Cervoni—as Conrad has suggested—was a 'monster'; so much a monster, he might have been the family devil's very incarnation.

Now, monsters require special treatment. There was a story popular among young readers in Victorian times—it was entitled *Seagull Rock*—in which one of these unfortunate creatures was induced by special treatment to perform an act of heroic gratitude. Monsters may well possess, like certain wild beasts, instinctive virtues. It is true that the classic monster, Caliban in *The Tempest*, abused his benefactor's benevolence; yet he did so under great provocation: he had only acted, in Blake's phrase, 'from instinct'; as Prospero, exalted philosopher as he was, ought to have understood. Instead of that, he sentenced Caliban like a common magistrate, and converted him from a natural creature into a criminal. Caliban conspired. Dominic maltreated Cesar; Cesar likewise conspired.

He was more astute, however, than Caliban and his conspiracy was a success. The notion came to him probably when he was knocked down on the eve of the *Tremolino's* final voyage. On this occasion, upon being knocked down, he went clean over into the harbour. Dominic gave him a rope's end to hang on to, while he resumed his conversation with Conrad that had been interrupted by the incident. After a while he got up from the deck on which he had been seated, and hailed a boatman on the quay. He directed him to fish Cesar out of the harbour, and the latter returned on board 'shivering, streaming with filthy water, with bits of rotten straws in his hair and a piece of dirty orange-peel stranded on his shoulder. His teeth chattered; his yellow eyes squinted balefully at us as he passed forward'.

Conrad thought it his duty to remonstrate. 'Why are you always knocking him about, Dominic?' he asked.

iv

The subsequent voyage was an important one, played for a high stake; and, before venturing upon its most dangerous stage, it was found necessary to 'look into Barcelona for certain definite information'. This was duly obtained from the Custom-house officer on a piece of paper which, after officially poking into a 'layer of oranges' in the hatchway, he slipped into Dominic's hand as he was going ashore. A 'few hours afterwards, being off duty, he returned on board again athirst for drinks and gratitude,' and asserted, while enjoying them, that the guarda-costa they feared was well out of the way, 'lying at anchor, with her sails unbent, painting yards and scraping spars'. He departed, 'smirking reassuringly over his shoulder'.

But Cesar had been missing all day. At last, after Dominic had gone ashore to seek him, he was seen returning without his coat which, it was assumed, he had sold for pocket money. Where he had been was a puzzle, and nothing could induce him to say. He only gnashed his teeth; and did not 'shrink an inch before the sweep of Dominic's arm. He went down as if shot, of course. But this time . . . when picking himself up, he remained longer than usual on all fours, baring his big teeth over his shoulder and glaring upwards at his uncle with a new sort of hate in his round yellow eyes.'

The question as to where he had been during that long day ashore was answered on the following morning when, after stealing out of Barcelona at dusk, they were well on their course. This was the really dangerous part of the enterprise, but everything seemed as it should be. The wind was favourable, but gusty, and the balancelle, sailing at her maximum speed, seemed 'to hardly touch the great bursts of foam over which she darted'. Several sail were in sight and, among them, Conrad curiously remarked one in particular. The craft appeared directly in their wake, where the 'press of canvas she carried made her loom up high like a grey column standing motionless'. Conrad pointed her out to Dominic in a casual way; but he, standing in the stern, regarded her intently for a long time. At length, he gave Conrad a shock by saying:

'He has come out here to wash the new paint off his yards I suppose.'

The ship was the guardacosta, and they had been betrayed.

Conrad recovered his equanimity, however, when he considered the great speed the *Tremolino* was making, and the apparent impossibility of her being overtaken by her pursuer. The balancelle could easily keep her distance until night-fall, and then they could haul off to seaward and consider the situation.

For all that, there remained an element of risk, a spice

of romantic adventure—a spice indeed; for what could be more thrilling to a young gun-runner like Conrad, who had read Marryat, than a chase at sea?

The weather had grown stormy, with blustering winds and squalls of rain and hail, and this, as Dominic remarked, was in the guardacosta's favour, as she was three times the size of the *Tremolino*.

But Dominic spoke absently; his 'thoughts seemed to stumble in the darkness of some not solved enigma'.

There were, at that time, aboard the *Tremolino* as she was swept onward in the hurricane, four distinct states of thought and feeling. There was Conrad's: excited, but unquestioningly reliant in the presence of his great monitor (such characters seem, on occasions, to take upon themselves the attributes of fate). There was Dominic's fierce bitterness as he cogitated within the darkness of his hood. There was the gloomy preoccupation, in general, of the men, who had discovered the nature of the pursuing craft as she was lit up by a gleam of sunshine. From that moment, they had 'no eyes and no thought', writes Conrad, 'but for the slight column-shape astern of us. Its swaying had become perceptible. For the moment she remained dazzlingly white, then faded away slowly to nothing in a squall, only to reappear again, nearly black, resembling a post stuck upright against the slaty background of solid cloud.'

Finally, there was Cesar's state of mind.

At length, Dominic emerged from his dark cogitations. As if he were a sort of nautical Sherlock Holmes in a night-sitting, he had been puzzling out the problem of the guardacosta—how she came to be where she was when they sighted her—and he explained to Conrad that, but for a fortunate miscalculation, she would have been lying in ambush for them on the other side of Cape San Sebastian, which they were now approaching, ' "and"—he snapped his teeth like a wolf' close to Conrad's face— ' "she would have had us like—that".'

The ship had come out 'on information'. This could not be doubted. But in what conceivable circumstances could that information have been given? 'Why?' cried Dominic. 'How? What for?' (He did not ask, 'By whom?') 'We always paid them so well on shore. . . . No! but it is my head that is going to burst.'

'No!' but he knew the truth was 'Yes'—that the answer to the questions, 'Why?' 'How?' 'What for?' was implicit in and was resolved by his unuttered, 'By whom?' *Cesar*; it was by *Cesar*, his own nephew, his blood-relation, a Cervoni! *Cesar, that spawn! Cesar* had given the information! *Cesar* had betrayed him and, through him, Conrad! As in a dream of an instant's duration, a whole scene of action takes place; so in Dominic's brain there was exhibited the appalling *dénouement*. An access seized him. He 'seemed to choke, tugged at the throat button of the cloak, jumped up open-mouthed as if to hurl curses and denunciation. . . .' Instantly he checked himself; the exertion must have been as a desperate wrenching hold upon the tiller of his will. But he regained control at once and, having sat down again on the deck, he was soon talking with Conrad quite calmly.

v

In all this time, the pursuing guardacosta had scarcely gained at all upon her quarry, and Dominic confirmed Conrad's assurance that they would get clean away. The fleet *Tremolino*, with her great sails outspread like vans, was as a bird-creature; one as native to its element, the sea, as the fabulous man-conveying roc was native to its Arabian skies, or like an angel, as Conrad has described the ship he loved so well. And as an angel of salvation he may well have regarded her in that perilous time—unmindful of 'Inexorable Fate'.

The end came quickly. The devil of the Cervonis—the devil who in Dominic's brother, Cesar's father, had masqueraded as ancestral loyalty—the devil whom Dominic had awakened in Cesar by continually knocking him down —was a circumspect, far-seeing devil. The vengeful demoniac had not failed to take into account the *Tremolino's* capacity for speed, and Cesar had managed on some clandestine occasion to cut the roping stitches of the mainsail. He had not, however, cut enough of them; not enough to prevent it from holding out even through the gusts and squalls—as long, that is to say, as the ship sailed directly on the open sea.

After Conrad's talk with Dominic, however, she approached the Cape, and it became necessary to stand in and steer close along the shore to avoid an adverse current. As they came round into the shelter of the bluff, the wind failed completely, the sails hung dead; the returning gust blew half of the mainsail clean out of the bolt-ropes.

The whole obstruction was thrown overboard and, in a 'fierce breeze and in much smoother water', the ship sailed on under the single sail that was left to her. But the guardacosta gained on her frightfully; and now the element of risk, the spice of romantic adventure, was changed in Conrad's imagination to stark realism. Even when the pursuer was hidden by the squalls, we 'felt her there', he writes, 'like a knife at our throats'.

An hour and more passed; in the course of which it came home to Conrad how intense was his feeling for the *Tremolino*.

'They will get the poor barky,' he stammered out suddenly, almost on the verge of tears.

Dominic answered in a whisper:

'*Il faut la tuer.*'

Conrad's heart began to beat violently. That was it! *She must be killed.*

Dominic continued:

'You love her well?'

'I do.'

'Then you must find the heart for that work, too. You must steer her yourself, and I shall see to it that she dies quickly, without leaving as much as a chip behind.'

So it was resolved. Dominic 'knew of a rock', where the *Tremolino* could be 'killed', even as the beautiful brig in Conrad's *Freya of the Seven Isles* was to be killed.

In the meantime, they had to exercise caution. There was treachery on board. They had not seen Cesar for some time—not since the beginning of the chase, in fact; but Conrad, upon leaving Dominic, saw the dreadful youth stretched out at full length 'face down' on the deck near the foremast. They must be wary, also, lest any suspicion of their project to wreck the ship should arise among the men. They must be vigilant. 'A knife drawn across the fore halyards', Dominic had whispered, 'would bring the foresail down, and put an end to our liberty in twenty minutes'. The gloom among the men had become total; their faces were 'all turned one way to watch the chaser'. None of them had eaten that morning, but they had been 'coming constantly to drink at the water-butt'.

Conrad hastened down to the cabin to get ten thousand francs in gold which he had secreted in his locker. He discovered that it had been rifled. When, in an undertone, he told Dominic, who alone knew of the cache, the strong man began to tremble violently. 'What did you want to do with it?' he asked.

' "Put it round my waist, of course," I answered, amazed to hear his teeth chattering.

' "Cursed gold!" he muttered. "The weight of the money might have cost you your life, perhaps." He shuddered. "There is no time to talk about that now".'

He stood waiting. Conrad was ready. The squall they expected came at last. The pursuer, 'overtaken by a sort of murky whirlwind', disappeared. The *Tremolino* bounded forward.

'*Prenez la barre, monsieur,*' said Dominic in an austere voice. Then he called loudly to the steersman; 'Let the signorino take the tiller, and you with the others stand by to haul the boat alongside quickly at the word.'

Having thus disposed of the men by diverting their attention, Dominic went forward, paused to look down at the prostrate Cesar, and dived out of sight under the foresail.

Conrad could see nothing ahead; the huge sail screened the view. But he had his orders and, when the word of command came in a whisper, he obeyed at once.

'Now, signorino!'

He bore hard upon the tiller. The faint call came again and, held straight to her course, the *Tremolino* sped onward in her voyage of death. Conrad set his teeth. At one moment, there was the 'rush and the soaring swing of speed: the next a crash, and death, stillness—a moment of horrible immobility, with the song of the wind changed to a strident wail, and the heavy waters boiling up. . . '. Conrad had a sight of the foreyard swinging fore and aft, the panic of the men, fallen in a heap, cursing, and hauling at the boat-line. Cesar was among them—Conrad saw the sweep of Dominic's arm. Next moment the tiller, which he had let go, 'caught him a crack under the ear', and he saw no more.

When he regained consciousness, which was a few moments later, he found himself in the dinghy, with Dominic's arm round his shoulders. The boat was driving before the wind, steadied by two men with their oars.

The country in which they landed was familiar to them, and they at once began to make their way inland. Dominic carried an oar; there was a stream they would have to cross and the pole of the punt was sometimes found missing. At the same time, he assisted Conrad, in his weak state, up to the higher ground. At the top of a ridge, where they paused to rest, Conrad, looking back over the empty shore, observed that not a 'chip' of the *Tremolino* remained above water, but 'in the centre of the thinning squall, phantom-like, under a frightful press of canvas, the unconscious guardacosta dashed on, still chasing to the northward'.

'Dominic,' Conrad cried, 'where's Cesar?'

'As if repulsing the very sound of the name, the *padrone* made that ample, sweeping, knocking-down gesture.'

But he did not speak at once. It seemed that words alone were not enough; there was required the concomitant of effective dramatisation. Dominic's preparations on this account were elaborate. He planted the oar he had laid down, upright in the soft soil. He then proceeded in a leisurely manner to roll up his right sleeve, baring his great forearm, which he extended before Conrad's face.

' "This", he began, with extreme deliberation, whose superhuman restraint vibrated with the suppressed violence of his feelings, "is the arm which delivered the blow. I am afraid it is your own gold that did the rest. I forgot all about your money. . . . I forgot, I forgot," he repeated disconsolately.'

'Cesar stole the belt?' Conrad stammered out.

'And who else? *Canallia!*' cried Dominic. 'He must have been spying on you for days. And he did the whole thing. . . .'

'And you drowned him,' Conrad said feebly.

'I struck once, and the wretch went down like a stone —with the gold. Yes. But he had time to read in my eyes that nothing could save him while I was alive. And had I not the right—I, Dominic Cervoni, *padrone,* who brought him aboard your fellucca—my nephew, a traitor?'

He pulled the oar out of the ground and helped Conrad carefully down the slope. When the fishing-hamlet they were making for came into view, he stopped.

'Do you think you can make your way as far as the houses by yourself?' he asked.

'Yes, I think so. But why? Where are you going, Dominic?'

'Anywhere. What a question! Signorino, you are but little more than a boy to ask such a question of a man having this tale in his family. Ah! *Traditore!* Whatever made me ever own that spawn of a hungry devil for our own blood! Thief, cheat, coward, liar. . . . But I was his uncle, and so . . . I wish he had poisoned me—*charogne!* But this; that I, a confidential man and a Corsican, should have to ask your pardon for bringing on board your vessel, of which I was *padrone,* a Cervoni, who has betrayed you —a traitor!—that is too much. It is too much. . . .'

He continued to vent the fury of his passion.

At last, he turned and walked away, repeating with violent gestures, '*Canaille! Canaille!*' Conrad, 'trembling with weakness and mute with awe', gazed after him until he vanished, with his oar on his shoulder, up a 'barren, rock-strewn ravine'.

The wrecking of the *Tremolino* is tragic, in the classical sense; while the scene of it in the Baie de Rosas beside Cap Creux has a nomenclatural irony of its own. The effects upon Conrad and upon Dominic were catastrophic. They were very different, of course. Dominic, a powerfully-formed character, was blinded morally by the shock caused by Cesar's treachery to his egotistical pride; in Conrad's words, his 'moral entity was destroyed'.

Conrad was bereft, in his own confession, of 'all that was in me of independent life'. By the wrecking of the *Tremolino* he had sustained a total loss; the loss of the ship that had afforded adventures and dangers which alone had made his life bearable by countering with their diverting influence his passion and its pain—the passionate love that had grown up within him for Doña Rita; the pain of what he felt to be its hopeless nature.

Away from the sea, in Marseilles, the pain could become maddening, as when on a recent occasion he had snatched desperately at a mere illusion of support at least, so it is related in *The Arrow of Gold*: he had searched a room, pulled out all the drawers, in the frantic hope that Doña Rita, who had been in there before departing, might have left something, or taken something away, as a sign to him. When the hope ceased, his 'unhappiness became dulled, as the grief of those who mourn for the dead gets dulled in the overwhelming sensation that everything's over, that a part of themselves is lost beyond recall, taking with it all the savour of life'.

When, later on, the hope—or ghost of hope—revived the trouble in his mind became unbearable: 'I remember once getting up at two in the morning to search for a little cardboard box in the bathroom, into which, I remembered, I had not looked before. Of course it was empty; and, anyway, Rita could not possibly have known of its existence.

'I got back to bed shivering violently, though the night was warm, and with a distinct impression that this thing would end by making me mad. It was no longer a question of "this sort of thing" killing me. The moral atmosphere of this torture was different. It would make me mad.'

The gun-running business had latterly fallen into disorganisation through mismanagement at headquarters, and had therefore become the more dangerous—the more dangerous the better from Conrad's point of view; a 'more potent influence', as he writes (in *The Arrow of Gold*), 'like the stronger intoxication of raw spirits'. Twice he escaped narrowly—on the second occasion when, 'sailing quietly at night,' as he relates, 'we found ourselves suddenly near a small coasting vessel, also without lights, which all at once treated us to a volley of rifle fire.

'A volley in the dark after all was not such a bad thing,' he comments bitterly. 'Only a moment before we had received it, there, in that calm night of the sea full of freshness and soft whispers, I had been looking at an enchanting turn of a head in a faint light of its own, the tawny hair with snared red sparks brushed up from the nape of a white neck and held up on high by an arrow of gold. . . . Often I dreamed of her with white limbs shimmering in the gloom like a nymph haunting a riot of foliage and raising a perfect round arm to take an arrow of gold out of her hair to throw it at me by hand, like a dart. It came on, a whizzing trail of light, but I always woke up before it struck. . . . It never had a chance. A volley of small arms was much more likely to do the business. . . .'

Besides affording such a homeopathic, if desperate, palliative for his love-sickness, the *Tremolino* herself had been a help in trouble; she had been an object of aesthetic devotion and pride.

But the *Tremolino* was gone. 'The lurid swiftness of it all', writes Conrad, 'was like a stunning thunder-clap'— and he really was stunned; reduced almost to an automaton.

He continues (in *The Arrow of Gold*):

'. . . one evening, I found myself weary, heartsore, my brain still dazed and with awe in my heart, entering

Marseilles by way of the railway station, after many adventures, one more disagreeable than another, involving privations, great exertions, a lot of difficulties with all sorts of people who looked upon me evidently more as a discreditable vagabond deserving the attention of gendarmes than a respectable (if crazy) young gentleman attended by a guardian angel of his own. I must confess that I slunk out of the railway station shunning its many lights, as if, invariably, failure made an outcast of a man. I hadn't any money in my pocket. I hadn't even the bundle and the stick of a destitute wayfarer. I was unshaven and unwashed, and my heart was faint within me. . . . I slunk on and on, shivering with cold. . . .

'Small objects of no value have the secret of sticking to a man in an astonishing way. I had nearly lost my liberty and even my life, I had lost my ship, a money-belt full of gold, I had lost my companions, had parted from my friend; my occupation, my only link with life, my touch with the sea, my cap and jacket were gone— but a small penknife and a latchkey had never parted company with me. With the latchkey I opened the door of refuge.'

THE BIOGRAPHER INTRUDES

In passing from *The Mirror of the Sea* to *The Arrow of Gold,* as I have done in my last quotation, I would observe that the two books belong to different categories. The former is autobiographical, avowedly so, and is as faithful to fact and circumstance, therefore, as Conrad could make it. So considerable, however, was the pull exerted by his imagination that, even in that work, allowance must be made for some fictional leeway.

The Arrow of Gold, on the other hand, is not an autobiographical work *per se*; it is an autobiographical novel;

yet one that is probably much closer to fact and circumstance than are ordinary autobiographical novels; for
example, *David Copperfield* or *Moby Dick*. It is assuredly,
from the biographical point of view, Conrad's most important novel.

He himself asserts in his preface to the collected edition
of his works,[4] that, in writing the book, he 'kept strictly
within the limits of unadorned sincerity' and 'invented
nothing'; and he wrote in Richard Curle's copy of *The
Arrow of Gold*, 'All the personages are authentic and the
facts are as stated.'[5]

Yet his language in this preface is elusive and carries,
evidently, a figurative rather than a literal meaning; the
words 'unadorned sincerity' having an essential, not a
formal signification. They would seem to imply that the
work is not a plain chronicle, but a substantial representa-
tion, of events and experiences distilled in the limbec of
memory, modified and collocated by the influence of
imagination—but not by the ingenuity of invention or
artifice. Accordingly, the work is, in the ideal sense,
sincerely true.

In writing *The Arrow of Gold*, Conrad virtually effected
the principle enunciated by Coleridge:

> 'Let each of us, then, relate that which has left the
> deepest impression on his mind, at whatever period in
> his life he may have seen, heard, or read it; but let him
> tell it in accordance with the *present state* of his intellect
> and feelings, even as he has, perhaps (Alnaschar-like),
> acted it over again by the parlour-fireside of a rustic inn,
> with the fire and the candles for his only companions.'

'The subject of this book', writes Conrad in the same
preface, 'I had been carrying about with me for many
years, not so much a possession of my memory as an
inherent part of myself. It was ever present in my mind
and ready to my hand, but I was loth to touch it from
a feeling of what I imagined to be mere shyness but

---

[4] Dent.
[5] *The Last Twelve Years of Joseph Conrad*. (Sampson Low.)

which in reality was a very comprehensive mistrust of myself.

'In plucking the fruit of memory one runs the risk of spoiling its bloom, especially if it has got to be carried into the market-place. This being the product of my private garden, my reluctance can be easily understood; and though some critics have expressed their regret that I had not written this book fifteen years earlier I do not share that opinion. If I took it up so late in life it is because the right moment had not arrived till then. I mean the positive feeling of it, which is a thing that cannot be discussed.'

Conrad's 'positive feeling' is tantamount to Coleridge's 'present state of the intellect and feelings', as above. It also corresponds, of course, to Wordsworth's *desideratum* of 'emotion remembered in tranquillity'.

The aim and object of writing in this memory-refracted manner is to obtain an ideal presentation of reality, to make reality visible and vivid by bringing out its significance, much on the principle of Conrad's own conception of such a thing. He says that the essential meaning of a story is not 'inside, like a kernel, but outside, enveloping the tale, which brought it out, only as a glow brings out a haze'.

In Conrad's sense the 'kernel' of *The Arrow of Gold* consists of the actual events, persons, and circumstances; the 'essential meaning' is in the story's atmosphere, as the essential meaning of an opera, for example, may be said to be in the musical rendering of the subject.

Thus, the essential meaning of *The Arrow of Gold,* from a biographical point of view, is in the romantic medium, or atmosphere, which is brought out by the story of Conrad's passion for Doña Rita, which is its real subject; the 'glow' of this subject brings out the romantic colours of Conrad's self-portraiture; whereas a mere chronicle of events, although more accurate, in a literal sense—as a photograph is more accurate than a portrait—would be merely 'photographic'.

That this passion for Doña Rita was the true subject of *The Arrow of Gold* is patent in this preface, in the words :

'What the story of the *Tremolino* in its anecdotic character has in common with the story of *The Arrow of Gold* is the quality of initiation (through an ordeal which required some resolution to face) into the life of passion. In the few pages at the end of *The Mirror of the Sea* and in the whole volume of *The Arrow of Gold,* *that* and no other is the subject offered to the public. The pages and the book form together a complete record; and the only assurance I can give my readers is, that as it stands here with all its imperfections it is given to them complete.'

Some of the characters in the story bear fictitious names; for example, Rita de Lastaola (Doña Rita)[6] and Mills,[7] who in *The Mirror of the Sea* is Henry C—. He has a fictitious personal appearance, also; as Henry C—, he is lanky; as Mills, 'bulky'. These modifications are not important, except in one case—Conrad, the narrator and chief actor in *The Arrow of Gold,* calls himself therein, 'Monsieur George'. It is the name, he explains, that he is known by among his Carlist associates, and it gives him freedom to expatiate in a seemingly ingenuous way, as under a domino.

This is a stumbling-block to the biographer while, at the same time, it tends to hinder the scenes presented from appearing what they actually are, intensive autobiography, integral influences and impressions 'acted over again' on Coleridge's principle.

After all, Conrad and 'Monsieur George' are identical; the 'same man', as Conrad himself avers; while the two narratives, representing his 'initiation into the life of passion' (the central subject of both) 'form together a com-

---

[6] Her real name is unknown.
[7] Conrad told Jean-Aubry that he had 'given Mills the physical appearance of his great friend, Marwood'. (*Marlow,* the name of Conrad's mouthpiece-character, perhaps had the same source.)

plete record'. In fact, a passage expressive of the subject has been carried over from the one narrative into the other and, as it refers to the actual 'arrow of gold'—Doña Rita's hairpin-ornament—it seems symbolically to transfix both.

In the climactic scenes that follow after Conrad arrives, from the Baie de Rosas, at the 'door of refuge', he, as 'Monsieur George', is the actor. He is also the spectator as he looks back on those scenes in the mirror of memory. But the reader sees him as the participator in those scenes in his own person, under his own name. It seems appropriate, therefore, that he should appear under his own name in the following compendious rendering of those scenes. I have, therefore, referred to him throughout simply as 'Conrad'.

vi

The 'door of refuge' at which Conrad arrived after the wrecking of the *Tremolino* belonged to a house on the Prado. This house was owned by Doña Rita, bequeathed to her by Henry Allègre, together with all his other possessions, and she continued to use it during her visits to Marseilles. It was here that Conrad lodged in the intervals of his voyages in the *Tremolino*.

There were other lodgers also—an old Italian and his two 'dancing daughters', and a Carlist Marquis. J. M. K. Blunt had been one of them but, being a realist, the man who 'lived by his sword' had admitted the fact that his suit of Doña Rita was hopeless and had departed.

The establishment was managed by Doña Rita's sister, Therese; an avaricious, half-demented creature who assumed the proprietorship in her own imaginary right. At the same time, she persecuted Rita with continual requests and admonitions compounded of avarice and false piety, manifesting the utmost solicitude regarding the state of her soul. The woman was more monstrous in a grotesque, sinister way even than Cesar Cervoni; for Cesar was a negatively evil character, reacting from a kind of moral 'inferiority complex', but Therese was positive in her malignity.

In any matter relating to her sister and benefactress, she was ruthless. In fact, she had been in league against her, and this for a long time, with another crazy reprobate, a Basque named Ortega. The man had become the dogging horror of Rita's existence. His persecution had started in her early girlhood when, an uncouth boy, he had pestered her with amorous advances; an experience which may well have produced the aversion to erotic sentiment which was so marked a trait in her character.

The effect upon Ortega himself, however, was very different. This unprepossessing degenerate—pale-faced, red-mouthed, side-whiskers that trembled with his red lips—was afflicted with the passion of a Tarquin. He pursued Doña Rita, in his later life, like a roaring lion. She was so well protected, however, after the time when Henry Allègre had included her among his art treasures, that Ortega could never get near her. At his death, Allègre had left her possessed of means, as it were a fortress of gold; in which she could have become her own protectress. She, however, had come out into the open, in the fervid political field, *por el Rey,* and Ortega had got on her tracks as she flitted about, by becoming a Carlist emissary.

Conrad had heard that Ortega was the dread of Doña Rita's life; her maid, Rose, had told him. One evening, soon after his return to Marseilles, as it happened, he fell in with the man himself: Ortega was on his way to Tolosa, where Doña Rita was reported to be. Conrad, therefore, determined to divert the wretch and, fearful of losing sight of him for a moment, beguiled him to the house on the Prado, to lodge him securely for the night.

In order to render Ortega's security doubly secure, he decided to post himself in a coign of vantage and to remain there vigilant until morning. While seeking such a position, he entered a room which had been for a long time disused. To his amazement, it was brilliantly lit up.

It was a very large room, which Allègre, with consummate luxury and art, had had specially prepared as the private apartment of Doña Rita. She had ceased to use it, but—perhaps out of respect for her benefactor's memory, which was profound—she had left it unchanged.

The light in the room as Conrad entered from outer darkness, seemed dazzling. It proceeded from the candles of an eight-branched candelabra and, amid the 'splendour of marbles and mirrors, of cut crystals and carvings', he caught a glimpse of 'woman's apparel scattered about', while the 'faintest possible whiff of a familiar perfume' made his 'head swim with its suggestion. . . .'

'The silence was profound. Suddenly a voice began to speak:

' "Haven't you tormented me enough today?" it said. . . . "Can't you make up your mind to leave me alone for tonight?" '

It was the voice of Doña Rita. She had heard Conrad enter, but, owing to the position of the sofa on which she lay, was unable to see him, and she had mistaken him for Therese entering in her nightdress to torment her. This was no uncommon occurrence when Therese wanted to talk about Rita's soul and money—the redemption of the one and the condemnation of the other; or, rather, it was probably the other way about—but her pious and avaricious effusions were mixed.

Conrad, meanwhile, stood lost in a state of fascinated abstraction. His astonishment at discovering Doña Rita in the room was succeeded by other feelings. He experienced a deep sense of relief; a profound assurance of security for Rita and himself. She was now, he felt, safe, since she was with him—and he himself was safe because his own existence and hers were indivisible. He was now in a position to protect her. Ortega was there as a ravenous wild beast in the house—there was also Therese, his coadjutor—but Conrad had no fear. Neither was he perturbed by the thought that Ortega would be armed, while he himself carried no weapon.

He had, in fact, a strong disinclination to carrying arms; a congenital disinclination; yet if it had not been for Doña Rita's unexpected return from Tolosa, he would have been obliged, not only to provide himself with a weapon, but

also to use it. It was from the fear of that contingency—
and his fear had been appalling—that he had now been
delivered; for, unable to endure any longer the thought of
the tracking and hounding of the woman he loved, he had
determined to kill Ortega. He had intended to lure him
into some obscure place, kill him quickly, and stand his
trial for murder.

But the burden of his resolve had passed, with the horror
of it, and even the repugnant desire. The sweet tones of
Rita moved Conrad to his very soul; his eyes ran full of
tears. He was 'suddenly at peace with all mankind, with
all nature. He felt as if he 'couldn't hurt a fly'. A gush of
joy welled up in him. He moved round the head of the
couch, and stood and gazed:

'In the wide fireplace on a pile of white ashes the logs
had a deep crimson glow; and turned towards them
Doña Rita reclined on her side enveloped in the skins
of wild beasts like a charming and savage young chieftain
before a camp fire. She never even raised her eyes,
giving me the opportunity to contemplate mutely that
adolescent, delicately masculine head, so mysteriously
feminine in the power of instant seduction, so infinitely
suave in its firm design, almost childlike in the freshness
of detail: altogether ravishing in the inspired strength
of the modelling. That precious head reposed in the
palm of her hand; the face was slightly flushed (with
anger perhaps). She kept her eyes obstinately fixed on
the pages of a book which she was holding with her
other hand. I had the time to lay my infinite adoration
at her feet. . . .'

Conrad's state of happy exaltation, however, was
abridged; for Rita, at length, looking up and beholding
him, took him in her amazement for a vision, perhaps
imagining he had been drowned at sea and she saw his
apparition. But when she realised that it was his actual
presence, she uttered a 'low, awed, "No",' which 'chilled
his blood like an evil omen'.

Nor less chilling, in this sense, was her comment when he told her about the loss of the *Tremolino*:

'I could feel almost happy that it is all over, if you hadn't had to lose your love. Oh, *amigo* George, it was a safe love for you.'

But his true love—his love for Rita, *unsafe,* hopeless—was to receive a more direct discouragement when, re-marking on the circumstance that Therese had not told her of his unexpected return to the house, he said, 'It's very clear she did not mean us to come together again.'

'Neither did I, my dear,' said Rita.

'What do you mean by speaking like this, in this tone, in these words?' Conrad exclaimed. 'You seem to use them as if they were a sort of formula. Am I a dear to you? Or is anybody? . . . Or everybody?'

Rita betrayed her distress at his outburst; but a 'fit of wickedness' came upon Conrad, and he pursued his inter-rogations wildly. 'What are the motives of your speeches?' he inquired. 'What prompts your actions?' And he seems, running on in this way, inwardly to have torn himself to pieces before the fascinating Rita, the woman representa-tive of all women, the cynosure of love, herself un-approachable as its North Star.

After a pause, he continued:

'Why aren't you in Tolosa? You ought to be in Tolosa. Isn't Tolosa the proper field for your abilities, for your sympathies, for your profusions, for your generosities—the king without a crown, the man without a fortune!'

He came down to self-pity at last and, as it happened, mentioned Therese.

'For goodness' sake don't let her come in and find you here,' said Rita—and that is all she did say; except when Conrad, sobered by the matter-of-fact remark, asked whether he should lock both doors:

'Do what you like as long as you keep her out. You two together would be too much for me tonight.'

After locking the doors, Conrad, approaching the couch, sank down on his knees and leaned his forehead on its edge. 'That penitential attitude', he tells us, 'had but little remorse in it. I detected no movement and heard no sound from her. . . . no forgiving hand came to rest on my bowed head. I only breathed deeply the faint scent of violets, her own particular fragrance enveloping my body, penetrating my very heart with an inconceivable intimacy, bringing me closer to her than the closest embrace, and yet so subtle that I sensed her existence in me only as a great, glowing, indeterminate tenderness, something like the evening light disclosing after the white passion of the day infinite depths in the colours of the sky and an unsuspected soul of peace in the protean forms of life.'[8]

When, after getting to his feet, Conrad looked at Doña Rita, he was startled—as innocently and ingenuously startled as when, on a bygone evening, she had recoiled from his impetuous embrace. Her face was 'flushed, her teeth clenched, her nostrils dilated, and in her narrow, level-glancing eyes a look of inward and frightened ecstasy'.

But presently he is comparing her to a phantom mist, while her 'real self' exists only in his own consciousness.

Rita made no response to this mystic notion, remaining silent; and he retorted:

'Just what I expected. You are a cold illusion.'

He felt that he had said something rather foolish, however, and, hastening to modify his conception of Doña Rita as a 'mist', asserted, on the contrary, that she was a 'woman of granite'.

'A doctor once told me', Rita remarked, 'that I was made to last for ever.'

But this prosaic response, this grappling hold of his 'granite' metaphor, was displeasing to Conrad, who, in his vivid, image-making mind, saw it, perhaps, as a rock in a mirrory ocean and Rita clinging to it. At the same time, he would rather have beheld her, no doubt, like Venus, all froth and foam and iridescent spindrift.

---

[8] In Conrad's *The Warrior Soul*, there is a curious variant of this conception: 'his passion appeared to him to flame up and envelop her in blue fiery tongues, from head to foot and over her head, while her soul reposed in the centre like a big white rose.' Cp. the 'kernel' and the 'haze' in Conrad's story-significance conception.

However this may be, he answered in an abstract way. 'But essentially it's the same thing,' he said. 'Granite, too, is insensible.'

Yet the 'woman of granite, built to last for ever', continued to look at the 'glowing logs which made a sort of fiery ruin on the white pile of ashes'.

'I will tell you how it is,' Conrad went on with effusive exposition. 'When I have you before my eyes there is such a projection of my whole being towards you that I fail to see you distinctly. It was like that from the beginning. I may say that I never saw you distinctly till after we had parted and I thought you had gone from my sight for ever. It was then that you took body in my imagination and that my mind seized on a definite form of you for all its adorations—for its profanations, too. Don't imagine me grovelling in spiritual abasement before a mere image. I got a grip on you that nothing can shake now.'

'Don't speak like this,' said Doña Rita. 'It's too much for me. And there is a whole long night before us.'

'You don't think that I dealt with you sentimentally enough perhaps?' Conrad continued. He assured her that he was thinking of her in terms of the most exalted sentiment; 'as clear a flame as ever burned on earth'. 'Is it my fault', he cried, 'that what I had to give was real flame, and not a mystic's incense? It is neither your fault nor mine. And now whatever we say to each other at night or in daylight, that sentiment must be taken for granted. It will be there on the day I die—when you won't be there.'

'She continued to look fixedly at the red embers; and from her lips that hardly moved came the quietest possible whisper: "Nothing would be easier than to die for you".'

This declaration exasperated Conrad. He had asked for the bread of love and been offered a stone—a gravestone. Rita had talked of dying for him—leaving not a ghost— not a *mist*—behind! 'How dare you offer me this char-

latanism of passion!' he cried. 'What has it got to do between you and me who are the only two beings in the
world that may safely say that we have no need of a sham
between ourselves? . . .'

The nocturnal dialogue went on. At length, a request
from Conrad that Rita would not go out of the room until
he told her that she might, startled her.

'What do you mean?' she exclaimed. 'Is there something
in the house then? This is most extraordinary! Stay in this
room? And you, too, it seems? Are you also afraid for
yourself?'

Conrad wished to avoid answering these questions.
Anxious to spare Rita the knowledge that Ortega was in
the house, he repeated a trick that had previously availed;
this was when Rita had asked why he had entered the
room. He had avoided answering that question by side-
tracking it. This time, he was not so successful.

He had seized on Rita's enquiry, 'Are you also afraid
for yourself?' and was dilating—apropos the subject of
being afraid—on his own peculiar aversion to carrying a
weapon. 'I shall go through life', he declared, 'without
as much as a stick in my hand.'

Rita suddenly sat up. 'Don George,' she said, 'I insist
upon knowing who is in my house.'

'You insist! But Therese says it is *her* house.'

The riposte was merely exasperating. 'Had there been
anything handy, such as a cigarette box, for instance.'
says Conrad, referring to a habit of Doña Rita's when pro-
voked, 'it would have gone sailing through the air spouting
cigarettes as it went.'

He compromised by saying that it was a Jacobin who
was in the house.

She complained that he was jesting. Suddenly they were
interrupted. A sound was heard—a faint, indefinite sound,
like a 'metallic rattle'.

This strange occurrence, which was not without its effect
upon Conrad himself, made Rita the more solicitous concerning the 'Jacobin'.

Conrad explained in a whisper (they had both lowered

their voices) that he had brought the Jacobin home with him.

'What for?'

He prevaricated, and she enquired precisely why—for what reason—had he brought the Jacobin into her house.

'I don't know—from sudden affection.'

Conrad was not thinking what he was saying; he was lost in contemplation. 'All I wanted', he says, 'was to keep her in her pose, excited and still, sitting up with her hair loose, softly glowing, the dark brown fur making a wonderful contrast with the white lace on her breast. All I was thinking of was that she was adorable and too lovely for words. I cared for nothing but that sublimely æsthetic impression. It summed up all life, all joy, all poetry! It had a divine strain. I am certain that I was not in my right mind. . . .'

Rita herself recalled him.

'George, come to yourself,' she said in her hushed tone.

'No, it was not from affection,' Conrad whispered, taking up what he had said about the Jacobin, 'it was for the love of you that I brought him here.'

He went on to tell her of his dread intention of murdering the man. In the meantime, the strange metallic sound recurred; and, now, as Rita's mind was trembling on the verge of discovery, of apprehending who it was that Conrad had brought into the house, he told her it was Ortega.

vii

The effect was terrific. Rita, recoiling in her whole being, behaved like a frenzied wild creature; while Conrad exerted his utmost powers to restrain and soothe her, striving at the same time to maintain the precautionary silence in the room. In this he succeeded comparatively well; for Rita's cries, as if she had retained an instinctive prudence, were not loud.

At length, the violent perturbations of her spirits sank to the weakness of a helpless child, and, suddenly still, . . .

she whispered as from an 'abyss of desolation', ' "O! George! No! No! Not Ortega".'

'Yes, Ortega. Well, what of it?' Conrad answered in a tone of complete assurance.

But all her 'moral economy' had 'gone to pieces. Everything was gone except her strong sense of life, with all its implied menaces'; she had become a 'mere chaos of sensations and vitality'.

The only others in the house (the Italian and his daughters being absent) were virtually maniacs: Therese controlled by avaricious greed, Ortega by lustful passion. Therese's greed was concentrated upon the legal acquisition of Doña Rita's house; Rita was the obstruction to this, and Therese, who could not brook an obstruction, would remove her as summarily as she would sweep away rubbish with her housekeeper's broom. All that was needed, she thought, was to bring Ortega in contact with the sororal obstruction. 'Mine—or dead' was Conrad's conception of Ortega's attitude towards Rita. Substitute 'and' for 'or', and we have Therese's standpoint regarding the house: *dead—and mine.*

And Therese would be piously complaisant about her intention. She would assure herself that Ortega had been sent; that Providence had delivered him into her house in order that her just claim to its possession should be properly established.

The spirit of Therese was certainly at work in the house, that night; and Conrad, recovering from the whirl into which his brain had been thrown, could almost smell the odour of her sanctimoniousness. He saw the 'contrasted heads of those two formidable lunatics close together in a dark mist of whispers compounded of greed, piety, and jealousy, plotting in a sense of perfect security as if under the very wing of Providence'.

Also, he saw Ortega with understanding, the 'figure he was, inspiring both pity and fear'. 'I could not deny', he says, 'that I understood, not the full extent but the exact nature of his suffering.'

In that moment of dreadful lucidity, he saw Therese

'pressing with fervour the key into the fevered palm' of the Carlist emissary who, by the forethought of Just Providence, had become her own agent and instrument. That key was the key of the fencing-room, which was usually kept locked, and the fencing-room was adjacent to the room in which Rita slept. The one room opened into the other by the door that Conrad had locked. On the wall of the fencing-room there hung, as decorations, various barbarous weapons, and Conrad deduced that Ortega had entered, and taken one of them down, and, in doing so, had dislodged another, which had fallen. This had caused the metallic rattle they had heard.

Conrad had now a 'sickening vision of the fellow crouching at the key-hole, listening, listening. . . .' It was imperative that Rita should not make a sound; for, though Ortega might have known she was there, if he were to hear her voice, or any other sensuous expression of the woman who had brought to him as a boy 'the curse of the gods', his 'madness would gain strength enough to burst the lock'. Conrad, therefore, watched Doña Rita with anxiety. She was motionless. At length, he watched the door-handle.

Conrad liked adventure, but the present affair had taken a trend which ran counter to his inclination.

'A horrid mistrust of the whole house', he writes, 'possessed me. I saw it in the light of a deadly trap. I had no weapon. . . . I wasn't afraid of a struggle as far as I, myself, was concerned, but I was afraid of it for Doña Rita. To be rolling at her feet, locked in a literally tooth-and-nail struggle with Ortega would have been odious.'

He glanced from the door-handle to look at Rita, and at that moment the word, 'Beloved' sounded 'weak, distinct, piteous, like the last request of the dying'.

It was almost immediately repeated, this time louder, and with such a note of agony as pierced to Conrad's heart. Then, there came, 'positively bellowed', 'Speak, perjured beast!'

A violent shaking of the door-handle followed; then a pause; during which Doña Rita betrayed consternation and dread as to what Ortega would say. She asked Conrad in a whisper what Ortega had said about her when they met.

'He raved,' said Conrad.

'Listen to me. It was all true!'

'I daresay, but what of that?'

Ortega began again, his voice 'stammering words without connection, pausing and faltering, till suddenly steadied it soared into impassioned entreaty, sank to low, harsh tones, voluble; lofty sometimes and sometimes abject.'

After this, the real violence began, with lulls of hopeless bewailing, desperate appeals. It was a violence of raving words accompanied by bangs as Ortega battered wildly at the door.

At one juncture, he remarked—deliberately, as it seemed—'Oh, you know how to torment a man, you brown-skinned, lean, grinning, dishevelled imp, you. Your eyes are hateful and your mouth is hateful, and your hair is hateful, and your body is cold and vicious like a snake— and altogether you are perdition.'

He 'drew a moaning breath' and went on, 'You know, Rita, that I cannot live without you. I haven't lived. I am not living now. . . .'

He proliferated his wrongs. Rita had stolen a boy's soul and passed from one rich pair of arms to another, with her 'tricks'. She had sworn time after time to be his wife.

Then, seized with a suspicion that she was escaping, he darted round into the hall with such celerity that, as if unable to stop in time, he precipitated himself against the other door. 'The shock seemed enough to stun an elephant.' There was silence, a 'low grunt', and Ortega resumed:

'You will have to be my wife . . . you swore you would be and so you will have to be.'

'Yes, every day, for two months,' said Rita in a tone of shrill merriment. 'Sixty times at least, sixty times at least.'

'Be quiet.' Conrad spoke so sharply that Ortega heard. 'Eh?' he said, and was still, listening. He concluded, apparently, that his ears had deceived him and, after a deep sigh, he began in a harsh, melancholy tone:

' "My love, my soul, my life, do speak to me. What am I that you should take so much trouble to pretend that you aren't there? Do speak to me," he repeated tremulously, following this mechanical appeal with a string of extravagantly endearing names, some of them quite childish, which all of a sudden stopped dead: and then after a pause there came a distinct unutterably weary: "What shall I do now?" '

It is conceivable that Ortega, exhausted in all his nerves, would now have collapsed had not Doña Rita behaved, as she did, with hysterical folly. 'Do!' she cried. 'Why, slink off home looking over your shoulder as you used to years ago when I had done with you—all but the laughter.'

This precipitated the climax. Ortega, 'struck dumb for an instant', replied in such scurrilous terms that Rita cried out wildly to prevent Conrad from hearing. Ortega rushed away, screaming to Therese that Rita had got a man in her room. 'Come down,' he yelled. 'Come down, you miserable, starved peasant, come down and see.'

His voice was terrible, with a 'shrill over-note' such as made Conrad certain that if Therese was 'in bed the only thing she would think of doing would be to put her head under the bed-clothes'.

Ortega then dashed back to the door and started shaking it violently.

'It was a double door, very tall, and there must have been a lot of things loose about its fittings, bolts, latches, and all those brass applications with broken screws, because it rattled, it clattered, it jingled; and produced also the sound as of thunder rolling in the big, empty hall.'

The reverberating racket was accompanied by shouting, bellowing. Fiercely Ortega raged. He shook the door with superhuman fury. The whole frenzied being of the man must have agonised in his struggles with that double door, more resistible (had he been Samson himself) than the twin pillars of the Temple of Dagon. He struggled with it as with the portals of his own hell. In fact, the hell of such a man shuts in by shutting out. Conrad makes us see and believe in such a hell, as in *Heart of Darkness* he conducts every Virgil of his readers down into a lower circle of the psychological inferno; for Kurtz, his perverted and lost idealist, is in worse case even than Ortega.

When the desperate exertions of his arms gave out, Ortega still went on shouting. 'He saw it all! He had been decoyed there! He had been decoyed in order to be exposed to this! By this shameless *Catin! Catin! Catin!*'

Doña Rita was laughing helplessly and hopelessly. 'Oh, my dear,' she said to Conrad, 'will you ever consent to speak to me after all this? But don't ask for the impossible. He was born to be laughed at.'

'Yes,' cried Conrad, now as matter-of-fact as Rita had been before. 'But don't let yourself go.'

A tremendously violent, long-sustained onslaught upon the door followed, to be succeeded, after a pause, by a feeble, brief rattling, and Ortega became still.

Suddenly he gave a cry. It was that 'miserable, canting peasant-woman upstairs'. It was she—no doubt, she had consulted her priests—who had made him a laughing-stock. But he would regain his self-respect. 'Let her die first,' he cried, and dashed away. The Atropos that Therese had let loose was returning upon herself. Ortega rushed down the hall. Doña Rita's 'contralto laugh rang out, loud, bitter, and contemptuous'; at the same time, Ortega screamed, 'It hurts! It hurts! It hurts!'

Conrad opened the door. As he did so, there came from the hall the sounds of a groan and a heavy fall.

At the foot of the stairs, Ortega lay on his back in a contorted, curiously flattened position. He was in his shirt-sleeves. One of his legs was raised, and one arm extended at full length on the white-and-black paving, with the palm of his hand upwards and the fingers rigidly spread out.

'He had taken on himself such a distorted shape', says Conrad with a characteristically grotesque fancy, 'that he might have been the mere shadow of Señor Ortega.'

'It was rather fascinating', he adds, using the word in its sinister sense, 'to see him so quiet at the end of all that fury, clamour, passion, and uproar. . . . I had a bizarre notion that he was not to be disturbed.'

Judging by his appearance, Ortega was beyond disturbance, whether produced by himself or arising involuntarily in the depths of his personal hell. In some obscure way he had sustained a gash in his side from the Abyssinian weapon that he had taken from the fencing-room. Elaborately barbaric, with a 'sharp edge and pointed end', it lay beneath him in a pool of blood.

viii

There came the sound of the front door being jarred against the chain, which was not ordinarily used, but which Therese had put up, that evening, to keep Conrad out of the house; for she thought he had gone out early in the evening. It was the old Italian lodger returning, with his two dancing daughters, from the ball. An old, burly, paterfamilias, with a long, white, pointed beard, in a tall hat and a 'respectable overcoat', he made a welcome sight to the nerve-racked Conrad, who let him in—but not without a warning, in his ear, as to what there was lying in the hall.

'Your daughters,' Conrad admonished him.

'Va bene, va bene,' the old Italian said kindly, and, with masterly speed and adroitness, ushered, almost bundled, the two girls through the hall. 'They had no time for more than one scared look over the shoulder.' In 'short-skirted costumes, white stockings, and low shoes, their heads powdered and ear-rings sparkling in their ears', they passed like a flash of revelry beside the ghastly shadow on the floor.

The appearance, however, was deceptive. It was not so ghastly. Señor Ortega was not dead, as Conrad had supposed. The truth was revealed by the old Italian, who, having returned after locking his daughters safely in his rooms, had examined Ortega's wound. The benevolent friend in need was practical in an efficient way—the fruit of venerable experience—and he asked no questions. A doctor whom Conrad had called in when Ortega was removed to a bed and his wound bound up, was similarly unobtrusive. He only asked as he was leaving, 'What was he up to, that imbecile?'

'Oh, he was examining this curiosity,' said Conrad, pointing to the Abyssinian knife.

'Oh, yes, and it accidentally went off,' returned the doctor, satirically, adding, 'I would bet there is a woman somewhere under this.'

Conrad now hastened to Doña Rita, who had not left her room. He found her standing in her nightdress, deathly pale and cold, rigid, apathetic. He hurriedly wrapped her in her long fur coat and tried to persuade her to lie down: but 'not after all this,' she said. 'I couldn't close my eyes in this place. Its full of corruption and ugliness all round, in me, too, everywhere except in your heart, which has nothing to do where I breathe. And here you may leave me. But wherever you go remember that I am not evil, I am not evil.' Conrad answered in his matter-of-fact tone, 'I also think you can't stay in this room.' She should remove, he told her, into his own room. She 'needn't hesitate. . . .'

'No,' she answered. 'It doesn't matter now. He has killed me. The little joy that was in me.'

'He tried to kill himself out there in the hall,' said Conrad; but in this he blundered; Doña Rita consequently refused to set foot in the hall. In vain he assured her that Ortega was no longer there. Eventually, Conrad lifted her in his arms and carried her through the hall himself.

When he had made her as comfortable as possible in his room, she recovered her spirit so much as to remark, when he took the 'arrow of gold' out of her hair: 'Ah! that poor philistinish ornament!'

Conrad told her how vividly that glittering arrow had haunted his dreams. And then he said what we have already read in *The Mirror of the Sea*:

'I dreamed of you sometimes as a huntress nymph gleaming white through the foliage and throwing this arrow like a dart at my heart. But it never reached it. It always fell at my feet as I woke up.'

Rita answered that she was no huntress and no nymph, but ónly a goatherd girl. 'Dream of her no more, my dear,' she said.

Despite the pain and sadness that her last words inflicted on him, he answered pleasantly, and afterwards tried to make her sleep.

'She lay down quietly. I covered her up, looked once into her eyes and felt the restlessness of fatigue overpower me so that I wanted to stagger out, walk straight before me, stagger on and on till I dropped. In the end I lost myself in thought.'

The passage is a remarkable signification of Conrad's vital power. It is a pre-signification also; for, as a writer in his last toiling, ailing days, he behaved precisely like that. Stationary at his desk, or in his arm-chair, his physical energy transubstantiated[9] he worked right on until he lost himself, as it were, in death.

But Doña Rita could not sleep. She was haunted by a horror of Ortega; a horror of herself. 'That voice in my ears,' she cried. 'All true. All true.' Conrad, aroused by her voice, acted with the bold inspiration of tender love and pity. He 'threw away the pillows from which she had risen and sat down behind her on the couch. "Perhaps like this",' he said, resting her head gently on his breast, and so he continued to sit motionless, keeping awake, listening to the ticking of the clock, which 'recorded the moments of her rest'.

But he, too, slept at last—to have a 'tumultuous awakening'. Doña Rita had flung herself out of his arms, and was standing beside the couch.

'Daylight,' she whispered. 'Don't look at me, George. I can't face daylight. No—not with you. Before we set eyes on each other all that past was like nothing. . . . Nothing could touch the Rita whose hand was kissed by you. But now! Never in daylight.'

---

[9] As on the Einsteinian principle that gravitation and force are interchangeable.

Conrad heard her with absolute dismay. A crisis had occurred, he felt; a deadly crisis. He had been changed, in a night, in the ordeals and ecstasies he had experienced in Rita's room. He had entered it a youth; he had left it a grown man; and a 'grown-man's bitterness, informed suspicions, resembling hatred, welled out of my heart'.

'All this means that you're going to desert me again!' he said, 'with contempt'. 'All right. I won't throw stones after you . . . are you going, then?'

He said more, letting himself go, pouring out indignation and scorn in the rage of his despair—even as Ortega had done. The floor seemed to 'heave up and down' before his eyes as Doña Rita moved, with firm steps, towards the door. In his frantic misery, he 'snatched up the arrow of gold from the table and threw it after her'.

'She never looked round. She walked to the door, opened it without haste, and on the landing in the diffused light from the ground-glass skylight, there appeared, rigid, like an implacable and obscure fate, the awful Therese—waiting for her sister. The heavy ends of a big black shawl thrown over her head hung massively in biblical folds. With a faint cry of dismay Doña Rita stopped just within my room.'

'The two women faced each other for a few minutes silently. Therese spoke first. There was no austerity in her tone. Her voice was, as usual, pertinacious, unfeeling, with a slight plaint in it; terrible in its unchanged purpose.

' "I have been standing here before this door all night," she said. "I don't know how I lived through it. I thought I would die a hundred times for shame. So that's how you are spending your time? You are worse than shameless. But God may still forgive you. You have a soul. You are my sister. I will never abandon you—till you die."

' "What is it?" Doña Rita was heard wistfully, "my soul or this house that you won't abandon."

' "Come out and bow your head in humiliation. I am

your sister and I shall help you to pray to God and all the Saints. Come away from that poor young gentleman who like all the others can have nothing but contempt and disgust for you in his heart. Come and hide your head where no one will reproach you—but I, your sister. Come out and beat your breast: come, poor Sinner, and let me kiss you, for you are my sister!"

'While Therese was speaking Doña Rita stepped back a pace and as the other moved forward, still extending the hand of sisterly love, she slammed the door in Therese's face. "You abominable girl!" she cried fiercely. Then she turned about and walked towards me who had not moved. I felt hardly alive but for the cruel pain that possessed my whole being. On the way she stooped to pick up the arrow of gold and then moved on quicker, holding it out to me in her open palm.

' "You thought I wouldn't give it to you. *Amigo,* I wanted nothing so much as to give it to you. And now, perhaps—you will take it."

' "Not without the woman," I said sombrely.

' "Take it," she said. "I haven't the courage to deliver myself up to Therese. No. Not even for your sake. Don't you think I have been miserable enough yet?"

'I snatched the arrow out of her hand then and ridiculously pressed it to my breast; but as I opened my lips she who knew what was struggling for utterance in my heart cried in a ringing tone:

' "Speak no words of love, George! Not yet. Not in this house of ill-luck and falsehood. Not within a hundred miles of this house, where they came clinging to me all profaned from the mouth of that man. Haven't you heard them—the horrible things? And what can words have to do between you and me?"

'Her hands were stretched out imploringly. I said, childishly disconcerted:

' "But Rita, how can I help using words of love to you? They come of themselves on my lips."

' "They come! Ah! But I shall seal your lips with the thing itself," she said. "Like this. . . .".'

It seems a happy ending; and for a time, as we read in the Note appended to the tale, the lovers were indeed happy—happy in a blissful, harmonious way. They betook themselves to an Alpine solitude near the sea, to a little house 'built of dry stones and embowered with roses'. Conrad writes that their state of mind was 'characterised more by a deep and joyous tenderness than by sheer passion. All fierceness of spirit seems to have burnt itself out in their preliminary hesitations and struggles against each other and themselves.' They were in 'exact accord', 'amazingly ingenuous in the practice of sentiment'; and 'less like released lovers than as companions who had found each other's fitness in a specially intense way'. They were as unreserved as children in the 'instant sharing of all thoughts, all impressions, all sensations'. Rita, having once 'renounced her honourable scruples', 'took good care that he should taste no flavour of misgivings in the cup'. She was 'as new to love as he was', but 'being older, it was she who imparted its character to the situation. As to the man, if he had any superiority of his own it was simply the superiority of him who loves with the greater self-surrender.'

ix

According to Stevenson, grief is selfish; but so, too, is happiness. Each is a condition of self-absorption. For a while, the happy pair, engrossed with each other, had no thoughts for anybody else. At length, however, Conrad remembered Dominic, wondering what had become of him and whether he could serve him in any way; and he journeyed to Marseilles in order to find out.

Dominic was away, and Madame Lenore, his inamorata —that 'bright-eyed, nonchalant, and passionate woman'— whom Conrad visited, would not tell him Dominic's whereabouts. She told him, however, that she was making arrangements to dispose of her café before departing to join him.

Later on, Conrad made another visit to Marseilles; this time, on financial business.

But these visits were hazardous. To leave an earthly Eden, once ensconced there, is not wise. Conrad's former visit to Marseilles had passed without harm. He had 'managed to sneak out of the town without being seen by a single soul that mattered', and so regained (with what delight!) his blissful seat. From the second visit, he returned, indeed, but not so safe. 'Inexorable Fate', which always loomed so imminently in his philosophy, entrapped him through his own fault. He ought, after visiting his banker, to 'have taken the very next train out of the town'; he did not do so.

The banker—no other, it would appear, than the old 'frozen-up, mummified Royalist', Monsieur Delestang— received him rather frigidly. He referred casually to the Carlist enterprise, it being the conversational topic of the day, for it had 'collapsed utterly, leaving behind, as usual, a large crop of recriminations, charges of incompetency and treachery, and a certain amount of scandalous gossip'. The banker himself had 'never believed in the success of the cause'; Conrad responded, with truth, that he himself had never cared whether it failed or succeeded.

After leaving the banker, he 'yielded to the temptation to discover what had happened to the house in the street of the Consuls after he and Doña Rita had stolen out of it like two scared yet jubilant children'. He found it in charge of a woman caretaker, put in by Doña Rita's agent; who told him that she had 'been in charge for the last four months; ever since the person who was there before had eloped with some Spaniard who had been lying in the house ill wth fever for more than six weeks'.

If now Conrad had got away, all would have been well; but he 'decided to have a bit of dinner at the Restaurant de la Gare where he felt pretty certain he would not meet any of his friends'. However, a hand was laid gently on his shoulder, and there stood behind him an old acquaintance, a member of the Royalist club, who had been on the watch for him. He was a young man with a cheerful countenance; but he wore a grave and anxious expression as he told Conrad, in a roundabout way, what, he felt, he ought to know; for, he assumed, he couldn't already be aware of it. He, Conrad, had vanished, he pointed out, at the very same time as Madame de Lastaola (Doña Rita) had vanished, and Captain Blunt—'an honourable man, a member of a good club'—on 'three distinct occasions when the name of Madame de Lastaola came up in conversation in a mixed company of men had expressed his regret that she should have become the prey of a young adventurer who was exploiting her shamelessly'. ' "In fact," the young man burst out excitedly, "it is *your* name that he mentions. And in order to fix the exact personality he always takes care to add that you are that young fellow who was known as Monsieur George all over the South amongst the initiated Carlists".'

Thus, it came about that Conrad would be obliged to use a weapon, after all, despite his aversion from carrying one; for the only possible course of action for him to take, in such circumstances, was to challenge Captain Blunt to a duel, and for this he at once made the appropriate arrangements, and returned to Doña Rita.

With her he spent three more days, priding himself on his 'impenetrability' before her and on their 'happiness without a shadow'. On the fourth day he left her.

But Rita, the 'woman of all time', possessed the gift that women of ancient times, deemed prophetesses, possessed; she 'must have had', says Conrad, 'the intuition of there being something in the wind, because on the evening of the very same day on which he left her . . . she was already ensconced in the house in the street of the Consuls, with the trustworthy Rose scouting all over the town to gain information'.

The duel was to take place in a walled garden in the Marseilles countryside. It was a hot summer's day but, in the sultry atmosphere, Conrad felt a tension, an 'earnestness of purpose' that 'lifted the business above the common run of affairs of honour'. This psychological tension was centred in the heart of J. M. K. Blunt. The American gentleman who 'lived by his sword' had evidently formed the intention that Conrad should die by his pistol. He **was** the thrall of jealousy, as Cesar had been the victim of resentment and Ortega of passion. Yet his very jealousy, *qua* jealousy, was perversion; according to Conrad, Blunt did not really love Doña Rita. Rather, he was a lover of himself, captivated by his own distinction of features, elegance of form, aristocracy of manner. Conrad had wounded his self-love by having been preferred by Doña Rita; accordingly, he would kill Conrad—at any rate, severely wound him. Blunt's animus against his rival had been exacerbated in another way—by considerations of the desirable beauty's fortune.

Before the duel began, Conrad defied rigorous regulations by approaching his adversary. He said:

'Captain Blunt, the result of this meeting may go against me. In that case you will recognise publicly that you were wrong. For you are wrong, and you know it. May I trust your honour?'

Blunt bowed slightly.

The word was given. Conrad fired. Blunt's pistol arm dropped powerless by his side; but he did not drop his pistol. He reached for it and grasped it with his left hand, took careful aim, and fired. The bullet penetrated the left side of Conrad's chest.

While he was being driven, at a walking pace, to the town, Doña Rita, from a brougham that had pulled up at the roadside, directed the carriage to follow hers.

Of this Conrad was told later; at the time, and for many days afterwards, he was in a 'hazy and nightmarish' state; in which, like the Ancient Mariner in his trance, he eventually heard two voices in the air.

'This is the second case', said the first voice, 'I have had in this house, and I am sure that indirectly it was connected with that woman. She will go on like this, leaving a track behind her, and then some day there will be really a corpse. This young fellow might have been it.'

'In this case, doctor,' said the second voice, 'one can't blame the woman very much. I assure you she made a very determined fight.'

'What do you mean? That she didn't want to. . . .'

'Yes. A very good fight. I heard all about it. It is easy to blame her, but, as she asked me despairingly, could she go through life veiled from head to foot or go out of it altogether into a convent?'

The voices continued and sank, and the 'shape of a man' went out of the room. Conrad heard the door open and shut, and his own voice bursting out with the words, 'Who is there?'

Mills appeared, approaching his bedside, and Conrad's mind reverted to the consciousness of time, the dimension of events and phenomena. 'How long is it since I saw you last?' he asked the man who, in the beginning, introduced him to Blunt; who, in his turn, introduced him to Doña Rita:

' "Something like ten months,' answered Mills' kindly voice.

' "Ah! Is Therese outside the door? She stood there all night, you know."

' "Yes, I heard of it. She is hundreds of miles away now."

' "Well, then ask Rita to come in."

' "I can't do that, my dear boy," said Mills with affectionate gentleness. He hesitated a moment. "Doña Rita went away yesterday," he said softly.

' "Went away? Why? . . ."

' "Because, I am thankful to say, your life is no longer in danger. And I have told you that she is gone because, strange as it may seem, I believe you can stand this news better now than later when you get stronger".'

x

Conrad fell asleep almost immediately. He awoke to mental anguish. For days Mills attended the bedside patiently, kindly. One day, Conrad asked him whether Doña Rita had ever talked to him about himself. 'She told me, amongst other things,' Mills answered, 'that till she met you she knew nothing of love. That you were to her in more senses than one a complete revelation.'

'And then she went away. Ran away from the revelation,' said Conrad bitterly.

'What's the good of being angry?' Mills said gently. 'You know that this world is not a world for lovers, not even for such lovers as you two who have nothing to do with the world as it is. No, a world of lovers would be impossible. It would be a mere ruin of lives which seem to be meant for something else. What this something else is I don't know; and I am certain that she and you will never find out.'

A few days later, he said:

'Before she left the house she gave me that arrow she used to wear in her hair to hand over to you as a keepsake and also to prevent you, she said, from dreaming of her. This message sounds rather cryptic.'

'Oh, I understand perfectly,' said Conrad. 'Don't give me the thing now. Leave it somewhere where I can find it some day when I am alone. But when you write to her you may tell her that now at last—surer than Mr Blunt's bullet—the arrow has found its mark. There will be no more dreaming. Tell her. She will understand. . . . Tell, me, Mills, what will become of her?'

'She will be wasted,' said Mills sadly. 'She is a most unfortunate creature. Not even poverty could save her now. She cannot go back to her goats. Yet who can tell? She may find something in life. She may! It won't be love. She has sacrificed that chance to the integrity of your life—heroically. Do you remember telling her once that you meant to live your life integrally—oh, you lawless young pedant! Well, she is gone; but you may be sure that whatever she finds now in life it will not be peace. You understand me? Not even in a convent.'

' "She was supremely lovable," said the wounded man, speaking as if she were lying dead already on his oppressed heart.

' "And elusive," struck in Mills in a low voice. "Some of them are like that. She will never change. Mid all the shames and shadows of that life there will always be the ray of her perfect honesty. I don't know about your honesty, but yours will be the easier lot. You will always have your . . . other love—you pig-headed enthusiast of the sea".'

'Then let me go to it,' Conrad cried. 'Let me go to it.'

He 'went to it as soon as he had strength enough to feel the crushing weight of his loss (or his gain) fully, and discovered that he could bear it without flinching. After this discovery he was fit to face anything. He tells his correspondent that if he had been more romantic he would never have looked at any other woman. But on the contrary. No face worthy of attention escaped him. He looked at them all; and each reminded him of Doña Rita, either by some profound resemblance or by the startling force of contrast.

'The faithful austerity of the sea protected him from the rumours that fly on the tongues of men. He never heard of her. Even the echoes of the sale of the great Allègre collection failed to reach him. . . . Then, years later, he was deprived even of the arrow. It was lost to him in a stormy catastrophe; and he confesses that next day he stood on a rocky, wind-assaulted shore, looking at the seas raging over the very spot of his loss and thought it was well. It was not a thing that one could leave behind one for strange hands—for the cold eyes of ignorance. Like the old King of Thule with the gold goblet of his mistress, he would have had to cast it into the sea, before he died. . . .'

But although Conrad thus jettisoned the relic of his lost love, the reality of it, acute and heavy in his heart, remained irremovable. Doña Rita had declared that he would never be able to forget her. She could not, in leaving him, pluck from his memory its rooted sorrow, even had she so desired. She had always intended to leave him in the end, and the happy state that the objectionable Blunt had broken into would have been, in any case, but temporary.

Rita, in virtue, perhaps, of the childlike quality of her nature, was evidently possessed of intuitive power, and this may well have been intensified in her communion with Conrad by the perspicacity of love. The amazing woman, redeemed by Conrad from the limbo of the unknown, ought to be collaterally associated with his fame. She exhibited in her act of self-immolation in abandoning him, a miracle of selfless love; the marvel of being able to detach herself from a lover through whom her own capacity for love, stemmed in her girlhood, had suddenly been released with accumulated force. Nor was that lover of any common or interior mould; the young Conrad, with his burgeoning genius, would have been no unfitting mate for such a woman; the 'woman of all time', an enchantress in person and personality; a Cleopatra surrendering her Antony. She foresaw that if she retained him, made him happy—so blissfully happy as their continued union would have made him—his development would be arrested, even as her own development, from a different cause, had been arrested, and, therefore—'heroically,' as Mills expressed it—she left him, beyond recall.

'Nothing would be easier', she had told him, 'than to die for you'; it seemed so easy to her in comparison with the thing she was going to do—to live for him, without him. She was 'supremely lovable', as Conrad declared from his stricken heart.

And she was supremely perspicacious: for had Conrad continued in his earthly Paradise, his own story would have had a 'happy ending', no doubt, and that would have been all; there would scarcely have been other stories, other novels, and Teodor Josef Konrad Nalccz Korzeniowski would never have become Joseph Conrad.

That is not to say, however, that Doña Rita inspired Conrad's work in the manner that Beatrice inspired Dante. Nor did Conrad's memories of her inform any of the women characters of his novels; as his memory of Dominic Cervoni produced men characters in their pages.

Conrad's heart-sorrow was too deep and too erosive to inspire, in that way. It produced a greater effect; it opened the way for inspiration. The impact of its arrow caused a shock, a psychological convulsion, which laid open the subliminal track of Conrad's genius. It set up in him a chronic state of disturbance, the very contrary to the static equilibrium of a tranquil mind.

The first actual effect it produced was to drive him back to the sea, in any ship, in any condition; to plunge desperately into the hard life of the sea; the probation, as it proved, to the still harder life—as he was to make it—of the pen.

Before he could find a ship, his uncle Tadeusz arrived, after a hurried, worried journey from Kiev, on a visit of investigation. All he knew, all he had learnt, about his nephew's wild doings and his duel with J. M. K. Blunt was contained in a telegram from one, James Fecht, notifying that Conrad had received a bullet wound.

The avuncular anxiety, on this account, was soon allayed, for the bullet wound was now healed. It gave place, however, to another form of anxiety; an anxiety emanating from a whole source of anxieties about Conrad in Marseilles. It concerned the state of his finances; for on that subject, also, there had been silence; an unwonted silence.

Tadeusz sustained a shock. Indeed, even if Conrad had been his own namesake grandfather, Teodor, or any other Utopian Korzeniowski, his finances could scarcely have been in a worse state, a more confused, more unbusinesslike condition. Tadeusz Bobrowski, as much as it was possible for that representative of his own level-headed family to lose control of his feelings, did so, lifting up his orderly and punctilious hands in a gesture of absolute exasperation.

However, he set all to rights in the space of a fortnight, and returned to Kiev. Conrad, in the meantime, had shipped aboard an English steamer, the *Mavis*; a cargo boat laden with coal for Constantinople. In her he left the port on 24th April 1878—not 'loath to depart'.

VARIOUS VOYAGES

(1878-83)

VARIOUS VOYAGES

(1878-83)

i

CONRAD, who remembered most things, was forgetful about dates—except historical dates, which he regarded in the nature of co-ordinates in a chart. He remembered the date of his departure from Marseilles because it happened to coincide with the close of the Russo-Turkish War and because, as the *Mavis* was steaming up the Sea of Marmora on her way to Constantinople, he saw the war's tail-end: the tents of the Russian Army at San Stephano.[1]

Conrad's carelessness in the matter of dates is homogeneous with the irregular, perfunctory way in which he treats particulars of place and circumstance in occasional reference to his travels. He took no notes, kept no diary—except during his Congo journey, and this was discovered by Mrs Conrad in the waste-paper basket. Being an impressionist—almost a Utopian in impressionism, to use Uncle Tadeusz' word—he was averse, by nature, from rendering chronological and detailed accounts. His autobiographical *The Mirror of the Sea*, the nautical companion to *A Personal Record*, includes nothing at all about the *Mavis* among its sporadic and rhetorical contents. Conrad's embarkation in that ship, nevertheless, was an event of maximum importance in his life; the starting-point of his graduation in the English Merchant Service; and the *Mavis* was to convey him (a long way round, it is true) to the country of his dreams, his hopes, his ambitions, and (to make up the Conradism) his aspirations.

---

[1] From a letter of Conrad to Joseph de Smet (a Belgian man-of-letters), 1911.

133

The *Mavis,* after discharging her cargo of coal at Constantinople, proceeded across the Sea of Azov, and at Yeisk, a sea-port in that remote region, she loaded up with linseed for Lowestoft.

During the succeeding long southward and westward-rounding voyage, we may conclude in the old phrase, that 'nothing remarkable fell out'; but, considering the hyperbole in which Conrad described his first sight of an Englishman, his failure to make even the slightest mention of his first sight of England seems lamentable. It may be that in the Straits of Dover where, presumably, it took place, he was in a lamentable state of mind—he could scarcely have been feeling very happy, after all that had taken place in Marseilles—and his recollection of the experience may have seemed unsuitable for description:

> *Patria dura parens, et saxis saevior albis*
> *Spumea quae pulsat littoris unda tui.*

Those white cliffs might have looked as savage—glistening and foaming—suggesting that the hard (*dura*) country to which they belonged, might not be altogether favourable. When, in due course, the ship was accompanied, mile after mile, by the low-lying, dun-coloured contours of Suffolk, the young traveller might have likened it to the 'dreary coast of Venezuela'.

At last, the great cliff of Lowestoft appeared, all jumbled over with old, ruddy-dark houses. The Captain pulls the cord, and the big-mouthed syren blares. He repeats the performance—so unnecessarily! Conrad, if he had read *Macbeth,* might well have commented, 'Had I three ears, I'ld hear thee.' Hundreds of ears had heard him. The road across the Swing Bridge was already being cleared and the crossing-gates slid along; the inner-harbour, Lake Lothing, is open. The outer-harbour, as the *Mavis* steams slowly in between the pier-heads, has the appearance as it broadens out of receiving her with open arms. Alas! when natural or artificial appearances seem to mock the feelings of sorrowing hearts.

ii

'My first English reading was the *Standard* newspaper, and my first acquaintance by the ear with it was in the speech of fishermen, shipwrights and sailors of the East Coast.'[2]

When, on 18th June 1878, Conrad stepped off the gangway of the *Mavis* on to the wharf at Lake Lothing, he was furnished with a few English words acquired during the voyage, and the few pounds he had been paid off with; if he had any more in his sailor's belt, it was not much more. His lack of English words was the worse, more vexatious deficiency; for words are the coins of communication, and to a man in Conrad's situation language—not 'silence', as the old adage has it—is 'golden'. In the currency of language Conrad was scarcely better off at Lowestoft than a beggarly mute. His French-English dictionary could teach him to read, but not to pronounce, the *Standard*: in these straits, he had recourse to those 'fishermen, shipwrights and sailors', above.

They rendered the East Anglian pronunciation, in which the Lowestoft accent is strong: but as Conrad's foreign accent was stronger—it persisted to the end of his days—this made no perceptible difference.

'Having unluckily no ear,' he tells his correspondent, 'my accentuation is uncertain. . . . In writing I wrestle painfully with that language which I feel I do not possess but which possesses me—alas! A devil of a language.'

Conrad's lingual wrestlings, begun at Lowestoft, are here evidenced in the meaning that he attaches to the word, 'accentuation'. It seems to be equivocal, implying confusion with the French sense of the word which, unlike the English, includes intonation as well as stress. Conrad may have meant that he was liable either to pronounce English words with a 'foreign accent' or, on the other hand, to pronounce them with the wrong syllabic stress. Actually, he was at fault in both respects. As an instance of the latter tendency, Ford Madox Hueffer relates that he would 'talk of Mr Cunninghame Graham's

---

[2] Letter to Joseph de Smet, 23rd January 1911.

book *Success* alternately as *Suc*cess and *Success* half a dozen times in the course of a conversation'.

However fallible in pronunciation, or accentuation, Conrad proved to be, he was, nevertheless, highly creditable to his instructor fishermen, whom (unlike the grammarian Professors in Cracow) he praised highly; 'sailors of the Norfolk shore; coast men, with steady eyes, mighty limbs, and gentle voice; men of very few words, which at least were never bare of meaning. Honest, steady men, sobered by domestic ties, one and all, as far as I can remember'.

And this eulogy is all that he has to say about his association with Lowestoft—all except a remark, in some letter or other, about his seeing a child digging on the sands.

On the other hand, there is nothing about Conrad at Lowestoft—no mention, even, in the Guide Book's 'Literary Associations'. Fitzgerald and George Borrow are included, and they were merely visitors to Lowestoft; whereas Conrad not only visited but landed at Lowestoft, which thereupon became his *Alma Mater Anglica*. It is never too late for the Town Council to erect a memorial.

iii

At the beginning of July, a letter arrived for Conrad from his uncle. It had probably been forwarded from Marseilles; for Tadeusz seems to have been under the impression that Conrad was still there, since he writes in the letter, 'if you wish to wait before signing on as a sailor in the French Navy, find some occupation while you are waiting'.[3] On the other hand, he says, as if he was aware of Conrad's departure, 'I am writing to M. Richard to send you 600 francs'.

Apart from the satisfactory '600 francs', the letter is apparently a continuation in writing of the kind of plain-spoken 'home truths' expressed by the uncle to the nephew during the former's visit to Marseilles.

Tadeusz had given Conrad in his previous letters many home truths; in the present letter they abound. This stable

---

[3] Ford Madox Hueffer states, under a misapprehension, that Conrad actually entered the French Navy.

character of a man wrote, as he spoke and acted, true to type. He both preached and practised home truths, and was a kind of home truth himself—as homely, by nature, in his sincere and sensible way, as he was true; the consequence is that his admonishments carried the greater weight. 'If you cannot find a ship at the moment,' he advises his romantic nephew, 'take to something—shopkeeping or anything else, but work . . . you won't otherwise get a penny from me. . . . I do not want to work for a lazy fellow.'

The Apostle Paul said, 'If a man will not work, neither shall he eat'; Tadeusz areads Conrad that if he won't work, his allowance will be stopped. He adds, 'If you learn what poverty is, that will teach you to value the money given you by others.' He protests that he has been unable to go to Marienbad, this year, in consequence of having had to pay for his nephew's follies.

However, it is never too late to mend:

'You wanted to be a sailor, and you must be responsible for the consequences; you have forfeited my confidence. Work now to regain it; you will win it back if you apply yourself steadily and pull yourself together.'

The letter was effective. The combination of plain-speaking, exhortation, and appeal—the effusion of an uncle who had become as his nephew's father and mother—was overpowering, breaking down Conrad's pride. Everything was now broken down in him; the way was open, in Tadeusz's words (in their reverse order), to pull himself together and apply himself steadily. Without delay, on 11th July 1878, he signed on in a barquantine[4] coaster, the *Skimmer of the Seas,* plying between Lowestoft and Newcastle.

'From Lowestoft to Newcastle and back again. Good school for a seaman,' writes Conrad, looking back on his North Sea voyages. Indeed, he went on learning in them both seamanship and English, taught by 'East Coast chaps, each built as though to last for ever, and coloured like a

---

[4] A three-masted vessel, with the foremast square rigged, and the main-mast and mizzen fore-and-aft rigged.

Christmas card. Tan and pink—gold hair and blue eyes—with that Northern straight-away-there look'.

The 'good school', however, was no more than his nautical preparatory school and, after skimming the shallow seas for the space of six weeks, he considered himself qualified for what he wanted, deep-water and antipodean voyages. He therefore answered an advertisement in a daily paper—probably the *Standard*—of a London shipping agent.

It was his first composition written in English and, unless his literary self-consciousness began to appear sooner than he thought, it was the first composition in which he sedulously sought the *mot juste*.

One cannot help bewailing, in this connection, that among the immortal contributions laid up for posterity by American millionaires, Conrad's first MS. in English has not been preserved.

However, a good many of Conrad's MSS. have been thus treasured up, although few of so early a date as September 1878, when the writer of the initial one, having said in it that he would call on the shipping agent in a few days, went by train to London. He records his impressions after arriving at Liverpool Street Station:

'Straight from the railway carriage I had walked into the great city with something of the feeling of a traveller penetrating into a vast and unexplored wilderness. No explorer could have been more lonely. I did not know a single soul of all these millions that all around me peopled the mysterious distances of the streets. I cannot say I was free from a little youthful awe, but at that age one's feelings are simple. I was elated. I was pursuing a clear aim, I was carrying out a deliberate plan of making out of myself, in the first place, a seaman worthy of the service, good enough to work by the side of the men with whom I was to live; and, in the second place, I had to justify my existence to myself, to redeem a tacit moral pledge. Both these aims were to be attained by the same effort. How simple seemed problems of life then on that hazy day of early September in the year 1878, when I entered London for the first time.

'From that point of view—Youth and a straight-forward scheme of conduct—it was certainly a year of grace. All the help I had to get in touch with the world I was invading was a piece of paper, not much bigger than the palm of my hand—in which I held it—torn out of a larger plan of London for the greater facility of reference. It had been the object of careful study for some days past. The fact that I could take a conveyance at the station never occurred to my mind, no, not even when I got out into the street, and stood, taking my anxious bearings, in the midst, so to speak, of twenty thousand hansoms. A strange absence of mind, or unconscious conviction that one cannot approach an important moment of one's life by means of a hired carriage? Yes, it would have been a preposterous proceeding. And indeed, I was to make an Australian voyage and encircle the globe before ever entering a London hansom.

'... I had vowed to myself not to inquire my way from anyone. Youth is the time of rash pledges. Had I taken a wrong turning I would have been lost; and if faithful to my pledge I might have remained lost for days, for weeks, have left perhaps my bones to be discovered bleaching in some blind alley of the Whitechapel district, as it has happened to lonely travellers lost in the Bush. But I walked on to my destination without hesitation or mistake, showing there, for the first time, some of that faculty to absorb and make my own the imaged topography of a chart, which in later years was to help me in regions of intricate navigation to keep the ships entrusted to me off the ground.'

Conrad's destination, he discovered, was a small, dusty office, in which there sat a man with a grey beard, a big nose, silver-rimmed spectacles, and a head of curly white hair. He was eating a chop when Conrad entered, and he went on eating it while he listened to the young applicant's broken English. Then—still eating the chop—he explained that his advertisement had been misapprehended; his business was to find ships for would-be premium apprentices, not to find ships for men who wanted, as Conrad did, a berth before the mast: an 'Act of Parliament made it a penal offence to procure ships for sailors'. On principle, therefore, he could do nothing.

He resembled an 'apostle in the Baroque Italian style', with his head of curly white hair; but Conrad's distress was evident, and the apostolic-looking shipping agent, tempted by commiseration, both transgressed his business principles and circumvented the law. He told Conrad he could get him a job as ordinary seaman on a very fine 'wool clipper', the *Duke of Sutherland,* which made voyages to and from Australia.

He was as good as his word and, on 15th October, Conrad embarked. He arrived at Sydney about the end of January and returned, in the same ship, a year later.

He is silent about this voyage, as he was silent about his early voyage in the *Mont-Blanc,* and this, in all probability, for the same reason—that the experience was a disagreeable one; better disregarded—at any rate, no fit subject for *The Mirror of the Sea.* Yet, as if in token of its disagreeableness, he relates a vestige—the incident of an encounter with a Sydney pickpocket who suddenly, one night, dashed up the ship's gangway, and left Conrad, who denied him refuge, floored.

There is also a trace of the *Duke of Sutherland* in *The Nigger of the Narcissus:* [5]

'. . . the old *Duke of S*— (she's dead, poor thing! a violent death on the coast of New Zealand).'

Conrad did not re-embark in the ship. He was probably in a state of nervous exhaustion due, as Jean-Aubry writes, to his 'limited knowledge of English, the fact that he was

---

[5] One of Conrad's fellow seamen in the *Duke of Sutherland* was James Waite—the name he bestowed on the amazing negro in *The Nigger of the Narcissus.* Also he met while in Sydney the handless French sailor, the original of a character in his short story, *Beware of the Dollars.*

a sailor before the mast who, up till then, had sailed under less hard conditions, the *necessity of drawing upon his solitary pride for the nervous force necessary to resist the fatigue of work,* often extremely exhausting for one of his temperament and antecedents'.

The italics are mine, the words being so truly expressive. Pride is always solitary, and Conrad was the more isolated aboard the *Duke of Sutherland* by his limited knowledge of English. This would occasion difficulties in his understanding of instructions and orders, and bring down upon his innocent head the wrath of the poop, or even of the quarter-deck, couched in terms afflicting to his spirit and imposing great strains on his self-control. As for his fo'c'sle companions, perhaps the democratic element in his Polish aristocratic temperament enabled him to alleviate their natural antipathy for the alien interloper. We vainly look in *The Mirror of the Sea*; where nothing is included reflecting humiliations of Conrad's personal dignity.

Severe tensions also, no doubt, were imposed upon his nerves; for, although before joining the *Duke of Sutherland* he had become sufficiently familiar with yards on high that swayed and jerked, yet there were times in a deep-water ship when a seaman on a mast had need to be as nerveless as a monkey on a tree.

As for the 'fatigue of work', there were times—days, nights, weeks, even—when the muscles and the nerves must become, whether numbed or aching, mechanical, and the brain blind; the will automatic : the whole physical contrivance driven relentlessly with desperate motion. Witness page after page of Conrad's *The Nigger of the Narcissus*.

For a month or more after quitting the ship, Conrad, apparently, lived in idleness. He was then in London— or, rather, Middlesex, lodging at 6 Dynevor Rd., Stoke Newington—where, perhaps, he relaxed his mind and stretched his limbs as, after leaving the *Mont-Blanc,* he had done in Paris, but his outlook would have been very different—as different as the atmospheres of the respective places. No doubt, he thought often of Doña Rita. He had told her that when he was away from her she appeared to him with the more intense realism. He would also have dreamt of her, and this not only in sleep but when his eyes, perhaps, like Coleridge's made 'pictures' when they were closed. He was now far from her—not only in space— spaces unknowable, untraversable—but also in time; distant as far as his life's end. It would always be so and he would see her always; her abstract image in the semblance of actual space—the desperate heart-plunging vacuity of the *not there.*

Recollections of Dominic also would have haunted him; Dominic with his great, dramatic presence and his ironical speech, or silence. Such sad, disturbing thoughts, whatever forms they may have taken, were associated, no doubt, with, what he expressed in a letter to his uncle, an extreme yearning to revisit the Mediterranean.

Along with this, he was troubled by a hankering, and probably remorseful, desire to see his uncle. But when he suggested in a letter that they should meet at Odessa in the year following, Tadeusz forbad the visit, replying, 'I do not want you to come to Russia before you have been naturalized as an Englishman.'

His objection was the danger that, if Conrad set foot on Russian, or Russian-Polish, territory unnaturalized, he would be apprehended for being the son of a political malefactor. In further correspondence, in which Conrad proposed again and again to visit his uncle in the Ukraine, Tadeusz responded always with the same prohibition, and kept on advising his nephew to be naturalized. Conrad had thought of applying for French naturalization, but his uncle objected because it would entail military service. Tadeusz became more and more insistent—and if this obstreperous nephew of his would not become an Englishman, let him become an American, or an Austrian, or a Swiss; on no account ought he to remain a Russian or a Russian-Pole.

But Conrad still delayed; he took no steps in the matter, although it might be thought that he would have rushed at the chance of becoming an Englishman. It will readily be apprehended, however, that the sensitive and imaginative young man may well have been obstructed by his conscience. He had been told before he left Poland to embark on the international ocean, that he was no less than a deserter of his country, and this damning insinuation, uttered like an anathema in a sacrarium, sank deep into his adolescent mind. The diverting excitements and, latterly, toils and fatigues of his life had kept him from dwelling upon it, but the impression it had left was permanent and potential; now, in the spell of desuetude, as I surmise, it had come to the surface, sprung by his uncle's message about naturalization, and, in a state of conscientiousness as extravagant as his 'creations', Dr Monygham, Heist, Falk, and Lord Jim, he had thoughts such as these: If I did not intentionally desert my country, I am still culpable, since I was exceedingly glad to get out of it. I left it because it was hopeless, irreparable, like a wreck on a shoal. Yet to abandon one's country in despair is contemptible. To disown one's country by becoming naturalized in another country would be real desertion, base treachery; more than that, it would be rank hypocrisy; it would mean being neither one national nor the other—a horrible hermaphrodite; it would mean nothing at all; for one cannot change one's country, any more than one can change one's father or mother; it is one's very *fatherland*.

Indeed, such distracting objections, bizarre and morbid though they appear, may easily have beset the lonely, heart-sick youth, perplexed between his desire and old implanted guilty feelings; for no other reason for his continual deferment of fulfilling his uncle's proviso that he should become naturalized as an Englishman before going to Poland, seems conceivable. Nor would these imaginary qualms and scruples be surprising in Conrad's special circumstances, considering his character and progeniture; for Uncle Tadeusz, with his astute integrity, was doubtless right in attributing the aberrations of the son to the father and the Utopian Korzeniowski strain.

But Apollo himself, and all his forebears themselves, were the sons of their fatherland, and in Poland patriotism, the veneration of the fatherland, was a religion—at least, it inspired the fervour of a religion, and of much more than most religious worship. It had, accordingly, developed a form of conscientiousness which, driven downwards by the subjugation and repression of its Czarist Devil, became as neurotic as the conscientiousness of the old extremist Puritans, with their 'razor's edge to walk on'. Hence, perhaps, the frequency with which the guilt-complex motif emerges in the stories—*Falk, Lord Jim, Nostromo, Under Western Eyes, The Shadow Line,* and *Victory.*

iv

Conrad managed to revisit the Mediterranean, as he had wanted to do. He got a berth in a steamship, the *Europa,* which left London on the 12th December 1879 to make a veritable cruise, touching at Genoa, Leghorn, Naples, Patras, Cephalonia, Messina, and Palermo. But there was small pleasure in the experience; in fact, it would appear from Uncle Tadeusz' replies to his nephew's letters to have been positively insufferable.

Conrad returned to London on 30th January 1880, and one of the first things he did then was to write to his uncle; he had already written to him at Patras, and was disappointed to find no reply.

Tadeusz answered that the letter from Patras had never arrived; then, after expressing the uneasiness he had felt at Conrad's apparent silence, he wrote:

'Your unpleasant experiences on the *Europa* do not make me very uneasy, although they may have given you some pain. Such things appear quite normal when you know human nature. They hurt you because they are undeserved and because you consider yourself exploited.'

Conrad was now wretched. He had left the *Europa* with bitter, angry feelings against her Captain; he was ill with fever; he had no money—'absolutely without money', attests Jean-Aubry—and his uncle, who was himself in financial difficulties at that time, could not come to his assistance.

Conrad wrote letter after letter to his uncle; the following reply seems to be in answer to more than one:

'I thoroughly sympathise with your mishap in connection with that madman of a Captain Monroe, but if he is mad his commission ought to be taken from him; on the other hand, if he cannot legally be considered insane, his commission is valid. I do not understand the way the English reason, but one cannot change them and one must adapt one's self to them. I suppose the *Europa* is now in port and that you have the certificate from your First Mate who has become a Captain and that you have passed your exam or that you will pass it. Never doubt that I wish you every kind of good, and that you have my blessing. Francoise prays for you night and morning.

'What I had to say about your naturalization I have already said in my last letter. It is impossible to live for ever like a bird on a branch; one must have, sooner or later, a legal standing, and it is better to do it when you are free than under pressure of circumstances. You would not be a "Nalecz", my dear boy, if you did not change your plans. I say that because you have told me of Mr Lascelle's offer to make you his secretary and to engage you to help him with his railway business. As for me, I should not be your uncle nor the man I am if I did not say straight out that it is hopeless to throw yourself from one profession to another. Changes of that kind make men into those kinds of wasters who, as we say at home, have no fireside, and achieve nothing for themselves. . . . Think over the matter for yourself. Is it sensible to link your fate to a man—however great he may be—who is a businessman or a politician? It is far more dignified and sensible to stick to a profession which one gets to understand more and more by working at it. You have chosen to be a sailor, you can enlarge

your career through trading, and I am sure that you will
succeed. . . . That is my advice, but act in your own
way, for in everything that concerns your career I leave
you complete freedom, being ignorant of the circumstances in which you live. I have never been anything
of an adventurer myself, and it is that fact which makes
me wish regular employment for you.'

Conrad continued to stay in London (at Stoke
Newington) for some six months—however, he managed
to live; perhaps Mr Lascelle, alluded to in the
epistle of Uncle Tadeusz, gave him employment, thus
discovering that he would make a good secretary. Enigma
after enigma; for how could a man who had learnt English
for only eighteen months, as in Conrad's case, make a
good secretary? However, such prodigies occur. There was
an admirable political-press reporter who had learnt shorthand in six weeks. It is true that it was his own self-
constructed shorthand—perhaps, it was also Conrad's self-
constructed English; it must have been so, since he
dispensed entirely, as he declares, with the verbal
mechanism of grammar.

At any rate, he was proficient enough in English by
the beginning of January 1880 to take and pass his Marine
Board examination for third mate. His examiner, a tall,
spare, white-bearded man, with a quiet, kindly manner,
his 'old thin hands loosely clasped resting on his crossed
legs . . . began by an elementary question in a mild voice,
and went on, went on—'

He went on for the space of three hours, and Conrad
became light-headed, at last, under this 'third degree' kind
of interrogation. 'Some very queer thoughts passed
through my head', he writes, 'while I was considering my
answers: thoughts which had nothing to do with seamanship nor yet with anything reasonable known to this
earth.' Eventually there fell a silence, which also seemed
to 'last for ages' (for Conrad had lost his sense of the pro-
portion of time); and during this silence the gentle old
man wrote out the examinee's pass-slip 'slowly with a

noiseless pen and extended the scrap of paper . . . without a word'.

The door-keeper told Conrad as he went out that he didn't 'think this ever happened with any of the gentlemen before'.

Conrad himself attributes the inquisitorial torture by time to something in his appearance that produced an unfavourable impression. But the fact is that a Polish examinee at the Marine Board was an unheard-of phenomenon; Conrad himself was the first Pole to become, as he eventually did, the captain of an English ship. The examiner, confronted by the unusual entrant—bizarre, ceremonious manner, voice, and bow— may naturally have felt perplexed and a little uncertain as to whether he ought to be admitted into the Service; whether, indeed, he ought to let him pass—in other words, whether this *rara avis* ought not to be prudently and ex-pediently plucked. Accordingly, taking up an easy position, with crossed legs, he proceeded at a leisurely pace to consider the question, while negligently pursuing his questions, perhaps hoping that, even at the last moment, up to the very last question, the dilemma might be solved for him, so that he could conscientiously *not* admit him into the Service.

Outside the building, Conrad was affected with another kind of light-headedness; he 'walked on air'. He may also be conceived to have *written on air* a letter announcing the good news to his uncle. Tadeusz replied:

'My dear boy and Lieutenant,

'Two days ago I received your two letters telling me of the happy result of your examination. You have filled me with joy. The sheet of paper on which the "Messieurs du Board Office" have written such terrible threats in event of your not fulfilling your duties has been my recompense, and I owe it to you. I sympathise entirely with your joy, which comes from two sources: (1) you have proved to your uncle and to the whole world that you have not eaten unearned bread during

these four years; (2) that you have been able to overcome the drawbacks of being a foreigner without back-
ing. You are also indebted to Captain Wyndham,[6] to
Professor Newton and to all your comrades who rejoice
over your success.

'There are honest folk everywhere—think of Solary
and Richard—only one must find them. From the very
start you have met them on your path and you are
bound to love them and to help others when they need
it. You see, there are many more honest folk than bad
ones. I congratulate you, *Monsieur l'officier de second
Rang de la Marine de la Grand Bretagne!*'

When Conrad wrote further to the effect that he had
given up all thought of going to Canada, the avuncular
joy became full:

'I see with pleasure that the "Nalecz" in you has been
modified by the influence of the "Bobruszczuki",[7] as your
incomparable mother used to call her own family before
she flew away to the nest of the "Nalecz". This time I
rejoice over the influence of my family, not, however,
without recognising in the "Nalecz" a spirit of initiative
and enterprise superior to that which runs in our veins.
From the blend of these two famous races should emerge
a character so steadfast and so energetic that the whole
world will be astonished at it.'

Uncle Tadeusz was nothing if not fair and, in this instance, his fairness to the Nalecz Korzeniowskis was
tempered with generosity; yet the 'Nalecz spirit of initiative and enterprise' is too rationalistic, too level-headed
a description of the Nalecz Korzeniowski constituents in
the 'blend'—which were, rather, in the nature of a ferment,
a cause of unrest and turmoil. It is the temperament of
genius; for, as Nietzsche asserts, 'Except your soul be full
of chaos, you cannot produce a dancing star.' Conrad was

---

[6] Captain Wyndham, author of a handbook on seamanship and
Conrad's first coach in navigation, etc.

[7] Bobruszczuki is a play upon the family name and the Polish
word for a beaver, bobrusz.

aware that the Nalecz element was in his veins and, in his earlier life, he let it ramp. Later on, when the Bobrowski side of his nature asserted itself, under his uncle's influence, he grew afraid of it. It was a devil, a family devil, like the Cervonis' (but every family has one of some kind or other); he grew afraid of it indeed:

'Yes! I too would like to hold the magic wand giving that command over laughter and tears which is declared to be the highest achievement of imaginative literature. Only, to be a great magician one must surrender oneself to occult and irresponsible powers, either outside or within one's own breast. We have all heard of simple men selling their souls for love or power to some grotesque devil. The most ordinary intelligence can perceive without much reflection that anything of the sort is bound to be a fool's bargain. I don't lay claim to particular wisdom because of my dislike and distrust of such transactions. It may be my sea-training acting upon a natural disposition to keep good hold on the one thing really mine, but the fact is that I have a positive horror of losing even for one moving moment that full possession of myself which is the first condition of good service.'

Uncle Tadeusz, however, knew better than he wrote; he had no illusions about the nature of the Nalecz characteristics. He was shrewd and matter-of-fact, but the forecast in his letter of Conrad's astonishing achievement was as prophetic as Apollo's 'eager boat with eagle's wings'.

Conrad's own elation at obtaining his certificate subsided as he discovered that it did not act like an *Open sesame* to admit him directly into a third mate's berth. Like a tyro of a briefless barrister, or patientless doctor (in former times)—or an unpublished author, for that matter —the brand new ship's officer must possess his soul in patience—and perhaps starve his body in the process. Yet he had not so long to wait as most of such novices have to do—not longer than three months. Three years before, he had written to his uncle asking him to intervene after his dispute with M. Delestang, to get him a certificate of apprenticeship and good service in the *Mont-Blanc* and the *Saint Antoine*; the certificate duly arrived, and probably was very influential. At any rate, on the 23rd August 1880, Conrad embarked as second mate in the *Loch Etive,* a clipper of 1,200 tons, bound for Sydney. He recalls his sensations, on the occasion, especially that of the 'peace of the sea'; a complex apprehension of sanctuary and security in escape to restless adventure.

The Mate, Mr P—, liked to pile on sail, which made the ship, and the Captain in his cabin, *jump.* Coming on deck, the Captain never wanted to reduce sail—for he, too, had the speed vice—but, knowing that there was too much of it, he waxed extremely irritable with the Mate on the subject, in order to divert his own conscience.

The Mate fell ill, and Conrad consequently came in for extra work, as well as the Captain's irritability; conditions that he accepted and endured with an even mind because he had become entirely devoted to his profession and rejoiced in the advantages of initiative the new responsibility gave him.

Also, he had formed a fervid admiration for the Captain, who, as he says, 'had a great name for sailor-like qualities', and he rather sympathised with his irritability, as it was really directed upon the ship rather than upon himself, because he could not get as many knots out of her as he had been able to get out of a ship he had formerly commanded. He eventually abandoned the attempt, dying on board, 21st September 1894.

The *Loch Etive* arrived at Sydney in November, and returned (round Cape Horn) in April of the next year; when Conrad left her.

He wrote, as usual, to his uncle about his sea experiences, this time with happy enthusiasm. Tadeusz responded in kind, but expressed a hope that his nephew, without loss to his career, could arrange before reembarking to meet him at Wiesbaden, where he was going for a cure in September. At the same time he sent him money to enable him to pass his next two examinations.

Conrad was now cured of his affectionate nostalgia—even Doña Rita, apparently, was out of his mind; his 'Blue-Eyed Dream', materialising, monopolised his thoughts: his desire and will were directed and concentrated upon the one object, the 'one thing in the world', as he saw it—to become the Captain of an English ship. He accordingly bent all his energies into increasing his knowledge as a navigator, and excused himself from meeting his uncle at Wiesbaden.

Tadeusz was hurt:

'Last post brought me your letter of 10th June.

'It is all the more welcome as it breathes ardour and enterprise, in spite of the failure of our plans for meeting. Perhaps the disappointment affects me more than it does you. I do not mean to reproach you in saying that. When one is young one believes more in the future, one is certain of striking a favourable bargain with Fate. As for me, I have closed those accounts. You believe we shall see each other again, and I—I doubt it. I want it to be so, I hope it will be so, but at the same time I see how uncertain of fulfillment my plans are. Meanwhile, I assure you that this melancholy is not due to my health growing worse, it is merely a reasonable judgment upon life.'

Tadeusz, an excellent writer himself, goes on to compliment his nephew on his literary style (in Polish), and suggests that he should contribute to the Warsaw *Wedrowiec* (*The Traveller*) some literary sketches of his Australian voyage: 'It would form a tie with your own country,' he writes, 'and it would be an act of piety to your father who wished to serve and did serve his country with his pen.'

Response to the suggestion would have greatly pleased Uncle Tadeusz, and kindness—which involves gratitude—to such a man, is a prudent virtue, an insurance policy against incident remorse; but the resolute devotee to his nautical ideal could afford no time for this. By what specific means he was advancing towards his objective is obscure. However, towards the middle of the year (1881), he apparently made a voyage in a ship named the *Anna Frost* (particulars unknown), in which he sustained some kind of accident, and had to lie up in hospital for a few days. His uncle in his next letter thanks God that he has 'escaped', and sends him £10, by request, which, he says, will not be deducted from his allowance, but is sent to him as a 'distressed seaman'. He refers to some 'risky speculation', admonishing his nephew to remember that he is a 'Nalecz' and that his grandfather 'wasted his property in speculation' and his uncle 'got into debt and many other awkward fixes through the same cause'.

v

At length, after many vain endeavours to obtain a berth, Conrad was appointed second mate in an old, crank barque of 425 tons, at a wage of £4 per month. The Captain was an old bent man, with a brave spirit, a kindly heart, but a somewhat poor intellect; the old, cranky barque was his first command.

Tadeusz (23rd September 1881) was gloomily critical of this appointment. However, the spirit of common sense with which he was so richly endowed induced him to look on the 'bright side of things' whenever there was a 'bright side' to be seen. If none were visible, he was not comfortless; he had another aspect to look from: while he invariably returned thanks to Heaven for good things, if a thing were not good he attributed it either to the Nalecz Korzeniowskis or to Fate; the other side of Uncle Tadeusz's outlook on a bad thing, or prospect was the *fait accompli*:

'Anyhow, it is all settled now,' he writes. 'Well, leave in good health, return in triumph. *Deus te ducat, perducat et reducat,* as our ancestors used to say to those who went to the wars, and as I say now to you, bidding you farewell and embracing you from the bottom of my heart.'

The letter then proceeds into a long passage about Panslavonic politics, showing that Tadeusz was as shrewd in those complicated matters as he was wise in the direct conduct of ordinary life. The passage 'shows', remarks Jean-Aubry, 'both Tadeusz Bobrowskis' prophetic insight, and how keen Conrad's preoccupations and anxieties regarding things Polish must have been at this time'. Apparently, Conrad continued to have his country on his conscience. If it was so, the burden was soon to be lifted—temporarily, at any rate.

This came about through the extremely decrepit condition of the *Palestine,* which proved to be excellent as a training ship; while, as a conveyance to scenes of wild adventure and hair-breadth escapes, she could scarcely have been bettered—or worsened, from Uncle Tadeusz's point of view. Old, bent, twisted Beard, also the worthy captain of an unseaworthy ship—was admirably fit, from Conrad's point of view. All things considered, the glass was set fair for trouble.

And so it fell out. The story is faithfully told in *Youth* by the voice of Marlow, Conrad's representative mouthpiece. Only, the *Palestine* is the *Judea* in the narrative; Captain Beard retains his own name.

On 21st September 1881 the *Judea* (or *Palestine*) left the Thames, in ballast, working out under canvas, with a North Sea pilot on board. She took a week to arrive in the roadstead of Yarmouth, where she rested awhile. Proceeding thence, she encountered a violent gale, the notorious gale of October 1881: 'It was wind, lightning, sleet, snow, and a terrific sea.'

The seas smashed the ship's bulwarks, flooded her deck, and eventually shifted her cargo. The gale lasted for two or three days. After floundering about on her side during that time and after, she fell in with a tug which towed her to Newcastle. There, undergoing repairs, waiting for her cargo to be loaded, and replacing members of her crew who had deserted, she remained for a month. On the night before she was ready to sail, and was already lying out at the buoys near the dock gates, a steamer barged into her, splintering the bulwarks and breaking braces.

Just before the crash, after the baleful red flashing of the steamer's head-light, Conrad had shouted down the cabin, 'Come up, quick!' The Captain came up quick, with his wife in his arms; a dear old body who, during a visit to the ship, had been mending Conrad's shirts and socks. At the word of alarm, immediately followed by the crash, the old man had caught up 'that old woman—the woman of his life'.[8] He bundled her to the deck, across the deck, and down the ladder into the boat that was fast there. Somehow the painter came adrift, and 'away they went together'. There were no oars in the boat. Nobody heard the Captain shouting, nor had anyone observed what had happened: so deep was the darkness on deck, so tumultuous the excitement, so rapid and precipitate were the old man's movements, though encumbered, in salvaging his human treasure. At length a question was asked, 'Where is the Captain?' Then, from somewhere out in the darkness of the dock, a doleful voice was heard, hailing, '*Judea*, ahoy!'

Captain and Mrs Beard were recovered by the aid of a water-man, Mrs Beard returning to the deck with the cheerful remark, 'I suppose it does not matter my losing the train now.'

'"No, Jenny—you go below and get warm," he growled. Then to us: "A sailor has no business with a wife—I say. There I was, out of the ship . . .".'

The repairs necessitated by the blundering steamer took up another fortnight. At last, with a cargo of good Hartley coal—fifty tons of it—and a crew of eight men and two boys, the *Judea* (or *Palestine*) sailed, bound for Bangkok.

---

[8] When, years afterwards, the old woman died, the Captain, more bent than ever, 'could not rest', as he told Conrad, who had met him, and took odd jobs of piloting, etc. 'His eyes', says Conrad, 'were perfectly angelic. This is not a sentimental exaggeration. . . .'

The weather was beautiful, sunny, halcyon—appropriately so, since it was January, the month of that sea-calming bird; the wind was favourable and, as the old barque got on her course, with her wind-filled sails, buoyantly gliding along, she had that aspect once seen in such a craft, in such weather, never to be forgotten, of eager, effortless motion.

The splendid weather lasted during the passage southward and through the Channel, and for three hundred miles to the westward of the Lizard; then the wind changed and freshened. After two days it blew a gale.

'The *Judea* 'hove to, wallowed on the Atlantic like an old candle-box. It blew day after day: it blew with spite, without interval, without mercy, without rest. The world was nothing but an immensity of great foaming waves rushing at us, under a sky low enough to touch with the hand and dirty like a smoked ceiling. . . . Day after day and night after night there was nothing round the ship but the howl of the wind, the tumult of the sea, the noise of water pouring over her decks. There was no rest for her and no rest for us. She tossed, she pitched, she stood on her head, she sat on her tail, she rolled, she groaned, and we had to hold on while on deck and cling to our bunks when below, in a constant effort of body and worry of mind.'

They took to the pumps:

'We pumped all the four hours. We pumped all night, all day, all the week—watch and watch. She was working herself loose, and leaked badly. . . . And while we pumped the ship was going from us piecemeal : the bulwarks went, the stanchions were torn out, the ventilators smashed, the cabin-door burst in . . . she was being gutted bit by bit. The long-boat changed, as if by magic, into matchwood where she stood in her gripes. . . . And we pumped. . . . The sea was white like a sheet of foam, like a cauldron of boiling milk. . . . There was for us no sky, there were for us no stars, no sun, no universe—nothing but angry clouds and an infuriated sea. We pumped watch and watch, for dear life; and it seemed to last for months, for years, for all eternity, as though we had been dead and gone to a hell for sailors. We forgot the day of the week, the name of the month . . . the sails blew away, she lay broadside on under a weather-cloth, the ocean poured over her, and we did not care. We turned those handles, and had the eyes of idiots . . . we turned incessantly, with the water to our waists, to our necks, over our heads.

'And there was somewhere in me the thought: By Jove! This is the deuce of an adventure—something you read about; and it is my first voyage as second mate —and I am only twenty—and here I am lasting it out as well as any of these men, and keeping my chaps up to the mark. . . . I had moments of exultation. Whenever the old dismantled craft pitched heavily with her counter high in the air, she seemed to me to throw up, like an appeal, like a defiance, like a cry to the clouds without mercy, the words written on her stern : "*Judea*, London. Do or Die".'

The deck-house forward was blown away. In the ruins, 'sitting in his bunk, surrounded by foam and wreckage, the cook was jabbering cheerfully to himself, out of his mind.' All they could do for him—there was no time for gentler treatment—was to pitch him head-first into the cabin, leaving those below to pick him up at the bottom of the stairs.

The wind fell, the sky cleared, the sea moderated; but the leak increased and, 'boats gone, deck swept clean, cabin gutted, stores spoilt, ship strained', the men, 'without a stitch but what they stood in', demanded to be put back. The ship was "bouted', but the wind changed at once, so that they had to beat up every inch of the way. However, they managed to reach Falmouth.

The ship repaired, and a new crew—the third—obtained, the *Judea* tried again, got as far as the roads, and was towed back to the inner harbour; where she stayed, becoming at last a laughing-stock: the barque that is going to Bangkok; 'small boys, pulling about in boats, would hail "*Judea* ahoy!" and if a head showed above the rail shouted, "Where are you bound to?—Bangkok?" and jeered.'

At length, her cargo was discharged into a hulk alongside, and she was put into dry dock, and her copper was stripped. The aged craft was found to be in a bad way; it was no wonder she leaked. She was far gone in that serious deficiency-ailment which old ships were prone to; all the oakum had gone out of her lower seams. She was re-caulked, recoppered, returned to the hulk, and her cargo reshipped.

Now, all the stores of the *Judea,* and the beds of the crew and officers, had been shared by the rats on board, which were numerous. The rat is a very intelligent rodent, and is a great lover of ships. It is also faithful to an old craft as long as it can do well out of her. It was the more remarkable, therefore, that, when the *Judea* had thus been made seaworthy and there was no longer any danger of shipwreck, while there remained plenty of food aboard, the rats suddenly left her. This took place on a fine moonlight night, and Conrad witnessed their departure. 'Rat after rat appeared on our rail, took a last look over his shoulder, and leaped with a hollow thud into the empty hulk.'

The interlude was advantageous; it released Conrad's thoughts inwards; aroused his mnemonic imagination.

His first acquaintance with English literature had been in reading, in MS., his father's translation of *The Two Gentlemen of Verona*; which happened a little before he read to Apollo the proofs of his translation of *Les Travailleurs de la Mer,* as related: he now read, at odd moments, and amid a din of caulkers' mallets, the works of Shakespeare throughout. The impressions left on his mind were, no doubt, deep, although no traces of them are apparent in his writings; such Shakespearean traces as there are, for example, in the writings of such a Shakespeare lover as Robert Louis Stevenson. This, however, is not strange. Stevenson read Shakespeare aesthetically—as aesthetically as the great Christian Father, for example, read Cicero—that is to say, for the style. Conrad, who despised Stevenson because he was a 'stylist', and was himself either heedless or else unaware of perpetrating solecisms—especially assonances—would have been influenced principally by the psychological content.

After Shakespeare, Conrad read Byron—at any rate, in part; whether or not he was influenced by that doyen of period-romanticism. This was in consequence of five days' leave and a trip to London:

> 'It took me a day to get there, and pretty well another to come back; but three months' pay went, all the same. I don't know what I did with it. I went to a music hall, I believe, lunched, dined, and supped in a swell place in Regent Street and was back to time with nothing but a complete set of Byron's works and a new railway rug to show for three months' work.'

In the meantime, another letter had arrived from Uncle Tadeusz, this one expressing deep solicitude: Fate and the absence of his nephew's own cool judgment had caused him, in the writer's opinion, to accept such a wretched ship as the *Palestine*; although he had done so to avoid being a burden to his uncle by staying on in London, and also to qualify for his next examination. But he, Tadeusz, did not want, for the sake of saving three to five hundred roubles, to see his nephew at the bottom of the sea, neither would it profit that young man to arrive at the Valley of Jehoshaphat in the rank of a second or third officer. Tadeusz is aware that he has no right to control his nephew who is now twenty-four years of age, but he implores him not to sail in such a wretched ship. Captain Beard and Conrad himself strike him as being 'desperate men who go out of their way to seek knocks and wounds', while the owner of the craft is a 'rascal who risks the lives of ten brave men for the sake of a blackguardly profit'.

Yet another letter arrived from Tadeusz during Conrad's stay at Falmouth; one expressing gladness at the evidence of his nephew's 'genuine energy, enterprise, and splendid health', and farewell blessings, with hopes of meeting at Cracow or Krynick at his return.

At last, 17th September 1882, the *Judea* set out from Falmouth, to the accompaniment, as one may conjecture, of 'cheers'. The weather, as at her departure from Newcastle, was fine and sunny and, this time, it lasted as she sailed on at the leisurely rate of three miles an hour, at length passing peacefully over the Line— ignored, it seems, by Neptune (at any rate, there is no record of his customary visit), but not ignored, as the event proved, by Inexorable Fate.

She proceeded into the Indian Ocean, and made north-ward toward Java Head. One day, Conrad smelt—as the decamping rats had smelt, in anticipation—burning. Next day, smoke was seen issuing from the main hold. Mean-while, she 'crawled on, do or die, in the serene weather. The sky was a miracle of purity, a miracle of azure. The sea was polished, was blue, was pellucid, was sparkling like a precious stone—as if the whole terrestrial globe had been one jewel, one colossal sapphire, a single gem fashioned into a planet. And on the lustre of the great calm waters the *Judea* glided imperceptibly, enveloped in languid and unclean vapours, in a lazy cloud that drifted to leeward, light and slow; a pestiferous cloud defiling the splendour of sea and sky'.

Water was poured in on to the coal. The smoke abated. On the second day more water was poured in, and four tons of coal were jettisoned. On the third day, the deck blew up.

Conrad was hurled through the burst after-hatch on to the coal, half buried in splintered wood. He scrambled out, with his hair, beard, and eyebrows burnt off.

A steamer providentially appeared, and took the burn-ing ship in tow. Captain Beard, tragically clinging to the hope of saving his 'first command', took the wheel him-self. But the fire spread and the ship became a raging furnace, so that they were compelled to man the boats.

Conrad was put in charge of the smallest, a '14-foot thing', with two other men; the boat was provisioned with a sack of biscuits, some tins of preserved meat, and a barrel of water. His orders were to keep close to the long-boat.

But the spirit, or dare-devil, of independence rose up in him:

'I thought I would part company as soon as I could. I wanted to have my first command all to myself. . . . I would make land by myself. I would beat the other boats. . . .'

There was no mast or sail in Conrad's boat, but he made a mast out of a spare oar and hoisted a boat awning for a sail, with a boat-hook for a yard. He was aware that she was overmasted, and the Captain warned him to be careful with the jury-rig; Mahon, the old Mate, 'wrinkled his curved nose and hailed, "You will sail that ship of yours under water, if you don't look out, young fellow".' But:

'I had the satisfaction of knowing that with the wind aft I could beat the other two. . . . Next day I sat steer-ing my cockleshell—my first command—with nothing but water and sky around me. I did sight in the after-noon the upper sails of a ship far away, but said nothing, and my men did not notice her. You see, I was afraid she might be homeward bound, and I had no mind to turn back from the portals of the East. . . .

'I need not tell you what it is to be knocking about in an open boat. I remember nights and days of calm, when we pulled, we pulled, and the boat seemed to stand still, as if bewitched within the circle of the sea horizon. I remember the heat, the deluge of rain-squalls that kept us baling for dear life (but filled our water-cask), and I remember sixteen hours on end with a mouth dry as a cinder and a steering-oar over the stern to keep my first command head on to a breaking sea. I did not know how good a man I was till then. I remember the drawn faces, the dejected figures of my two men, and I remember my youth and the feeling that will never come back any more—the feeling that I could last for ever, outlast the sea, the earth, and all men; the deceitful feeling that lures us on to joys, to perils, to love, to vain effort—to death. . . .

'And this is how I see the East. I have seen its secret places and have looked into its very soul; but now I see it always from a small boat, a high outline of mountains, blue and afar in the morning; like faint mist at noon; a jagged wall of purple at sunset. I have the feel of the oar in my hand, the vision of a scorching blue sea in my eyes. And I see a bay, a wide bay, smooth as glass and polished like ice, shimmering in the dark. A red light burns far off upon the loom of the land, and the night is soft and warm. We dragged at the oars with aching arms, and suddenly a puff of wind, a puff faint and tepid and laden with strange odours of blossoms, of aromatic wood, comes out of the still night. . . .'

The whole book is a lively revelation of Conrad's daredevil enthusiasms. According to ships' officers who had served with him in the Mercantile Marine, the proclivity persisted, so that he was apt to take risks with his ship: what kind of risks is suggested by the following quotation from *The Secret Sharer*; the story of how, by what precautionary finesse, a ship's Captain conceals in his cabin a fugitive from the law, to release him off an obscure island:

'I came out on deck slowly. It was now a matter of conscience to shave the land as closely as possible—for now he must go overboard whenever the ship was put in stays. . . . After a moment I walked over to leeward and my heart flew into my mouth at the nearness of the land on the bow. Under any other circumstances I would not have held on a minute longer. The second mate had followed me anxiously.

'I looked on till I felt I could command my voice.

' "She will weather," I said then in a quiet tone.

' "Are you going to try that, sir?" he stammered out incredulously.

'I took no notice of him and raised my tone just enough to be heard by the helmsman.

' "Keep her good full."

' "Good full, sir."

'The wind fanned my cheek, the sails slept, the world was silent. The strain of watching the dark loom of the land grow bigger and denser was too much for me. I had shut my eyes—because the ship must go closer. She must! . . .

'When I opened my eyes the second view started my heart with a thump. The black southern hill of Koh-ring seemed to hang right over the ship like a towering fragment of the everlasting night. On that enormous mass of blackness there was not a gleam to be seen, not a sound to be heard. It was gliding irresistibly toward us and yet seemed already within reach of the hand. I saw the vague figures of the watch grouped in the waist, gazing in awed silence.

' "Are you going on, sir?" enquired an unsteady voice at my elbow.

'I ignored it. I had to go on.

'. . . Was she close enough? Already she was, I won't say in the shadow of the land, but in the very blackness of it, already swallowed up as it were, gone too close to be recalled, gone from me altogether.

' "Give the mate a call," I said to the young man who stood at my elbow. . . .

'Then stillness again, with the great shadow gliding closer, towering higher. . . . Such a hush had fallen on the ship that she might have been a bark of the dead floating in slowly under the very gate of Erebus.

' "My God! Where are we?"

'It was the mate moaning at my elbow. . . . '

How long Conrad was pulling in his boat before he reached land in *Youth,* is obscure; all that is known is that he was in Singapore about fifteen days after leaving the

Judea. He remained in Singapore for about a month and then, at the beginning of May 1883, embarked as a passenger on a steamer bound for Liverpool. By the beginning of June he was back again in London.

vi

Conrad presented himself for his second examination on Tower Hill. The examiner, who had a 'simply execrable reputation for severity, 'short and sturdy', sat leaning on his hand, his elbow resting on the long table, which had an unrigged mast fixed to its edge. Motionless and with his hand shading his eyes, he had a grim and mournful aspect, and he put Conrad through an examination that became disquieting to the point of nightmare. Taking a suppositional ship at sea, in suppositional conditions, he ordered him to execute a suppositional manœuvre.

'Before I was half through with it', Conrad tells us, 'he did some material damage to the ship. Directly I had grappled with the difficulty he caused another to present itself, and when that too was met he stuck another ship before me, creating a very dangerous situation. . . .

' ''I wouldn't have got into that mess,'' I suggested mildly, ''I could have seen that ship before.''

'No you couldn't,' he said. 'The weather's thick.'

He proceeded, at length bringing the ship into the North Sea, with a 'lee-shore with outlying sandbanks'.

'Well?' he said.

'I will have to think a little, sir.'

' ''Doesn't look as if there were much time to think,'' he muttered sardonically from under his hand.

'No, sir,' Conrad said with some warmth. 'Not on board a ship I could see. But so many accidents have happened that I really can't remember what there's left for me to work with.'

Even an examinee, like the proverbial worm, will turn. Conrad had spoken, in Blake's sense, 'from instinct', and, whether or not Napoleon's maxim that the 'boldest policy is always the best policy' be valid in general, it certainly was so in this instance. The examiner, 'still half averted, and with his eyes concealed', made a 'grunting remark'.

'You've done very well.'

But the troubles of the ship were not yet over.

'Have I the two anchors at the bow, sir?' Conrad asked.

'Yes.'

'I prepared myself then, as a last hope for the ship,' he says, 'to let them both go in the most effectual manner, when his infernal system of testing resourcefulness came into play again.

' "But there's only one cable. You've lost the other".'

Conrad answered desperately that he would try fixing a hawser at the end of the anchor chain, and if it gave, which was quite likely, he could 'just do nothing. She would have to go.'

' "Nothing more to do, eh?"

' "No, sir, I could do no more."

'He gave a bitter half-laugh.

' "You could always say your prayers".'

The ordeal was over; Conrad had passed.

His feelings of elation at his success were mingled with an urgent, affectionate desire to meet his uncle at Marienbad, as had been in prospect. Tadeusz, however, had written:

'I would rather see you a little later, a free citizen of a free country, than that you should arrive earlier still a citizen of the world. But decide the question for yourself, arrange as you think fit; for after all it is your skin that is at stake.'

Conrad let this objection go by the board and, seven weeks later, on 24th July 1883, the reunion was effected. Uncle and nephew were together for a month, partly in Marienbad and partly at Toplitz, in Lubeck. They had not seen one another previously for five years, and the affection between them was very great. The quality of Tadeusz's attachment to his nephew is patent in his letters; and to Conrad himself his uncle had not only been intimately associated with his mother—a bond of association touching the very springs of being—but he had known his whole family. It is easy to conceive, therefore, of the heartiness with which they met and the congenial frankness of their intercourse: the ageing, over-anxious Polish squire, and the vital, care-free young ship's officer. Yet the still exuberant Tadeusz would have listened like Coleridge's 'three years child' to the youthful mariner's vivid recitals of the sea—but scarcely in silence without interjections, as Conrad's mouthpiece Marlow's auditors did, page after page, chapter after chapter.

And Tadeusz, for his part, in walks and talks, no doubt, would hold forth upon the subject of Polish politics, or Polish agricultural interests. There were also financial matters to be discussed, and Tadeusz rendered accounts of his nephew's funds with businesslike precision. They amounted to 3,600 roubles (about £300 in the currency of the day), which Conrad proposed should be invested in a transport agency—Barr, Moering & Co.—this through the suggestion of a friend, Adolf P. Krieger. (It was to this man that he eventually dedicated *Tales of Unrest*.)

When, at length, they parted, and Conrad returned to London, they exchanged letters, Tadeusz writing:

'Your letter gave me real pleasure. Everything you say I shall remember in my heart. . . . You are right in supposing that when I returned to Toplitz I was sad and depressed when in the evening I sat down at table opposite your empty chair. . . . As for going to sea again, the sooner you do so the better, and I hope you will naturalise yourself at the very earliest moment, and that the "filthy lucre" which has been put aside for it will not be used for any other purpose.'

On the 10th September 1883 Conrad embarked as second mate in the *Riversdale,* a sailing ship of 1,500 tons, bound from London to Madras. Jean-Aubry observes that the voyage seems to have suggested some scenes in the *Ferndale* episodes of *Chance*; but nothing is known about it, except that Conrad got at loggerheads with the Captain, L. B. McDonald, and threw up his berth at Madras. McDonald entered on his discharge certificate, against the particular, 'Character for ability', 'Very good'; but against 'Character for conduct', 'Decline'. ('This is the only example of an unfavourable comment', writes Jean-Aubry, 'in the thirteen certificates which were found among Conrad's papers.')

Unable, apparently, to obtain a new commission at Madras, Conrad proceeded to Bombay; where he was offered a berth on a British mail steamer. He refused it, however, because he disliked serving in a steamer.

One day, from the veranda of the Sailors' Home, the hospitable Mercantile Marine institution, he beheld, sailing into the harbour, a vessel which had all the majesty of a full-rigged ship and the graceful lines of a yacht. Her name was the *Narcissus*; an appropriate name indeed; the recollection of seeing her, at anchor, reflected—Narcissus-like—in the glassy waters of the harbour, may well have suggested to Conrad the title, *The Mirror of the Sea*.

The *Narcissus* of Conrad's masterpiece, the *Nigger of the Narcissus,* is associated with stormy seas rather than with calm reflections, and even when she did 'float on a smooth sea', resembling a 'sheet of ground glass', thunder squalls were 'growling angrily' on the horizon.

The book itself is of enthralling interest; the story of the mesmeric influence exercised on the crew by the great, dramatic personality of a dying negro; the action is lively, the sentences are short, following quickly one upon another—not 'multitudinous tandems', as H. G. Wells described Conrad's diction in other works. For all this, it was ignored by the British reading public for years. Conrad himself esteemed it dearly, even as he loved his great work, *Nostromo,* which was similarly ignored. What is apposite from a biographical point of view, however, is that the work presents obliquely in fictional form the kind of nautical and marine experiences that are directly presented in the autobiographical *Mirror of the Sea.*

In the actual *Narcissus,* a full-rigged ship of 1,500 tons, Conrad obtained the berth of second mate. But he made only one voyage in her. She left Bombay on 28th April and, after arriving at Dunkirk, was dismantled.

Conrad returned to London; where he passed the winter of 1884—mainly, no doubt, in reading for his final examination. In April, next year, he proceeded to Hull, to become second mate of the *Tilkhurst,* a ship of 1,500 tons; which sailed on the 24th for Cardiff. There he disembarked, to visit a refugee compatriot; with whose son, Spiridion Kliszczewski, he became friendly and corresponded during his subsequent voyage, in the same ship —the *Tilkhurst*—in which he had signed on again a few days after leaving her. This voyage was to Singapore, the ship sailing on 6th June.

'We had a very fine passage,' Conrad writes to Spiridion from Singapore; where he arrived on 25th September. From Singapore the *Tilkhurst* proceeded to Calcutta. In a letter to Spiridion from that place, Conrad, after referring to his forthcoming examination with remarkable assurance—taking it for granted that he will pass— broaches the real purport of his letter. It is a new enthusiasm :

'. . . I wish to start due North!

'In other words . . . my soul is bent upon a whaling venture.

'And now here I must pray you take also for granted that I am brimful with the most exhaustive information upon the subject. I have read, studied, pumped professional men and imbibed knowledge upon whale fishing and sealing for the last four years. I am acquainted with the practical part of the undertaking in a thorough manner. Moreover, I have the assurance of active help from a man brought up in the trade, and although doing well where he is now, ready to return to his former pursuit (of whales). Finally I have a vessel in view, on very advantageous terms.'

The ship would cost £1,500, and he has no capital. He cannot possibly ask his uncle for such a sum; but he could manage out of his allowance and from what he gets from his investment in the London Transport firm already mentioned, to pay a yearly premium on a life policy for

£2,000; and the 'interest on the loan', says he, 'I *suppose* I could raise on the security of the said policy. . . .' He asks his friend's advice, as a 'cool businessman', on the question of the feasibility of this scheme. Presumably, he received it; for the whole subject, whaling enthusiasm and all, fizzled out, a flash in the Nalecz Korzeniowski pan doused by Spiridion. In fact, after propounding it, Conrad adds soberly: 'Believe me, it is not the desire of getting much money that prompts me. It is simply the wish to work for myself. I am sick and tired of sailing about for little money and less consideration. But I love the sea: and if I could just clear my bare living in the way I suggested I should be comparatively happy.'

In the next letter to Spiridion (from Calcutta), he writes despondently about the political situation in England:

'Where's the man to stop the rush of social-democratic ideas? The opportunity and the day have come and are gone! Believe me: gone for ever! For the sun is set and the last barrier removed. England was the only barrier to the pressure of infernal doctrines born in continental back-slums.'

He concludes:

'I live mostly in the past and the future. The present has, you easily understand, but few charms for me. I look with the serenity of despair and the indifference of contempt upon the passing events.'

Milton, on the occasion of a political landslide—away from democracy, 'withdrew his eyes from external events'; but the young Conrad was more dolorous, even, than his literary predecessor, the young Stevenson; *Stevenson among the tombs.*[9]

vii

The homeward voyage of the *Tilkhurst* was as prosperous as her outward passage had been. It was the more pleasant

---

[9] Although Conrad subscribes his Polish name in these letters, he directs the replies to be addressed to 'Mr. J. Conrad'.

to Conrad because of her captain's personality—Captain Blacke was a 'man of singularly well-informed mind', as he is described in *The Mirror of the Sea*, 'the least sailorlike in outward aspect, but certainly one of the best seamen whom it has been my good luck to serve under.' Conrad 'thought no end of him', and the esteem was evidently mutual; for, when—about the middle of June—the ship arrived at Dundee, and Conrad was discharged, the Captain told him (a most unusual compliment from a Master to a second mate), 'If you happen to be in want of employment, remember that as long as I have a ship you have a ship too.'

But Captain Blacke never had another ship. He fell ill soon after, and Conrad saw him again but once, visiting him, by request, when he was dying. The description of the visit in *The Mirror of the Sea* is very moving.

Conrad's own health at this period was rather unstable. As Jean-Aubry shows, he drew largely on his nerves, or will-power, thus living above his strength, while his strength, in general, was relatively maintained in virtue of his 'open-air life and extreme sobriety'; but the fatigues and stresses of a sailor's existence—Baptistin Solary's *'métier de chien'*—had begun to undermine his constitution; incidentally, his sojourn in India had affected his liver. Also, he was downcast, as he had received melancholy news from his uncle, who was worried about his own affairs. Tadeusz, uneasy, also, about his nephew's insecure occupation, urged him, as a second means of livelihood, to increase his connection with Barr, Moering and Co., the transport agents.

Conrad even thought of leaving the sea and taking up a business life. He felt very desirous to visit his uncle in Poland; first, however, he would have to be naturalised and now, on 19th August 1886, after twelve years of procrastination, he became an English citizen. Tadeusz wrote, 'I clasp my Englishman to my breast as well as my nephew.'

There was also the matter of his examination and the time drew near. He felt quite equal to the ordeal; yet, judging from his former experiences of the examiners, he would want all the nerve-power or will-power he could muster.

This time, the examiner was 'short, plump, with a round, soft face in grey, fluffy whiskers, and fresh loquacious lips', and the examination itself might be described, almost, in the same terms, only it was not 'short'. It was long, yet not long enough for Conrad, who found himself very much in the position, at the close, of a man who, after entering a hospital with aversion, departs from it with reluctance. The examiner was most interesting, 'wandering off' after each question and answer into commentatorial 'bits out of his own life'; for example:

> 'What's your idea of a jury-rudder, now?' he enquired.
> 'I warned him that I had no experience of a lost rudder at sea, and gave him two classical examples of makeshifts out of a text-book. In exchange he described to me a jury-rudder he had invented himself, years before, when in command of a 3,000-ton steamer.'

'The examiner', writes Conrad, at length, 'had given himself up to the spirit of gossiping idleness. For myself, I was in no haste to leave that room. Not in the least. . . . I would never again see that friendly man who was a professional ancestor, a sort of grandfather in the craft.'

At about this time (in the year 1886), Conrad made his first attempt at writing fiction. *Tit-Bits*—that evergreen old pioneer among popular weekly papers—offered a prize for a short story, and Conrad wrote and sent in *The Black Mate*. It is—or, rather, was—to judge from the amended version (the original no longer exists), a very elementary composition intended to be funny after the vein of W. W. Jacobs; a writer whom Conrad, in due time, came to admire. There is a funny *dénouement* when it transpires that the 'black mate' has dyed his hair, and the inclusion of the story in *Tales of Hearsay* is very much on a par with the inclusion of the lines *On the University Carrier* in Milton's earlier poems.

It did not gain the prize; the receipt of which, as it

was a money prize, would have been very welcome; for Conrad's finances were low. That he was, after passing his examination, unable to get a command, his 'first command', was no more than what, considering previous delays in obtaining berths after examinations, he could have expected. But he could not afford such delay and, the chance offering, he became, on 16th February 1887, the first mate of the *Highland Forest*, a Glasgow ship of 1,000 tons, then lying at Amsterdam.

She was destined for Samarang, Java; but she was winter-bound and, though not 'in the frozen zone' yet 'miserably benumbed'; she was, also, empty, her cargo up-country on a barge, or schuyt, endlessly delayed; her environment:

'a flat foreground of waste land, with here and there stacks of timber, like the huts of a camp of some very miserable tribe; the long stretch of the Handelskade; cold, stone-faced quays, with the snow-sprinkled ground and the hard, frozen water of the canal, in which were set ships one behind another with their frosty mooring-ropes hanging slack and their decks idle and deserted, alike waiting for their winter-bound cargoes.'[10]

Conrad grew weary of waiting; of shivering in his cabin, in which the ink, despite the stove—a small one—froze on the swing-table; of 'scrambling over the Arctic waste-land'; of 'shivering in glazed tramcars'; of returning up the side of the frozen craft, sliding about on the deck, to descend into his vault-cold berth. It was a 'cruel winter'.

'. . . 'Tis bitter cold,
And I am sick at heart.'

The lonely mate—for there was no one else in the ship except a toothless shipkeeper—might well have quoted *Hamlet*—but no; his heart was warm with 'sacred fire': he never forgot, for 'five consecutive minutes', that he had been 'appointed chief mate'. The 'sacred fire' was better even than the 'high pile of blankets, which positively

---

10 *The Mirror of the Sea.*

crackled with frost' as he 'threw them off in the morning'.

In his journeys to the town, Conrad waited upon the agent in endeavours to accelerate delivery of the cargo—endeavours which became, at length, a mere hopeless routine. The agent, Mr Hudig—a big, swarthy Netherlander—always received him, in his warm office, with the warmest cordiality; he was, nevertheless, as baffling as the binding frost.

'He always began by showing me into a chair before I had time to open my mouth, gave me cordially a large cigar, and in excellent English would start to talk everlastingly about the phenomenal severity of the weather.'

Mr Hudig, who had 'black moustaches and a bold glance', and spoke such excellent English, seemed 'incapable of understanding any phrase pronounced in a tone of remonstrance or discontent', and he would throw out, in the haze of cigar-smoke, the genial suggestion, 'I suppose in the end it is you they will appoint captain before the ship sails'. When Conrad, with due modesty, replied that they would not consider he had had enough experience, the good-natured Hudig would demur. ' "You know very well how to go about business matters," he used to say, with a sort of affected moodiness clouding his serene round face.'

At last, the cargo arrived. It was duly stowed, amid the thaw that had set in. The Captain appeared, walked up and down, contemplating the lay of the ship fore and aft in the water; then squatted down on his heels in the slush, to observe the draught of water under her counter. This solicitous ship-master was Captain John McWhirr, who is magnified in his practical carefulness in Conrad's supremely great short story, *Typhoon*.

He questioned Conrad concerning the levels at which the proportional weights of the cargo were disposed; for ships, like horses, have peculiarities or idiosyncrasies, this especially in regard to the way they are loaded. The Captain found that Conrad, insufficiently acquainted with this individual craft, had not apportioned enough of the weight to the upper part. She had been made much too

stable; the consequence was, as the Captain admonished
Conrad, that she would roll; and after they put to sea,
which was on the following day, his words came true with
a vengeance. At length :

'Down south, running before the gales of high lati-
tudes, she made our life a burden to us. There were days
when nothing would keep even on the swing-tables,
when there was no position where you could fix yourself
so as not to feel a constant strain upon all the muscles
of your body. She rolled and rolled with an awful dis-
lodging jerk and that dizzily fast sweep of her masts on
every swing. It was a wonder that the men sent aloft
were not flung off the yards, the yards not flung off the
masts, the masts not flung overboard. The Captain in
his arm-chair, holding on grimly at the head of the
table, with the soup-tureen rolling on one side of the
cabin and the steward sprawling on the other, would
observe, looking at me : "That's your one third above
the beams. The only thing that surprises me is that the
sticks have stuck to her all this time".'

This was a remarkably mild expression of reproach in a
ship-master. Inexorable Fate, apparently, took a sterner
view. A piece of a spar, carried away in the gale, struck
Conrad on the back, and sent him 'sliding on his face for
quite a considerable distance along the main deck'. Thereupon followed 'queer symptoms', as the Captain, who
treated them, used to say; 'inexplicable periods of power-
lessness, sudden accesses of mysterious pains'.

This led to 'sick bay'. At Samarang, where the *Highland
Forest*—moving as steadily into the harbour as Birnam
Wood when it went to Dunsinane—arrived in June, Conrad mystified a doctor with his symptoms. The doctor
said, 'Ah, friend . . . you must leave your ship; you must
quite silent be for three months—quite silent.'

Conrad left his ship, and went—as silently as possible,
no doubt—to Singapore. There, in a 'great airy ward', he
lay for some weeks of 'mental worry, hard rolling,
remorse, and physical pain', sometimes watching the

'fronds of the palm-trees tossing and rustling at the height of the window', in contrast with the 'dreadful cold and snow of Amsterdam'.

viii

Conrad, whose illness was, apparently, some sort of rheumatism, recovered sooner than expected and, on 22nd August 1887, two months after leaving the *Highland Forest*, he embarked as second mate in the s.s. *Vidar* (800 tons); no doubt preferring a steamer, as Jean-Aubry suggests, because he knew his strength, after convalescence, unequal to the more exacting requirements of a sailing ship.

Jean-Aubry had the good fortune, in 1924, to meet Conrad's old *Vidar* Commander, 'Captain C—', who told him:

> 'The first time I met Conrad was at the Shipping Office of Singapore about the middle of August 1887. He pleased me at once by his manners, which were distinguished and reserved. One of the first things he told me was that he was a foreigner by birth, which I had already guessed from his accent. I replied that that did not matter in the least as he had his certificate. (It was quite difficult at that time to find officers in the East who were not over fond of the bottle.) The *Vidar* belonged to an Arab called Syed* Mosin Bin S. Ali Jaffree. He had been a rich man, but he had been nearly ruined by his two sons-in-law. I had navigated these waters for the past ten or twelve years, and I had got to know that Arab well. I respected him. Some of his creditors were on the point of making him bankrupt; the Chartered Bank had seized the ship, but they could not sell because I was a creditor with a prior claim—for wages, docking-costs, etc. During one voyage among the islands I collected several thousand guilders from his debtors, and on his instructions I placed them with a bank, which, after a creditors' meeting, made an

---

* Syed signifies descent from Mahomet, conferring high rank.

arrangement; there was a sale, and the steamship *Vidar* became in part my property.'

Also, Conrad writes in *The Shadow Line*, describing the ship he had just left:

'. . . She traded among dark islands on a blue reef-scarred sea, with the Red Ensign over the taffrail and at her masthead a house-flag, also red, but with a green border and with a white crescent in it. For an Arab owned her, and a Syed at that. Hence the green border on the flag. He was the head of a great house of Straits Arabs . . . and he had a great occult power amongst his own people. . . . He had to employ white men in the shipping part of his business, and many of those he so employed had never set eyes on him from the first to the last day. I myself saw him but once, quite accidentally on a wharf—an old, dark little man blind in one eye, in a snowy robe and yellow slippers. He was having his hand severely kissed by a crowd of Malay pilgrims to whom he had done some favour, in the way of food and money. . . . Excellent (and picturesque) Arab owner. . . .'

Conrad became on intimately friendly terms with his new captain; who therefore may well have related to him the story of his salving the good Arab's ship, in her dangerous position, from the Chartered Bank.[11] He probably told it, along with other reminiscences, while the s.s. *Vidar* plugged steadily along on the shallow sea and among the 'thousand islands' of the Malay Archipelago.

With that sea and with those islands, Captain C— had been acquainted for ten years and more: he had navigated the dangerous estuaries and tortuous rivers between dense, dark forests; bargained on landing-stages, or in tiny houses, with Malay princes, Chinamen, Eurasians, and English or Dutch sea-trader adventurers; the motley merchant-princes and businessmen of that self-contained but heterogeneous world.

Conrad himself was to be in it, if not of it (he was

---

[11] So, in *Victory*, Heyst financially salves Morrison's brig.

always, wherever he was, constitutionally detached); he observed its natural effects, the brilliant, violent changes of light on sea and river and forest-clad country; the panorama of its inhabitants: their forms, colours, physiognomies, bearing, gestures, and all the minutiæ of the clothes, the ornaments, and the weapons that they wore.

All these impressions, appearances, and aspects he duly expressed in those of his novels in which he had taken the Malay Archipelago for his literary province—*Almayer's Folly, An Outcast of the Islands, Lord Jim, The Rescue,* as also such shorter stories as *Karain* and *The Lagoon.* He expressed them as he himself had seen them with more than ordinary vividness; but his own experiences were enriched and substantiated by those of the Captain which, though less vivid and intensive, had had, like a photographic plate, the longer exposure. Conrad also derived much of his future romantic material from James Allen and John C. Niven, the first and second engineers of the *Vidar.* Captain C— testified to the fidelity with which Conrad had presented the character of Almayer, and to his insight into the characters of such Arab personages as Abdulla, Babalatchi, and Lakamba, as re-presented (in different guises) in his Archipelagian novels. Although Conrad denies that he had entertained, at this stage, the slightest notion of becoming an author, Captain C—, nevertheless, told Jean-Aubry that when he 'went down to the cabin to talk to his first mate' (Conrad had then been promoted) 'he usually found him writing'. He may have been writing letters, of course; but Jean-Aubry notes 'We have traced only one letter written by Conrad from the *Vidar.*'

As for the itinerary of the steamer, Jean-Aubry gives the details with admirable conciseness:

'She was not sailing under the British, but under the Dutch flag, and she was registered at Banjarmassim, one of the chief ports of Dutch Borneo. Her course was to sail from Singapore through the Carimata Strait, from South Borneo to Banjarmassim, then between the Isles of Pulo Laut and the coast of Borneo. She coaled at Pulo Laut, touched at Dongola on the western coast of the Celebes, returned to Coti Broeuw, and finally reached Bulungan on the east coast of Borneo, whence she returned by the same route to Singapore.'

Jean-Aubry says also, 'there was a profitable trade in natural products; in rubber, cane, gutta percha, gum, resin. The *Vidar* took as a rule three weeks over this voyage. Besides the captain and Conrad, the crew consisted of two European and one Chinese engineer, a second mate Mahamat, eleven Malayans, and eighty-two Chinamen. Conrad made, between 22nd August 1887 and 5th January 1888, five or six of these voyages from Singapore to Bulungan in Borneo, which is the place to which he gave the name of "Sambir" in *Almayer's Folly* and *An Outcast of the Islands*. Its river he called the "Pantai".'

The substitution of fictitious place-names for actual ones, as in this case of 'Sambir' for Bulungan, is characteristic of Conrad, who always distinguished his own literary function from that of a reporter or chronicler; since they are occupied with time and space, the actual and the literal, but he, as an imaginative writer, with another dimension.

On the other hand, he did not always change, or modify, the names of actual people in representing them as characters in his novels. Thus he did not change the name of Almayer; an Eurasian-Dutch trader, the crucial character in his literary career. Before stating the reason in Conrad's own words, it is due to the sensitive reader to warn him that it is one of those cases in Conrad's style of jarring and jingling assonances: 'If I had not got to know Almayer pretty well, it is almost certain there would never have been a line of mine in print.'

Conrad heard a good deal about Almayer both at sea and in port—at sea, from 'deck passengers (mostly wandering traders of good repute) as they sat all over the ship—each man fenced round with bundles and boxes—on mats, on pillows, on quilts, on billets of wood';

in port, at Singapore, at Pulo Laut, at Dongola, in Celebes when the Rajah came on board and 'drank bottle after bottle of soda-water on the after-skylight' with the Captain, who smiled; while the Rajah—a rare thing with Malay Rajahs—'Laughed audibly'.

The subject of Almayer and his house (or 'folly', as it was called derisively) was a topic of endemic and inexhaustible humour. It was the kind of humour which is excited in some people by the spectacle of a man running after his hat; if the chase is prolonged and the hat continually evades the man just as he is, or thinks he is, on the point of getting hold of it, the humour is the more excited. Conceive the hat eventually rising and ascending while the man gazes upwards in despair—despair that is, etymologically, *wanhope,* the ghost of hope; conceive that he is so gazing eternally, and you have the image of Almayer; Almayer as Conrad saw him—not funny at all.

He was a weak character with an invincible opinion of his own high qualities and capabilities and an unquenchable ambition; a sort of paradoxical parody of Milton's motto, 'In weakness I am made strong.'

His trading-station was situated on a river-reach some forty miles up the forest-bound 'Pantai', and there, from the bridge of the *Vidar,* which was 'moored to a rickety little wharf', Conrad first beheld him. It was at daybreak, a dank tropical daybreak, the air saturated with chill moisture; but Almayer was 'in pyjamas' and a 'thin cotton singlet with short sleeves'. He was 'moving across a patch of burnt grass, a blurred shadowy-shape with the blurred bulk of a house behind him, a low house of mats, bamboos, and palm-leaves with a high-pitched roof of grass'.

That house had once been handsome, and proudly cared for, but had fallen into such a state of dilapidation that it vies, in Conrad's description, with such an 'abomination of desolation' as Hood's *Haunted House*; while everything else about the place—the offices, booths or go-downs, etc. —was in the same slatternly state of neglect. Almayer's wife, an Arab woman, had also deteriorated, and this to such an extent, according to *Almayer's Folly,* as to have become actually dangerous. Almayer himself, however, remained among the ruins of his life like Horace's 'man', unshaken, or, like Milton's '*Atlas*', 'unremov'd'. He had never lost his belief in himself; but he bewailed himself continually.

'I suppose you haven't got such a thing as a pony on board?'

Almayer, after wandering about in the chilly fog, as related, had come close to the ship's side on the jetty and, with a 'harassed countenance' and a 'heavy, pained glance', a curl of his thick black hair dangling over his forehead, had been engaging Conrad in melancholy, scarcely more than monosyllabic, talk. What he wanted was the pony— for what purpose appeared inconceivable, since in the 'whole settlement at which he used to shake daily his impotent fist, there was only one path that was practicable for a pony: a quarter of a mile at most, hedged in by hundreds of square leagues of virgin forest'. However, as he had ordered the pony and wanted it, it would cheer him, Conrad thought, to be reassured of its safe arrival. Conrad himself was feeling somewhat depressed, and his own voice had become modulated, during the conversation, to a minor key.

Yet Almayer remained looking at him with his melancholy eyes as if incredulous. This 'pathetic mistrust in the favourable issue of any sort of affair', writes Conrad, 'touched me deeply'. The truth was that, although Almayer had maintained his belief in himself, he had lost faith in everything outside himself; if, like Horace's 'man', he had stood amid the fallen rubble of the world undismayed, it would have been largely from lack of interest. He even lost interest in the pony when he was assured it had arrived. Any sediment of doubt on that score was dispelled:

'Suddenly the pony leaped upon the fore-hatch. His little hoofs thundered tremendously; he plunged and reared. He had tossed his mane and his forelock into a

TMC12*

state of amazing wildness, he dilated his nostrils, bits of foam flecked his broad little chest, his eyes blazed . . . he was fierce, terrible, angry, warlike, he said ha! ha! distinctly, he raged and thumped—and sixteen able-bodied Kalashes stood round him like disconcerted nurses round a spoilt and passionate child.'

Upon being swung from the derrick across the deck, the pony went limp, relaxed in a 'nerveless and absolute immobility'; yet as it went swaying past the front of the bridge, Conrad observed an 'astute gleam in his dreamy, half-closed eye'.

Almayer was asked to take hold of the rope before they lowered away, and he gathered it in a casual but perfectly efficient manner, until the 'pony's hoofs touched the wharf', when he 'gave way all at once to a most foolish optimism', letting fall the rope. He was knocked flat, while the pony got away. Almayer got up.

'Where do you think he will get to?' cried Conrad. 'Are there any fences anywhere in this fog? Can he bolt into the forest? What's to be done now?'

'Almayer shrugged his shoulders.'

Conrad conceived a very different idea of Almayer from that of the traders who derided him. They regarded him as a pitiful failure who made himself ridiculous by refusing to accept the fact; Conrad regarded him not, indeed, as tragic in the classic sense but tragic none the less—in a more subtle sense. He describes, himself, what it was in Almayer that impressed him so deeply and so strangely, as it did, so that it came to haunt his imagination, driving him, at length, after four years, to begin writing about the man; thence to carry his MS. about with him from sea to sea and port to port, adding line upon line, chapter upon chapter, as occasion offered, until the work was finished.

Here is the peroration of a speech he thought of delivering to Almayer's Shade in case he should eventually meet it in the Elysian Fields:

'I believed in you in the only way it was possible for me to believe. It was not worthy of your merits? So be it. But you were always an unlucky man, Almayer. Nothing was ever quite worthy of you. What made you so real to me was that you held this lofty theory with some force of conviction and with an admirable consistency.'

In fact, Almayer's vanity was as heroic as that of Nostromo, the dynamic *Capataz de Cargadores* of Costaguana.

Other characters prominent in Conrad's Archipelagian novels are Captain Tom Lingard, Jim Lingard, and Willems.

Captain Lingard, as Conrad represents him, was a well-meaning, adventurous trader who interested himself in Malay political affairs—which usually took the form of feuds and fights—and was known among the various chiefs and their peoples, as he came and went in his formidable armed brig, as the *Rajah Laut*, the King of the Sea. Extremely fortunate in his business, he was as unfortunate in his good intentions; at any rate, in his exploits in *The Rescue* and *Almayer's Folly*.

In *The Rescue* he betrays the trust of a noble Malay prince and his sister as a consequence of salvaging the schooner-yacht of an inane, inanely ungrateful English nobleman, and of becoming infatuated with his aristocratic wife, the yacht having arrived (directed by Inexorable Fate) on a mud bank. In *Almayer's Folly*, after providing Almayer with his Malay wife, trading-station, and ambition, which he has inflated, with a promise to fulfil it, he leaves him, disappears in Europe on some business connected with the purpose, and is no more heard of.

The character of Lingard was created out of traits perceived by Conrad in an actual Lingard, the Captain of a trading-schooner plying between the same Eastern Dutch ports as the *Vidar*. Captain Lingard's nephew, Jim Lingard, became the hero of *Lord Jim* but only in respect of his 'swaggering manner'—the effect, perhaps, of an 'inferiority complex' due to his having married a Malayan woman; a derogatory proceeding; so deemed, although, as if in reversal of this judgment in another court, he was provided by her with numerous children.

Willems, the 'outcast' of *The Outcast of the Islands,* was in actual life a Dutch sailor who, having taken to drink, became a dependent of Almayer; a 'hanger-on', as the term is. The idea of the story was suggested, in Captain C—'s opinion, by the salvage, during one of the *Vidar's* voyages, of a runaway Malayan slave from a sinking canoe. The work ranks below *Almayer's Folly,* which itself is not high in the Conradian scale. The *Outcast* is lurid and melodramatic, and might be described, if the neologism be not too barbarous, as *televisionary.* Conrad's literary power when he wrote these books was unequal to the wealth of Archipelagian material that he had acquired. It was not until he came to write *The Rescue* that his realistic cargo was distributed technically in a masterpiece.

The wealth of potential knowledge that Conrad carried away from these Eastern voyages, although they lasted only four months, was prodigious. One would describe it even as Shakespearean; for Shakespeare acquired and absorbed his own potential material in some such impressionable way. Only the state of childhood is truly impressionable; it is as if the cranium of creative genius lies open like a new-born babe's. Conrad himself not only possessed such impressionable genius; he preached the gospel of being impressionable. After deploring the miserable state of the 'totally unimaginative, of those unfortunate beings in whose empty and unseeing gaze (as a great French writer has put it) "the whole universe vanishes into blank nothingness",' he continues:

'The ethical view of the universe involves us at last in so many cruel and absurd contradictions, where the last vestiges of faith, hope, charity, and even of reason itself, seem ready to perish, that I have come to suspect that the aim of creation cannot be ethical at all. I would fondly believe that its object is purely spectacular: a spectacle for awe, love, adoration, or hate, if you like, but in this view—and in this view alone—never for despair! Those visions, delicious or poignant, are a moral end in themselves. The rest is our affair—the laughter, the tears, the tenderness, the indignation, the high tranquillity of a steeled heart, the detached curiosity of a subtle mind—that's our affair! And the unwearied self-forgetful attention to every phase of the living universe reflected in our consciousness may be our appointed task on this earth. A task in which fate has perhaps engaged nothing of us except our conscience, gifted with a voice in order to bear true testimony to the visible wonder, the haunting terror, the infinite passion and the illimitable serenity; to the supreme law and the abiding mystery of the sublime spectacle.

'*Chi lo sà?* It may be true. In this view there is room for every religion except for the inverted creed of impiety, the mask and cloak of arid despair; for every joy and every sorrow, for every fair dream, for every charitable hope. The great aim is to remain true to the emotions called out of the deep encircled by the firmament of stars. . . .'

ix

Conrad's reason for berthing in a steamer rather than in a sailing-ship proved very valid; in consequence of the easier life and shorter voyages in the *Vidar*, he quickly recovered his health. Despite his dislike of steamers, in general, he always retained a great kindness for this particular one: on board of her he not only acquired, as has been shown, the main material for the development of his genius but, together with that, and—what was efficacious in bringing it out—he laid up for himself treasures of memory. Thus, more than thirty years afterwards, he wrote to Mr Niven, the engineer:

'You could not really have believed that I had forgotten any time in the *Vidar*. It is part of my sea life to which my memory returns most often, since there is

nothing to remember but what is good and pleasant in
my temporary association with three men for whom, I
assure you, I have preserved to this day a warm regard
and sincere esteem.'

And yet, child of unrest that he was, Conrad was not
constituted for happiness in the *Vidar,* or anywhere else;
it was not in him to enjoy peace. Calm with him was
liable to become *dead calm;* the *doldrums*—the doldrums
disturbed, as they are in their equatorial region, by vari-
able winds: Conrad was disturbed by fluctuating moods
—weariness, depression, vague uneasiness. He himself
discloses what he felt. After declaring how fortunate he
was in every way on board the *Vidar,* he writes:

'And suddenly I left all this. I left it in that, to us,
inconsequential manner in which a bird flies away from
a comfortable branch. It was as though all unknown I
had heard a whisper or seen something. Well—perhaps!
One day I was perfectly right and the next everything
was gone—glamour, labour, interest, contentment—
everything.'

He attributes his state of mind to the 'green sickness of
late youth,' and to the 'shadow-line' of approaching man-
hood, when the 'still young are inclined to commit rash
actions, such as getting married suddenly or else throwing
up a job for no reason'.

Certainly there is such a state as the 'shadow-line', the
equator in life's sphere, and there are other lines of latitude
as well; Conrad was traversing one of them, as Madame
Delestang noticed, in Marseilles.[12]

Apart from this 'green sickness', or 'shadow-line', however, there remains as the basic cause of Conrad's leaving

[12] At the period, Conrad was thirty years old; he died about
thirty-three years afterwards. The date, therefore, proved very
nearly equatorial, and the curious question arises—Is such a circumstance, in general, significant? In that case, the 'shadow-line' in
a man's life, if determinable, might denote the man's 'expectation
of life'. The consideration may be commended to the attention of
the Life Insurance Companies.

the *Vidar*, his constitutional restlessness. He left ship after ship and when, eventually, he lived in England, he left house after house in quick succession. Only at his desk could he find peace, but even at that quiet anchorage his mental equilibrium was precarious; if his pen happened to fall to the floor, he would sit for some time drumming with his fingers in helpless exasperation.

Jean-Aubry holds that Conrad left the *Vidar* mainly because the 'want of variety in these regular voyages, the routine work on board, began to weigh upon him'—and that seems to be the conclusion of the whole matter. Conrad could 'endure hardness', in the Pauline phrase— the hardness of toiling at the pumps, of being bandied about on a craft pitching and rolling as in a watery earth-quake, of struggling on a yard with an ice-hard sail; but— less hardy, in one respect, than a bus-driver or a bank clerk—he could not endure monotony. He could not endure it because, lacking the diversion and distraction of exciting interests and adventures, it left his mind open to the entry of sorrows, dissatisfactions, nostalgia. The 'prophetic soul' is cognizant of its own needs, and the desire for travel to the wide spaces of the earth, early raised up in Conrad, with his tragic temperament, his sensitive nature, and his vivid imagination, was providential. It was necessary for him to keep 'on the run' in this way—to live strenuously and 'dangerously', in the Nietzschean sense, until the time came—now fast approaching—when he would be able to live imaginatively in what he himself describes as the 'hard slavery' (but not monotony) 'of the pen'.

When, on 5th January 1888, the *Vidar* arrived at Singa-pore, Conrad determined to throw up his berth. Good Captain C— 'stared hard', as well he might, upon being notified of this sudden, surprising decision; neither could Conrad render a reason. However, the shrewd shipmaster was a psychologist, although he had not attended the Academy of Freud; gradually a smile 'came to lurk under his thick iron-grey moustache', and 'I do believe', says Conrad, 'he understood my case'.

At any rate, he provided his ex-officer with an excellent testimonial.

Conrad's intention was now to return to Europe in the hope of obtaining a ship. Yet he felt pretty hopeless—not, indeed, in despair, for it was against his philosophy to yield to despair; he was at a loose end; figuratively, at the end of the rope he himself had cut. He felt as though he were falling through a void; the void, in his own expression, of 'life-emptiness'.

From this deplorable situation he was suddenly delivered. A demand had arisen, circulated from Bangkok, for a shipmaster to replace one who had died at sea, and Conrad was offered the position. Avidly he accepted it. It was his First Command; the position for which he had waited for a year; the consummation of ten years' unrelaxed efforts, of toils, privations, humiliations; it was that apogee of a quarter-deck to which he had always aspired. He was no longer under the 'shadow-line'; the jaded and gloomy young man had become a boy again; the boy who in his romantic dreaming was a man, a sailor, a Captain in the English Mercantile Marine.

In fact, he had become young enough to take the appointment at its 'face value' as a smile of fortune— forgetful once more, as in the voyage of the *Palestine,* of Inexorable Fate; which, like Milton in Tennyson's poem, as it proved, 'somewhat grimly smiled'.

He was the more elated because there was to be no delay; his instructions read :

'This is to inform you that you are required to proceed to-day in the s.s. *Melita* to Bangkok and you will report your arrival to the British Consul which will show that I have engaged you to be Master of the *Otago* in accordance with the Consul's telegram on a voyage from Bangkok to Melbourne, wages at fourteen pounds per month and to count from date of your arrival at Bangkok, your passage from Singapore to Bangkok to be borne by the ship. Further to receive a passage from Melbourne to Singapore if you are not kept in the ship.'

The memorandum was addressed 'Captain C. Korzeniowski', dated 19th January 1888, and signed 'Henry Ellis', the Marine Superintendent at Singapore. The actual agent of the appointment, however, was a Captain Patterson, the original in *The Shadow Line* of the most likeable, most memorable of all Conrad's characters (speaking personally); the middle-aged, humanely experienced shipmaster, Captain Giles. Ellis, the Marine Superintendent, appears in *The Shadow Line* under his real name. Captain C— of the *Vidar* is also in the book, under the name of Kent.

To his ship, in that authentically autobiographical story,[13] Conrad, in the s.s. *Melita,* at once proceeded. He scarcely gave a thought to Captain Patterson's parting words, 'I expect you'll have your hands pretty full of tangled-up business', and scouted a previous remark of that weighty ocean-sage, about the Gulf of Siam, 'The Gulf. . . . Ay! A funny piece of water—that.' He also remained immune to the exceptionally morose behaviour of the *Melita's* Captain, the 'first really unsympathetic man', he says, 'I had ever come in contact with'. Only, the voyage seemed long, he was so very eager to see his ship.

At last, on the fourth day, 'that imbecile', as he calls the Captain of the *Melita,* called and beckoned him up on the bridge. Conrad perfunctorily ascended the ladder; whereupon the disagreeable captain grasped him by the shoulder and slewed him round a little, pointing with his other arm, at the same time. 'There! That's your ship, Captain,' he said.

'I felt a thump in my breast,' says Conrad in *The Shadow Line,* '. . . as if my heart had ceased to beat. There were ten or more ships moored along the bank, and the one he meant was partly hidden from my sight

---

[13] 'That piece of work is not a story really but an exact autobiography.'—(Letter to J. B. Pinker, 1917.) 'The very speeches are (I won't say authentic, they are that absolutely) I believe verbally accurate.'—(Letter to Sir Sidney Colvin, 27th February 1917.) Also, Conrad first entitled the work *First Command.*

by her next astern. . . . Yes, there she was. Her hull, her rigging filled my eye with a great content. That feeling of life-emptiness which had made me so restless for the last few months lost its bitter plausibility, its evil influence, dissolved into a flow of joyous emotion. At the first glance I saw that she was a high-class vessel, a harmonious creature in the lines of her fine body, in the proportioned tallness of her spars. Whatever her age and her history, she had preserved the stamp of her origin. She was one of those craft that in virtue of their design and complete finish will never look old. Amongst her companions moored to the bank, and all bigger than herself, she looked like a creature of high breed—an Arab-steed in a string of cart-horses. . . . I knew that, like some rare women, she was one of those creatures whose mere existence is enough to awaken an unselfish delight. One feels that it is good to be in the world in which she has her being.'

The ship was all this, there is no doubt—of herself; but, in ulterior respects, she might have been either Coleridge's or Poe's nightmarish bark—or both; for certainly she had such horrors aboard. Conrad found her to be the seat of disorder, rancour, stupidity.

Concerning the disorder, Captain Giles's 'tangled-up' remark proved to be, to say the least, euphemistic.

Conrad was a poor hand at business matters, although he contrived to meet his own responsibilities as a ship-master; but even if he had been a chartered accountant, or possessed the financial finesse of a Governor of the Bank of England, he could scarcely have been equal to the situation in which he found himself when confronted with the professional effects of the late Captain of the *Otago*.

Item, 'Some suspiciously unreceipted bills.'

Item, 'A few drydock estimates hinting at bribery.'

Item, 'A quantity of vouchers for three years' extravagant expenditure.'

The above were discovered muddled up in an old violin

case. Also, an account-book filled up with poems, as described by Jean-Aubry, of a 'joyful and indecent character'.

Jean-Aubry, whose Conradian researches ranged so far and wide, includes in his great work the reply to a letter which Conrad had sent to Messrs Henry Simpson and Sons, of Port Adelaide, the owners of the *Otago*. It is dated 5th April 1888, and begins:

'Dear Sir:

'Your favours dated Bangkok 2nd and 6th February, latter with P.S. dated 7th on the eve of sailing, duly reached me and have been interesting as detailing the melancholy circumstances under which you took charge of the barque *Otago*.

'The accounts which you enclose are no doubt at all in order but I have no means of comparing them with other documents as the late Captain never favoured me with a scratch of the pen from the time of leaving Newcastle in August last and the acting Master Mr Burns only wrote me a brief note acquainting me with his Captain's death. Therefore, I am at a loss to know what business was done by the ship after she arrived at Haiphong, whether she earned or whether she lost money. In fact, other than your documents, I have no record whatever of receipts and expenditure. Will you, therefore, please inform me whether any freight was obtained between Haiphong and Bangkok and if so, how much and generally what business was done by the ship for the ten months previous to your assuming command?'

Judging from this letter, the late Captain of the *Otago* would seem to have been as inattentive to his owners as the famous Captain of the *Pequod*, in *Moby Dick*, was contemptuous of his own employers.

Another particular which made Conrad's 'hands pretty full' was the absence of ship's stores—extra gear; spare sailcloth, rope, etc.; while in the matter of the ship's medicine-chest, it will transpire how great a cause of trouble its deficiencies became. A cause of present trouble was that the river where the ship lay was pestilential; already there was fever on board, while she could not get to the sea, the best remedy, because the cargo had been delayed.

The first to succumb was the steward. He was replaced by a Chinaman, introduced by a local hotel-keeper, who became the original of the malicious Schomberg in *Falk* and *Victory*. The Chinaman left the ship after three days, with Conrad's emergency fund, amounting to £32. Soon after, Mr Burns, the Mate, was down with fever, and was removed to hospital.

Mr Burns was a malcontent. After the death of his old Captain, at the age of sixty-five, he had entertained full expectations of being appointed Captain in his stead. Although he was not professionally qualified for such a position, he had navigated the ship to Bangkok and that, in his own estimation, was sufficient warrant of his competency. At first, in the violence of his disappointment, he threatened to resign but, as he had a wife and child in Sydney, he forebore.

As for the second mate, he apparently was a mere cypher stupid, and of no help at all in the surrounding difficulties.

During the unsuccessful chase of the absconding Chinaman, Conrad had made the acquaintance of the Captain of a German ship anchored near the *Otago*. Captain Hermann proved a cordial friend in need, and afforded Conrad some respite from his worries. Every evening the jaded Captain of a fever-infected ship would betake himself into the midst of a happy family circle, and smoke a pipe with the worthy German in company with his wife and children. Jean-Aubry suggests that one of the children was the original of the 'silent heroine of *Falk*'; the young woman whose substantial charms satisfied a hunger worse than famine endured in Antarctic wastes.

x

At last, after a fortnight, the *Otago* escaped down the river to the sea. But Mr Burns had left the hospital so ill that he had had to be carried on board in a litter, and most of the crew were still sick. The second mate proved as futile as he was stupid. Only Ransome, the cook, who was a first-rate sailor, but could not act in that capacity because he had a weak heart, was a great support to Conrad in running the ship. Mr Burns, morose and gloomy in his cabin, solaced his disappointment by talking to his new Captain about the old one.

He displayed a photograph of the old man:

> 'There he sat,' Conrad writes in *The Shadow Line*, 'with his hands reposing on his knees, bold, squat, grey, bristly, recalling a wild boar somehow; and by his side towered an awful, mature, white female with rapacious nostrils and a cheaply ill-omened stare in her enormous eyes. She was disguised in some semi-oriental, vulgar, fancy costume. She resembled a low-class medium or one of those women who tell fortunes by cards for half-a-crown. And yet she was striking. A professional sorceress from the slums. It was incomprehensible. There was something awful in the thought that she was the last reflection of the world of passion for the fierce soul which seemed to look at one out of the sardonically savage face of that old seaman.'

To sport with this appalling Amaryllis in the shade was preferable, to the old Captain, to bothering about his unloaded ship, which he left sweltering at anchor, and her crew gasping for three weeks in a pestilential hot harbour. Not even the atrocious Mr Vanslyperken in Marryat's *Snarleyyow* (and perhaps he, too, was working in the deep hold of Conrad's recollections), wooing the widow Vandersloosh in the stuffy parlour, on the 'little fubsy sofa', is a more 'awful' imagination. But the scene ends abruptly.

Suddenly he 'came on board in the middle of the night and took the ship out to sea with the first break of dawn. Daylight showed him looking wild and ill. . . .'

He proceeds to drive his unballasted craft as recklessly as the Flying Dutchman himself, beating up against a fierce monsoon, 'blowing away sails, straining the spars, exhausting the crew', whose remonstrances he meets with a grim taciturnity. Usually shut up in his cabin, he played the violin.

He was, however, slowly dying; and as the days went by the distracting sounds gradually grew less, till at last only a feeble scratching could be heard outside the door. One afternoon, the water-tanks being low and the ship having not gained fifty miles in a fortnight, Mr Burns, the Mate, burst into the cabin, and yelled close in his ear that he was 'going out of the world', that they could not wait until he was dead, and that he must put the helm up. ' "So I am going out of the world—am I?" snarled the man on the couch. "Yes sir—you haven't many days left in it. One can see it by your face."

' "My face, eh? . . . Well, put the helm up and be damned to you".' When the Mate informed him that this had been done, the old man 'gave him a look of savage spite, and said these atrocious words in deadly, slow tones :

' "If I had my wish, neither the ship nor any of you would ever reach port. And I hope you won't".'

After his death his fiddle cannot be found, but only the empty case. He must have thrown it over the side. 'It's my belief,' cried Mr Burns, after emphasising this conclusion, 'he would have tried to take the ship down with him if it had been in human power. He never meant her to see home again.'

The ship's store of quinine proves to have been faked, and the new Captain suffers agonies of remorse because he had neglected to examine it properly. Mr Burns, who is reduced to a state approaching madness, accuses the dead Captain :

'I always thought he would play us some deadly trick,' he exclaims, seated 'hunched up, emaciated, and demented in his cabin, and resembling an intense, animated, and loquacious skeleton, with long flaming red moustaches and spectral eyes'.

'The great thing to do, sir,' he said again and again, 'is to get the ship past 80° 20' of latitude.'

It is the position, outside the Gulf of Siam, where the
terrible old man lies buried, and the ship had been showing a queer inability to get past it. 'Fitful light airs had
played with her literally as catspaws; and when they
failed, she was manipulated by mysterious currents; but
never could she pass that latitude, never get out of sight
of the barren islet of Koh-ring.'

Mr Burns knew the reason. The trick with the quinine
was preparatory to the game the evil old man was going
to play them.

He had still, however, to reckon with Mr Burns. ' "It
won't be very long now before I can come up on deck,"
he muttered, "and then we shall see".'

'You have not known him,' he tells the Captain. 'I
have, and I have defied him. . . . I faced him in that
cabin. . . . If he had had his way, we should have been
beating up against the Nord-East monsoon, as long as
he lived and afterwards too, for ages and ages. Acting
the Flying Dutchman in the China Sea! Ha!'

From the flying Dutchman suggestion, the atmosphere
changes to that of the 'Ancient Mariner'. It was dead calm.
The 'sails hung motionless . . . the very folds of their sag-
ging surfaces moved no more than carved granite'. The
Captain's remorse deepens. He would have held the men
justified in tearing him 'limb from limb'. (Hanging the
empty quinine bottles about his neck like the dead body
of the albatross about the neck of the Ancient Mariner.)
They do not even curse him with their eyes. Their for-
bearance, however, heaps coals of fire upon his head.

He tramps the silent deck day and night, while the 'sun
climbs and descends, the night swings over our heads as
if somebody below the horizon were turning the crank'.
Occasionally he goes below to visit Mr Burns; who feeds
himself determinedly and seems engaged in some 'arduous'
(and probably supernatural) 'mental operation' (no doubt,
of combating the dead Captain). One night, the Captain
entertained an idea of daunting pessimism :

'As I emerge on deck the ordered arrangement of the stars meets my eyes, unclouded, infinitely wearisome. There they are: stars, sun, sea, light darkness, space, great waters; the formidable Work of the Seven (*sic*) Days, into which mankind seems to have blundered unbidden. Or else decoyed. . . .'

On a night that appeared extraordinarily dark, when the 'only spot of light in the ship' was where, as in *The Ancient Mariner*:

'The steersman's face by his lamp gleamed white', the fever-wasted men worked the ropes. As the Captain saw them:

'The shadows swayed away from me without a word. Those men were the ghosts of themselves, and their weight on a rope could be no more than the weight of a bunch of ghosts. . . . They wandered feebly after me from rope to rope, stumbling and panting. . . . I stood amongst them like a tower of strength, impervious to disease and feeling only the sickness of my soul. . . . I raised my voice not much above a whisper, and, noise-lessly, an uncomplaining spirit in a fever-wasted body appeared in the light aft, the head with hollow eyes illuminated against the blackness. . . .'

The thick darkness becomes flooded and saturated with an uncanny rain, in which the Captain, walking the poop —which he knows to be deserted—suddenly stumbles over 'something big and alive. Not a dog—more like a sheep, rather. But there were no animals in the ship.

'How could an animal?'

The eerie suggestion is that of what the spiritualists call an 'apport'—something fallen, or dropped, out of the un-known—and seems associated in some obscure way with the woman who had been photographed beside the old Captain, and gave the impression of a 'low-class medium'. Although Conrad himself disclaimed any belief in the supernatural, he could certainly suggest it.

It was indeed a nightmare voyage!

Eventually, however, the spell is broken (whether or not as a consequence of the interposition of Mr Burns) and the ship arrives at her destination, an 'Eastern port'. There, at the 'Officers' Sailors' Home', the harassed young Captain repairs to Captain Giles, who performs the function of a kind of purgative Greek chorus.

Captain Giles was 'stout and pale, with a great shiny dome of a bald forehead, and prominent brown eyes'. He was an expert in intricate navigation, but did not 'look like a sailor at all'. He had the 'appearance of a man from whom you would expect sound advice, moral sentiments, with perhaps a platitude or two thrown in on occasion'.

And that, indeed, is precisely what the excellent ex-shipmaster meted out on the present occasion. First, however, he had to deal helpfully with a young man who, 'prone in a long chair, opened as they approached, one horrible fish-like eye'.

'I remember his first coming ashore here some years ago,' commented Captain Giles. 'He was a nice boy. Oh! These nice boys!'

'Things out East are made easy for white men,' he explained. 'The difficulty with these nice boys' was how 'to go on keeping white.'

Conrad's difficulty, however—the thing that was troubling him—was very different; he was still thinking about the unfilled quinine bottles and the deaths of suffering men. He was worried by his conscience.

Captain Giles did not advise him, like the Lord Advocate in *Catriona*, to 'throw his conscience overboard'; but he said sagaciously:

'A man must learn to stand up to his conscience like everything else.'

xi

The *Otago*, which had taken three weeks to travel the eight hundred miles or so from Bangkok, remained at Singapore for three weeks, disembarking her sick crew, as many as survived, taking in fresh stores—with special attention to the medicine chest—and generally recuperating as well as might be, before proceeding to Sydney.

She sailed some time in March 1889, and made up for the past by having a very good passage, justifying in every way the high estimate Conrad had formed of her at first sight. Mr Burns, continuing on board on the way to see his wife and child, was still too weak to leave his cabin. No doubt, Conrad endeavoured to cheer him; with kindly dissimulation, perhaps, humouring him by agreeing that he had been too masterful for the malevolent old Captain. Yet if—on this hypothesis—Mr Burns had saved the ship, and so returned good for evil to his ungrateful owners for whom he had already navigated her out of the dying clutches of the old man, he might have regarded himself, from his own odd standpoint, as being the more unjustly dealt with.

The *Otago* reached Sydney in the beginning of May; when Conrad's regained high spirits were subdued by a letter from his uncle. Tadeusz's health had declined, and a cure abroad was prescribed, but he could not afford the expense. He yearns to see his nephew, and asks anxiously whether his English naturalization has yet been sanctioned in St Petersburg, adding 'I hope in 1890 to have a railway station eight versts[14] from here[15] and I want to live to take advantage of it, for there I shall be nearer for M. le Capitaine.'

In Sydney, at this time, Conrad chanced to meet Mr B—, the old Mate of the *Duke of Sutherland*, who had been in the habit when going ashore of getting drunk.

The episode is not a pleasing one; but biographers cannot be choosers and, at any rate, Conrad himself apparently saw no harm in it; for he thus relates it in *The Mirror of the Sea*:

'He recognised me at once, remembered my name, and in what ship I had served under his orders. He looked me over from head to foot.

---

14 A verst is nearly two-thirds of a mile.
15 Odessa, where he was staying.

' "What are you doing here?" he asked.

' "I am commanding a little barque," I said, "loading here for Mauritius." Then, thoughtlessly, I added: "And what are you doing, Mr B—?"

' "I," he said, looking at me unflinchingly with his old sardonic grin, "I am looking for something to do."

'I felt I would rather have bitten out my tongue. His jet-black, curly hair had turned iron-grey; he was scrupulously neat as ever, but frightfully threadbare. His shiny boots were worn down at heel. But he forgave me, and we drove off together in a hansom to dine on board my ship. He went over her conscientiously, praised her heartily, congratulated me on my command with absolute sincerity. At dinner, as I offered him wine and beer, he shook his head, and as I sat looking at him interrogatively, muttered in an undertone:

' "I've given up all that."

'After dinner we came again on deck. It seemed as though he could not tear himself away from the ship. We were fitting some new lower rigging, and he hung about, approving, suggesting, giving me advice in his old manner. Twice he addressed me as "My boy", and corrected himself quickly to "Captain". My Mate was about to leave me (to get married), but I concealed the fact from Mr B—, I was afraid he would ask me to give him the berth in some ghastly jocular hint that I could not refuse to take. I was afraid. It would have been impossible. I could not have given orders to Mr B—, and I am sure he would not have taken them from me very long. He could not have managed *that*, though he had managed to break himself from drink—too late. He said good-bye at last. As I watched his burly, bull-necked figure walk away up the street, I wondered with a sinking heart whether he had much more than the price of a night's lodging in his pocket. And I understood that if that very minute I were to call out after him, he would not even turn his head.'

From Sydney, the *Otago* proceeded to Melbourne,

arriving at the end of June 1889, where, five or six weeks later, she left Port Adelaide bound for Mauritius. The weather was stormy; but the season was advanced, and there was no time to spare: Conrad, despite the warnings of both the pilot and the tug master, left in a violent southwest gale. He took the risky route (with leave obtained from his trustful owners) of the Torres Strait. In his article, 'Geography and Some Explorers' (*Last Essays*, 1926), he describes the passage through the Straits:

'It was not without a certain emotion that, commanding very likely the first and certainly the last merchant ship that carried a cargo that way—from Sydney to Mauritius—I put her head at daybreak for Bligh's Entrance, and packed on her every bit of canvas she could carry. Wind-swept, sunlit, empty waters were all around me half-veiled by a brilliant haze. The first thing that caught my eyes upon the play of green white-capped waves was a black speck marking conveniently the end of a low sand-bank. It looked like the wreck of some small vessel.

'I altered the course slightly in order to pass close, with the hope of being able to read the letters on her stern. They were already faded. Her name was *Honolulu*. The name of the port I could not make out. The story of her life is known by now to God alone, and the winds must have drifted long ago around her remains a quiet grave of the very sand on which she had died. Thirty-six hours afterwards, of which about nine were spent at anchor, approaching the other end of the strait, I sighted a gaunt, grey wreck of a big American ship lying high and dry on the southernmost of the Warrior Reefs. She had been there for years. I had heard of her. She was legendary. She loomed up a sinister and enormous *memento mori* raised by the refraction of this serene afternoon above the far-away line of the horizon drawn under the sinking sun.

'And thus I passed out of Torres Strait before the dusk settled on its waters. Just as a clear sun sank ahead of

my ship I took a bearing of a little island for a fresh
departure, an insignificant crumb of dark earth, lonely,
like an advanced sentinel of that mass of broken land
and water, to watch the approaches from the side of
the Arafura Sea.'

Jean-Aubry associates Conrad's stay in Mauritius with
'A Smile of Fortune', one of the stories in *'Twixt Land and
Sea*. The respective circumstances tally in so far as the
narrator of the story is, as Conrad was, a young shipmaster
in his first command, his Mate is Mr Burns, of *The Shadow
Line*, and his ship has come into the harbour at Mauritius
to get chartered and lade sugar.

He becomes enamoured of the illegitimate daughter of
a Dutch trader on the island. This man, Jacobus, is under
a moral cloud among the other Europeans in the town, because he has transgressed their peculiar—by no means
strict—conventional code, and this to such an extent that
he is constrained to keep his daughter sequestered from
childhood in his house and garden. She spends her days
in the garden, a tropical paradise, chaperoned by her aunt,
a repulsive and evil, if well-born, old woman, who poisons
her mind with the belief that all men are brutal miscreants.

The young Captain's acquaintance with the girl has
been instigated by Jacobus himself. His object is twofold
—to dispose, at an exorbitant rate, of a load of potatoes,
and also, as a kind of long-term policy, of his illegitimate
daughter. He wishes to inveigle the Captain into marrying
his daughter, that by this means he may re-establish his
moral position and thus become reconciled with his
wealthy and socially-outraged brother. The Captain, as it
happens, is in desperate need of cargo-bags, which are
virtually unprocurable, and one day the wily trader fans
his hopes of acquiring them, while he steers him into his
house.

Alice, in the garden, is seated in a wicker chair. She
betrays charms of a very peculiar kind. She attracts against
her own will, paradoxically, by being defensively offensive,
while her 'flimsy, dingy, amber wrapper' becomes her to

the last seductive degree. She sits dreamily, in the wicker chair, in a sultry-charmed atmosphere of gorgeous blooms and massive leaves, like a 'spellbound creature with the forehead of a goddess crowned by the dishevelled magnificent hair of a gipsy tramp'. The young Captain, rebuffed, ignored, insulted, fascinated, returns day after day to 'taste perversely the flavour of contempt' in her 'indolent poses, drink in the provocation of her scornful looks, and listen to the curt, insolent remarks uttered in that harsh and seductive voice'.

At length, he succeeds in breaking down the girl's obsession as to male depravity and, leaping into the breach, unresisted, showers 'kisses upon her face'. Jacobus puts in an appearance at the passionate moment. Alice, however, with a woman's prevision, and an instinctively adroit movement, has already freed herself and retired into the house.

After some preliminary small-talk about the state of the market, Jacobus broaches the subject of the potatoes he wants to sell and the Captain doesn't want to buy. The latter is now persuaded into buying them, his main reason for doing so being that he urgently desires to see the girl again. Jacobus consents to go at once down to the wharf and see the potatoes loaded into the lighter.

The garden is now clear (the old woman chaperone, on this occasion, was conceivably indisposed), and the Captain calls, 'Alice!'

But the summons was unanswered, and he did not call again; 'I had become aware', he says, 'of a great discouragement. I was mentally jaded, morally dejected.'

He sat down and, with his elbows spread on the low balustrade, took his head in his hands.

The evening closed upon the garden. The 'colours of the blossoms deepened, losing their glow one by one'.

At length:

'The girl, when I turned my head at a slight noise, appeared to me very tall and slender, advancing with a swaying limp, a floating and uneven motion which ended in the sinking of her shadowy form into the deep low chair. And I don't know why or whence I received the impression that she had come too late. She ought to have appeared at my call. She ought to have . . . . It was as if a supreme opportunity had been missed.

'I rose and took a seat close to her, nearly opposite her arm-chair. Her ever discontented voice addressed me at once, contemptuously:

' "You are still here."

'I pitched mine low.

' "You have come out at last."

' "I came to look for my shoe—before they bring in the lights."

'It was her harsh, enticing whisper, subdued, not very steady, but its low tremulousness gave me no thrill now. I could only make out the oval of her face, her uncovered throat, the long, white gleam of her eyes. She was mysterious enough. Her hands were resting on the arms of the chair. But where was the mysterious and provoking sensation which was like the perfume of her flower like youth? . . . I would never find again near her the strange, half-evil, half-tender sensation which had given its acrid flavour to so many days, which had made her appear tragic and promising, pitiful and provoking. That was all over.'

The title of the story—'A Smile of Fortune'—is ironical. Pertinently it should be, rather, 'A Frown of Fate'. It is true that the potatoes which the Captain bought so reluctantly and so dearly, fetched three times the amount in Melbourne where, at the time of the ship's arrival at the port, there was, as it happened, a potato famine; *that*—derived from an exultant remark of the Mate, Mr Burns—was the 'smile of fortune'. On the other hand, the Captain lost, through his visit to Mauritius, his peace of mind, his joy on the sea, his enchantment-inspiring power of seeing the Indian Ocean. All these attributes of illusion and efficacy were gone, or had declined, like the glowing colours of the blossoms in the empty garden of Jacobus, like the young Captain's illusionary feeling for the girl who had failed to answer his call. It was as if they had passed at the very moment when he, by his own infatuated selfishness, had touched a spring, a deep spring, in the girl's own heart and mind. Now her eyes were opened; her gorgeous Paradise was converted into a solitary cell, her anodyne of mental blindness into a desolation of sight. At first, perhaps, she would hope, seated in her wicker chair, and the gaze of her 'long eyes, a narrowed gleam of liquid white and intense motionless black, would not now be 'empty of thought'.

The consciousness of the ruin—the actual, *living* ruin—the collapse of his illusion had left, haunted the young man as the ship, laden with sugar and potatoes, after sailing at last, stood out to sea, and Mauritius, 'Pearl of the Ocean', receded and dwindled on the skyline. He would never see again that beautiful island, where the air is sweet and the climate is luxuriant and suave as the sweetness of its sugar canes. The ship would return there inevitably on her route. In vain the Captain in Melbourne had submitted to his owners a 'carefully-thought-out scheme' for her 'employment in the East and about the China Seas'; although 'greatly struck with the project', they thought it better that she should continue in the sugar trade.

After reading this letter, the Captain sat motionless for a long time. He then wrote to his owners again, and went ashore to the post; but he passed letter-box after letter-box, wandering on through the populous streets as if lost in a desert solitude. He could not bring himself to post that letter which, as the more practical penalty of the 'smile of fortune', contained in its terms the destruction of all his plans, the endangering of his future, the deprivation of the ship that he had come to love: the *resignation of his First Command.*

At last:

'There came a moment when the awful tenacity of Jacobus, the man of one passion and of one idea, appeared to me almost heroic. He had not given me up.

. . . Was it for his own sake or for the sake of the poor girl? And on that last supposition the memory of the kiss which missed my lips appalled me; for whatever he had seen, or guessed at, or risked, he knew nothing of that. . . . How could I go back to fan that fatal spark with my cold breath? No, no, that unexpected kiss had to be paid for at its full price.

'At the first letter-box I came to I stopped and, reaching into my breast-pocket, I took out the letter—it was as if I were plucking out my very heart—and dropped it through the slit.'

❀   ❀   ❀   ❀

Jean-Aubry's main reason for associating this erotic story with the voyage of the *Otago* is as follows:

'I feel certain that the adventure narrated in 'A Smile of Fortune', connected with the cargo of potatoes, actually happened as described, on account of an odd question which Conrad asked me one day when I was talking to him about this story. "Do you think", he said to me, "that Jacobus had seen something?" (He was alluding to the beginning of Chapter VI where Jacobus either surprised the young Captain in the company of his daughter, Alice, or at least might have caught them at a compromising moment.) When I confessed that for my part I could not decide, and, in my turn, asked him the same question, he answered, "I never knew"—an answer which suggests that the incident is as autobiographic as that of the cargo of potatoes.'

It may be so. On the other hand, there is such a strong resemblance between Alice and Doña Rita in their respective reactions—or, in psycho-analytical jargon, 'complexes'—in relation to 'sex', that the one might seem to have been an imaginative variant of the other. (A curious parallel is the 'something masculine' in both young women), as witness in *A Smile of Fortune*:

'She drank the water at a draught, with the avidity of raging thirst, and let herself fall on the nearest chair, as if utterly overcome. Her attitude, like certain tones of her voice, had in it something masculine: the knees apart in the ample wrapper, the clasped hands hanging between them, her body leaning forward, with drooping head. I stared at the heavy black coil of twisted hair. It was enormous, crowning the bowed head with a crushing and disdained glory. The escaped wisps hung straight down. And suddenly I perceived that the girl was trembling from head to foot, as though the glass of iced water had chilled her to the bone.[16]

' "What's the matter now?" I said, startled, but in no very sympathetic mood.

'She shook her bowed, over-weighted head and cried in a stifled voice but with a rising inflexion:

' "Go away! Go away! Go away!"

'I got up then and approached her, with a strange sort of anxiety. I looked down at her round, strong neck, then stooped low enough to peep at her face. And I began to tremble a little myself.

' "What on earth are you gone wild about, Miss Don't Care?"

'She flung herself backwards violently, her head going over the back of the chair. And now it was her smooth, full, palpitating throat that lay exposed to my bewildered stare. Her eyes were nearly closed, with only a horrible white gleam under the lids as if she were dead.

' "What has come over you?" I asked in awe. "What are you terrifying yourself with?"

'She pulled herself together, her eyes open frightfully wide now. . . .

' "Never mind! Don't care!" Then after a gasp, she spoke with such frightful rapidity that I could hardly make out the amazing words: "For if you were to shut me up in an empty place as smooth all round as the palm of my hand, I could always strangle myself with my hair".'

---

[16] Cp. Doña Rita's behaviour on p. 108.

xii

The *Otago* left Mauritius for Port Adelaide on 18th November 1888. Upon her arrival, Conrad found two letters awaiting him from his uncle. One informed him about his inheritance: 15,000 roubles, free of succession duty, was to be paid to him a year after his uncle's death. The other letter read:

'You do not tell me how long you think you are going to remain in Australia. You know that I do not wish to influence you, but for an old man who has not long to live, time is a matter of some interest, and also to know that he may possibly see again those who are dear to him. Cannot you ask Mr Krieger to inquire at the Russian Embassy if the formality in excusing allegiance to the Czar is an accomplished fact? I read in the Polish newspapers that his grace had been afforded to twenty-seven persons. Perhaps you are one of them? No names were given. Perhaps it is all settled. In that case, we can hope to see each other in the country.'

Deeply stirred and saddened by these letters and anxious to return to Europe, Conrad resigned his command.[17]

The owners, at Port Adelaide, replied on 2nd April 1889 to Captain J. Conrad Korzeniowski:[18]

'Dear Sir:
'Referring to your resignation of the command (which we have in another letter formally accepted) of our bark *Otago*, we now have much pleasure in stating that this early severance from our employ is entirely at your own desire, with a view to visiting Europe, and that we entertain a high opinion of your ability in the

---

[17] The discrepancy between the reasons of Conrad's resignation of his first command does not necessarily discount Jean-Aubry's contention that the potato-erotic passages in *A Smile of Fortune* are autobiographic.

[18] Included in Jean-Aubry's *Joseph Conrad Life and Letters.* (Heinemann.)

capacity you now vacate, of your attainments generally, and should be glad to learn of your future success.
Wishing you a pleasant passage home,
We are, dear Sir,
Yours faithfully,
Henry Simpson & Sons,
Owners of the Black Diamond Line.'

Conrad reached London probably about the end of May 1889, but he could not proceed to the Ukraine, as he wanted to do; the sin of his delay in applying for English naturalization when his uncle first, and repeatedly afterwards, besought him to do so, had found him out. The wheels of the Czarist Administrative official machine, cluttered with red tape, moved slowly in its process of releasing a Russian citizen from his allegiance. The dilatory formalities had been progressing, on and off, for the space of three years in Conrad's case, and had still some months to go.

Prevented thus from revisiting his native country because he remained a member of it, and also from returning to his element, the sea, the shipless ex-Captain of the *Otago* was homeless, for his lodging-house at Bessborough Gardens was no home.

He was driven down into himself—into an introspective crasis of impressions and recollections. He lived an indolent, desultory life. There was no longer any necessity for him to read treatises on navigation, the mathematics of the sea, and, in that sense, he was mentally cut off also from his congenial avocation. Whether, unlike most sailors (who prefer, or used to prefer, Bulwer Lytton to Captain Marryat, and nowadays would probably prefer Daphne du Maurier to Joseph Conrad), he read any sea-writers at this period, is unknown. At any rate, he read a good many books.

Out-of-doors, he sauntered about London, or paid frequent visits to Captain Freud, the Secretary of the London Shipmaster's Society, in Fenchurch Street.

Captain Freud was a humble, unobtrusive benefactor to

his fellow-men, whose name has become immortalised, as it happens, for Conrad writes in *A Personal Record*:

'Dear Captain Freud—it is impossible not to pay him a tribute of affectionate familiarity at this distance of years—had very sound views as to the advancement of knowledge and status for the whole body of the officers of the mercantile marine. He organised for us courses of professional lectures, St. John Ambulance classes, corresponded industriously with public bodies and Members of Parliament on subjects touching the interests of the service. . . . Together with this high sense of his official duties he had in him a vein of personal kindness, a strong disposition to do what good he could to the individual members of that craft of which in his time he had been a very excellent master. And what greater kindness can one do to a seaman than to put him in the way of employment? Captain Freud did not see why the Shipmasters' Society, besides its general guardianship of our interests, should not be unofficially an employment agency of the very highest class. . . .

'In my wanderings about London from West to East and back again (I was very idle then) the two little rooms in Fenchurch Street were a sort of resting-place where my spirit, hankering after the sea, could feel itself nearer to the ships, the men, and the life of its choice— nearer there than on any other spot of the solid earth. This resting-place used to be, at about five o'clock in the afternoon, full of men and tobacco smoke, but Captain Freud had the smaller room to himself and there he granted private interviews, whose principal motive was to render service.'

Many names are recorded in the great political histories of the world, but a name thus celebrated by a Master, whether in prose or rhyme, is as good as written in the Book of Life.

Conrad also often visited, in this slack time, the offices of Messrs Barr, Moering & Co., in Camomile Street, to talk with his friend, Krieger.

Thus the time passed; an idle, empty time, as it might seem; yet, beneath the surface, as with fallow fields, development was proceeding. One morning, instead of dawdling over his breakfast, as he was in the habit of doing, Conrad abruptly rose and, instead of leaving the breakfast things to lie indefinitely, he pulled the bell-rope. When the table was cleared he began to write the first chapter of *Almayer's Folly*.

Yet, as he declares:

'The conception of a planned book was entirely outside my mental range when I sat down to write; the ambition of being an author had never turned up amongst those gracious imaginary existences one creates fondly for oneself at times in the stillness and immobility of a day-dream: yet it stands clear as the sun at noonday that from the moment I had done blackening over the first manuscript page of *Almayer's Folly* . . . from the moment I had, in the simplicity of my heart and the amazing ignorance of my mind, written that page the die was cast. Never had Rubicon been more blindly forded, without invocation to the gods, without fear of man.'

Conrad's first book having actually taken ink and paper, in this way, it became his practice directly after breakfast to 'hold animated conceptions of Malays, Arabs and half-castes', who 'came with a silent and irresistible appeal. . . .

'I did not receive my visitors with boisterous rapture as the bearers of any gifts of profit or fame. There was no vision of a printed book before me as I sat writing at that table, situated in a decayed part of Belgravia. After all these years, each leaving its evidence of slowly-blackened pages, I can honestly say that it is a sentiment akin to piety which prompted me to render in words assembled with conscientious care the memory of things far distant and of men who had lived.'

He was now a 'haunted man who looks for nothing but words wherein to capture his visions', especially was he obsessed by his impressions and imaginations of Almayer, a weak man, wrestling irritably, and full of self-pity, with Inexorable Fate.

However, he could not afford to go on indefinitely entertaining his Bornean visitants in Pimlico; his finances consisted mainly of the money he had saved during his year's command of the *Otago,* and another berth was apparently unobtainable, even by the utmost endeavours of Captain Freud.

Conrad, therefore, instead of going on 'blackening' the pages of *Almayer's Folly,* began to write letters—which, as they were careful, purposeful letters, were themselves deterrent to 'animated conceptions', even if they did not absolutely exorcise those 'Malays, Arabs and half-castes'. Besides, the object of these letters was to get a practical, matter-of-fact job.

They were addressed to various people on the Continent, who were, for the most part, Conrad's own relations; those among them who belonged to the more exalted—at least, elevated—ranks of society: 'good' people, as they are vulgarly called.

It does not appear, however, that a man's grand, or 'good', relations—especially a Merchant Service sailor's, or even an officer's—can do very much for him, and Marlow (Conrad's mouthpiece) relates in *Heart of Darkness* what the response to those letters, in general, proved to be. He puts it in a nutshell, in a sentence: 'The men said "My dear fellow", and did nothing.' The women replied in similar, if feminine, terms, and did no more. Among them there was, in Brussels, however, an 'aunt'— she was actually, according to Jean-Aubry, a 'maternal grandmother's first cousin'—who wrote, 'It will be delightful: I am ready to do anything, anything for you. . . . I know the wife of a very high personage in the Administration, and also a man who has lots of influence with', and so on, and so up.

She was Mme Marguerite Poradowska, a Frenchwoman

who had married a Pole; she was also a novelist.[19] She was perfectly sincere, and her spontaneity, the cordial atmosphere of generous intentions, raised and fixed Conrad's hopes in the direction of Belgium.

Brussels was, at that time, the lodestar and the rendezvous of all sorts of people—adventurers, stockbrokers, big-businessmen, small money-grubbers, and missionaries. Above them all, astutely eminent, arose the figure of Leopold II: he it was who in 1878 accepted the explorer Stanley's plans for the civilisation and development of Central Africa, which the British Government had rejected. The gifted monarch, as a Continental ruler, was out of his proper sphere; and Stanley acted as a providence, enabling him to rise in the financial world to the position of a Magnate; one of the richest men in Europe and even in America. Where Stanley saw only civilisation, Leopold envisaged a more solid sort of enlightenment; he sponsored the *Comité d'Etudes du Haut Congo,* which became the *Association Internationale*

---

[19] Mme Poradowska—a woman of great personal beauty—published several novels, as well as translations from the Polish. She and Conrad were in frequent correspondence; which was now accelerated. In this Conrad incessantly refers to her literary work, its development, and publication in periodicals—especially the *Revue des Deux Mondes*—and in book form, invariably writing of it on the top note of praise. In the same vein he expresses deepest affection and devotion, with anxiety regarding her health; while some passages, abstracted from their general context, might seem to verge even on the erotic. His own affairs—health, spirits, movements and, later on, literary endeavours—he discloses intimately; but always appears more concerned and interested in her personal and literary well-being than in his own. Occasionally he writes about himself, his moods varying from the crest of elation to the trough of despondency; sometimes, with bitter pessimism; sometimes, with hilarious burlesque.

But the extant letters (of Conrad) are best treated in quotation and exposition as a whole and, as they are chiefly important in connection with his later, literary life, and the present endeavour is far spent, I defer the subject to my (projected) complementary volume.

These letters have been translated and fully edited, by John A. Gee and Paul J. Sturm, in *Letters of Joseph Conrad to Marguerite Poradowska,* 1890-1920. (New Haven, Yale University Press; London, Humphrey Milford, Oxford University Press, 1940.)

du Congo. The Royal Croesus-to-be beamed upon Stanley with his gold-lustre, gave him his blessing, and sent him back to 'Darkest Africa' over which the sun of gold would rise. Stanley's mission was to let in the light; he was a minister of civilisation; an excellent practical administrator; but light, according to Shakespeare, 'thickens' and, according to Sir Oliver Lodge, matter is formed at the edges of light; so, in 'Darkest Africa', the light of civilisation coalesced, congealed, and coagulated into rubber, 'red rubber', as it came to be called in E. D. Morel's invective— or was it in De Vere Stacpoole's *The Pools of Silence?* Whichever author coined the phrase, their books are alike terrible, and if American comics had been published in those days, the accounts of Congo natives bereft of their hands, if those hands had failed to deliver their quota of rubber, would have furnished a suitable story. These books, having performed their function, are now forgotten, or they probably will be when they have passed out of living memory; but Conrad's *Heart of Darkness*. which treats of the same subject, the same iniquity, will not be forgotten.

In that extraordinary masterpiece, Conrad shows up the inane cruelty and rapacious mismanagement that abused Stanley's African enterprise after he had left it to the Leopoldian wolves (it naturally appalled Stanley himself when he came to hear of it). In 1890, however— the year of Conrad's epistolary search for employment— these African horrors had not become publicly known; at least, it was so in England, whatever some people in Belgium may have heard of them; perhaps cognizant of them in a sort of comatose, wishfully-oblivious way, as is natural to most people, feeling secure in the bed of their comfortable minds and disliking to be disturbed. Let us add, the less to appear contumelious, that the natives of the Congo were included among Kipling's 'lesser breeds' in those times; and breeds of low elevation as they were accounted, like the lower animals—being helpless also—are the more easily dissociated from the mind—at least, their tortures are. Thus, even lovers of animals can sleep peacefully in their beds, oblivious to the torment, and averse from the topic, of the gin-trap.

Thus, then, did Leopold and his 'Merchants of Light' *civilise* the Congo barbarians—in some such manner, in fact, as Julius Caesar *pacified* the Belgae, and thus the Belgian public were as ignorant of the means employed in 'Darkest Africa' as the populace of ancient Rome were ignorant of conditions in remotest Gaul.

Besides, rubber from the Congo brought money into the country; which Leopold and his fellow exploiters of black labour invested, to the common benefit as well as their own. At length, the publication, in 1890, of Stanley's *Darkest Africa* aroused and excited (to adopt Jean-Aubry's adjectives) the 'scientific, journalistic, political and commercial' world. The sensation descended in the most popular way to the man in the street, the woman in the house, even the boy in the school. The biographer recalls it in England, because there appeared in *Scraps,* a comic paper, an illustration of a man, his wife, and family, who had converted their suburban back garden into 'Darkest Africa' by erecting tents and wearing ducks and pith helmets.

According to *Heart of Darkness,* Conrad conceived the idea of going to the Congo upon seeing a map of those parts in a shop window. It was on such a map (as already related) that, when he was about nine years old, he had put his finger on a space then blank, and exclaimed, 'When I grow up I shall go there.' Whether or not the shop-window incident occurred before he sent his solicitous letters to the Continent, and whether or not Mme. Poradowska's influence was already active in Belgium, is obscure. At any rate, it was through Krieger and Barr, Moering & Co. that he actually went to the Congo; they introduced him to M. de Baerdemaecker of Ghent, *aide-de-camp* to King Leopold, who recommended him to Albert Thys, the acting-manager of the newly-formed and enterprising *Société Anonyme Belge pour le Commerce du Haut- Congo*; writing 'among other things: "His general education is better than most sailors and he is a perfect gentleman".'[20] Thys engaged to give him the command of one of the company's Congo river-steamboats as soon as there was a vacancy.

This was in September 1889. Three months went by, and Conrad was still waiting for his appointment, when a letter arrived from Uncle Tadeusz expressing the hope that his nephew's projected visit to him need no longer be delayed. Conrad, thereupon, arranged matters, in correspondence with Thys, very conveniently: there was no prospect of the appointment at present, and he would be given long enough notice when there was one to enable him to return from Poland and be ready to proceed to the Congo in good time.

He set off a few weeks later, breaking his journey at Brussels to pay a visit to the generous-hearted Mme. Poradowska—also to the Secretary of the Congo *Société* —and arrived at his destination, Kazimierowka in Polish Ukraine, on 16th February 1890.

Conrad stayed with his uncle for nearly two months; during which time, as a Polish gentleman became Captain in the English Mercantile Marine, he was an object of interest—also, no doubt, of admiration—to many visitors; although some among the older people who had censured him in the past as a renegade may have tendered their congratulations with somewhat mixed feelings. In the meantime he kept in touch with Thys, the acting-manager of the Congo *Société*, and upon his return to London he found a letter awaiting him to the effect that the expected vacancy had occurred and that he would be able to replace the Captain of a Congo steamboat who had been killed in a scuffle with the natives. He 'flew round to get ready', and before forty-eight hours had passed was crossing the Channel, and in a few more hours was in Brussels; a city, says his mouthpiece, Marlow, 'that always made him think of a whited sepulchre'.

He might well have thought of it in this way in view of the evil thing that, like the vampire emanating from

---

[20] Jean-Aubry.

the tomb of Dracula, came out of it; the 'obscene beast', as Conrad himself calls it, that materialised in Darkest Africa. But he was not yet in view of that abominable thing, as later he came to be. The city looked bright, not white in any sepulchral sense. Everybody he met was cheerful; they were 'going to run an over-sea empire, and make no end of coin by trade', and the office building of the Company (to which Conrad was on his way) was the 'biggest thing in the town'.

He came to the street in which the Company carried on business.

'A narrow and deserted street in deep shadow, high houses, innumerable windows with venetian blinds, a dead silence, grass sprouting between the stones, imposing carriage archways right and left, immense double doors standing ponderously ajar.'

There was, it would seem, nobody there; the eyes that had once looked through those innumerable windows, the hands that had once closed the ponderous double doors, had departed as if into the sepulchre. Conrad beheld, upon reaching the office building itself, two silent female figures, 'knitting black wool, as impassive as Fate'.[21]

But the acting-manager, described as 'pale plumpness in a frock-coat',[22] received him with a handshake, talked to him, gave him his contract to sign, engaging his services for three years, and informed him that he had scarcely a fortnight to make his preparations before departing to the equatorial regions.

xiii

On 11th May 1890 Conrad embarked, at Bordeaux, in the steamer *Ville de Maceio*, bound for Boma in the Congo Free State. The following letter to his cousin, Charles Zagorski, is illuminating:

---

[21] *Heart of Darkness.*
[22] ibid.

Freetown, Sierra Leone.
22nd May, 1890.

'My very dear Charles:

It is just a month to-day since you were scandalised by my hurried departure from Lublin.* From the date and address of this letter you will see that I have had to be pretty quick, and I am only just beginning to breathe a little more calmly. If you only knew the devilish haste I had to make! From London to Brussels, and back again to London! And again to Brussels! If you had only seen all the tin boxes and revolvers, the high boots and the touching farewells; just another handshake and just another pair of trousers!—and if you knew all the bottles of medicine and all the affectionate wishes I took away with me, you would understand in what a typhoon, cyclone, hurricane, earthquake—no!—in what a universal cataclysm, in what a fantastic atmosphere of mixed shopping, business and affecting scenes, I passed two whole weeks. Two weeks spent at sea have allowed me to rest and I am patiently waiting for the end of this trip. I shall reach Boma no doubt on the 7th of next month and then leave Boma with my caravan to go to Leopoldville [at Stanley Pool].

As far as I can make out from my "service letter" I am destined to the command of a steamboat, belonging to M. Delcommune's exploring party, which is being got ready; but I know nothing for certain as everything is supposed to be kept secret. What makes me rather uneasy is the information that 60 per cent. of our Company's employees return to Europe before they have completed even six months' service. Fever and dysentery. There are others who are sent home in a hurry at the end of a year, so that they shouldn't die in the Congo. God forbid! It would spoil the statistics which are excellent, you see! In a word, it seems there are only 7 per cent. who can do their three years' service.

* Conrad had broken his return journey from Kazimierowka to visit him.

. . . Yes! But a Polish nobleman, cased in British tar! *Nous verrons!* . . .[23]

He arrived at Boma on 12th June (not on the 7th, as in his letter). But his ultimate destination was Stanley Pool, about two hundred miles farther on, and, on the first stage of his journey, he proceeded in a small boat thirty miles up the Lower Congo to Matadi, where four factories—English, French, Portugese, and Dutch—had been set up in the African wilderness. Thus far had the enterprising industrialists been able to go, but no farther; mountains surrounded the place, and the river there had shallowed out, before it plunged into rapids—rapid after rapid. 'Accursed land,' had written Albert Thys, 'set there as a barrier by Nature herself to impede all progress.'

Aut viam inveniam aut faciam. The industrialists were making a railway. It was only begun, and Conrad would have to tramp the rest of the journey; two hundred and fifty miles and more up and down mountains, 'down and up chilly ravines, up and down stony hills ablaze with heat, through forests, through or over rivers, through long grass, through burnt grass'.

Most of these words are taken from *Heart of Darkness,* but they might equally well have come from a diary which Conrad kept from 13th June to 1st August.[24] The caravan with which he was going was to start in fifteen days' time. The interim, especially because of the company he had to keep, appeared as an 'eternity'. 'Think just now', he notes, 'that my life amongst the people (white) around here cannot be very comfortable; intend avoid acquaintances as much as possible'. Another entry, 'prominent character-

---

[23] 'Letter in Polish, communicated by the addressee's daughter'—Jean-Aubry.

[24] Included in *Last Essays* (Dent) as *A Congo Diary*. Written in pencil in two black penny note-books; the second note-book containing only technical matter: aids to local navigation, rough outline-maps, lists of stores, etc. Now preserved in the Library of Harvard University. (Particulars taken from Richard Curle's Introduction to *Joseph Conrad's Diary. The Blue Peter,* October, 1925.)

istics of the social life here; people speaking ill of each other'.

There was, however, an exception:

'Made the acquaintance of Mr Roger Casement'[25] which I should consider as a great pleasure under any circumstances and now it becomes a positive piece of luck. Thinks, speaks well, most intelligent and very sympathetic.'

This appreciation of Casement is expanded in a letter to Cunninghame Graham, in 1903, in Conrad's best style. After referring to the Leopold-Thys enterprise in Africa as a "gigantic and obscene beast', he writes:

'I send two letters I had from a man called Casement, premising that I knew him first in the Congo just 12 years ago. Perhaps you've heard or seen in print his name. He's a Protestant Irishman, pious too. . . . For the rest I can assure you that he is a limpid personality. There is a touch of the Conquistador in him too; for I've seen him start off into an unspeakable wilderness swinging a crookhandled stick for all weapons, with two bulldogs, Paddy (white) and Biddy (brindle), at his heels and a Loanda boy carrying a bundle for all company. A few months afterwards it so happened that I saw him come out again, a little leaner, a little browner, with his stick, dogs and Loanda boy, and quietly serene as though he had been for a stroll in a park. Then we lost sight of each other. He was, I believe, Bsh. Consul in Beira, and lately seems to have been sent to the Congo again, on some sort of mission, by the Br. Government. I have always thought that some particle of Las Casas'

---

[25] Sir Roger Casement became a fanatical patriot. In other respects, he was all that Conrad says of him; in an other's words, 'generous, careless of reward, indifferent to danger and death': a 'mixture of an Elizabethan and a Don Quixote'. At the time of his fatal plunge into Irish insurgency, his health was undermined and his nervous system wrecked in consequence of his work on behalf of the natives of the Congo and the Putumayo, whose wrongs he had shown up. He was hanged for treason in 1916, despite petitions for reprieve, to world-wide indignation.

soul had found refuge in his indefatigable body. The letters will tell you the rest. I would help him, but it is not in me. I am only a wretched novelist inventing wretched stories and not even up to that miserable game; but your good pen, keen, flexible and straight, and sure like a good Toledo blade, would tell in the fray if you felt disposed to give a slash or two. He could tell you things! Things I've tried to forget; things I never did know. He has had as many years of Africa as I had months—almost.'[26]

During his stay at Mapadi Conrad occupied himself with writing letters—especially to Mme. Poradowska—and by doing odd jobs—for instance, in his diary: 'Have been myself busy packing ivory in casks. Idiotic employment.'

On 28th June he started in a caravan of thirty-one men on the two-hundred-and-fifty-mile track to Kinchassa, where he was to take up his command of the steamboat. Crossing the river, after the first halt, they proceeded

---

[26] In this connection, Mr Retinger, in his *Conrad and His Contemporaries*, makes an astonishing statement:

'I am sure that the only outstanding characters he' (Conrad) 'became acquainted with during his voyages were John Galsworthy whom he adored, and Roger Casement whom he despised. In fact, I remember when after his trial and his condemnation during the War somebody, I believe it was Fisher Unwin, the publisher, circulated an appeal for pardon and asked Conrad's signature; he refused it with vehemence, telling me at the time that he once shared a hut on the Congo with Casement, and that he ended by utterly disliking the man.'

As Mr. Retinger's veracity may not be doubted, and as it is necessary, therefore, to believe (a test of 'faith', conventionally so called) in the amazing refusal, the only conceivable hypothesis seems to be that Conrad, as a naturalized Englishman in wartime, had become *ultra*-patriotic; 'more English than the English', as the saying is. In fact, Mr Curle, in *The Last Twelve Years of Joseph Conrad* (Sampson Low), asserts that very thing (Chapter X, page 186); a strain of his father's fanatical patriotism had apparently come out in him.

As for Conrad's eulogy of Casement in the above letter and Mr Retinger's assertion that he told him that he 'once shared a hut in the Congo with Casement, and that he ended by utterly disliking the man', they will not square; the disagreement is wrapt in obscurity.

towards Pataballa, where one arrives, writes Thys, 'sweating, panting, and aching in every limb'.

The region was mountainous and proved overpowering to a Belgian officer, Captain Harou, Conrad's travelling companion. He was corpulent, like Thys, and unhealthy, and he was seized with an attack of sickness; the beginning of recurrent attacks which necessitated his being carried, at intervals, throughout the journey.

They proceeded, marching about fifteen miles a day, through various landscapes, as already indicated, in vicissitudes of temperature from burning to chilling; much like the extremes between which the devils are hurried in Milton's Hell. In addition, there were the incessant, insistent mosquitoes, attacking—in particular the white men—by day and by night. On one night 'no mosquitoes' (sic), Conrad notes, 'owing to large fires lit all round our tent'.

He was 'getting jolly well sick of this fun'.

Yet, as a white man in the march, he bore but his own burden, not another's; whereas the native carriers sweated and ached under the pole from which depended the huge weight of the fat man in his hammock. They complained —not being speechless like the more unfortunate, still lower breeds in their woes—and Conrad was obliged to 'row' with them :

'At 2 p.m. put him' (Harou) 'in hammock. . . . Row with carriers all the way.'

'. . . a very hot day. Expect lots of bother with carriers to morrow. Had them all called and made a speech, which they did not understand—unable to comprehend the principle, no doubt, that "plumpness in a frock-coat", or a military jacket, is the black man's burden.' However, they 'promised good behaviour'.

Three days later :

'Put up at Gov^t shanty. Row between the carriers and a man stating himself in Gov^t employ about a mat. Blows with sticks raining hard. Stopped it.'

The climatic hardships natural to such a journey as

Conrad relates, together with scarcity of, and brackish, water, dirty camp-places, and the like, were relieved at sundry stages. Thus, at Manyanga, the travellers stayed sixteen days, hospitably entertained by the Manager of the Company, Reginald Heyn, an Englishman, and by his assistant. Conrad, whose health hitherto had been varying, fell ill there, as also did Harou. 'Most kindly care taken of us,' Conrad writes. At Luasi he with Harou called at the Mission, and he notes, 'the looks of the whole establishment eminently civilised and very refreshing to see after the lots of tumble-down hovels in which the State and Company agents are content to live'. At times, they obtained delicacies—chickens, eggs—at native markets. Other caravans passed them on the way, but, for the most part, the paths through the wilderness were deserted; on all sides an expansive or mountain-occluded solitude which, in some stages, was qualified, and the consciousness of it intensified, by the vicinity of invisible native villages. Their existence was inferred from the sight of calabashes suspended from the branches of palm trees 'for the "Malafu".'

The 'Malafu', indeed, might seem to have been somewhat active and, as it were, *malefic,* thereabouts, judging from the objects passed by the travellers—the 'dead body of a Backongo' (negro); 'another dead body lying by the path in an attitude of meditative repose'[27]; a 'skeleton tied up to a post'.

'At night when the moon rose, heard shouts and drumming in distant villages.'

This entry, in common with many others, is re-presented in *Heart of Darkness*: 'Perhaps on some quiet night the tremor of far-off drums, sinking, swelling, a tremor vast, faint; a sound weird, appealing, suggestive, and wild. . . .'

A characteristic description in the diary reads: 'General tone of landscape grey-yellowish (dry grass) with reddish patches (soil) and clumps of dark green vegetation scattered sparsely about. Mostly in steep gorges between the high mountains or in ravines cutting the plain.'

---

[27] Cp. the dead body lying on the sofa in *The Secret Agent*.

The following entries are strangely uncharacteristic of Conrad, who, in his works, shows no interest in *fauna* or *flora*:

'Bird notes charming. One especially a flute-like note. Another kind of "boom" resembling' (*sic*) 'the very distant baying of a hound. Saw only pigeons and a few green parroquets' (*sic*). 'Very small and not many. No birds of prey seen by me.'

The diary ends after recording an odd occurrence; a striking illustration of the well-known wound-surviving capacity of the African native:

'Chief came with a youth about 13 suffering from gunshot wound in the head. Bullet entered about an inch above the right eyebrow, and came out a little inside the roots of the hair, fairly in the middle of the brow in a line with the bridge of the nose. Bone not damaged apparently. Gave him a little glycerine to put on the wound made by the bullet on coming out.'

However, all the other African natives mentioned in the diary, except the carriers, had been shot effectually.

xiv

Conrad had written in his diary on 29th July 1890, 'Bad news from up the river. All the steamers disabled—one wrecked.' This wrecked steamer, the *Florida*, was the one he had been appointed to command. When, on 3rd August, he arrived with the caravan, at Kinchassa—which was the base harbour of the Upper Congo flotilla—she was being repaired. The repairs would occupy a considerable time, and Conrad took an opportunity that offered of becoming the Mate of a little steamboat, the *Roi des Belges*, whose Captain undertook to train him in local river navigation; hence the notes in the second note-book already referred to. The *Roi des Belges*, which Conrad describes as a 'tin sardine-box', was to leave on the day following his arrival.

The first duty of the new employee of the Company,

however, was to interview the 'Manager', as he calls him, although actually he was only a temporary sub-Manager, Camille Delcommune who, he says, 'did not ask me to sit down after my twenty-mile walk that morning'. And, as usual when Conrad took a dislike to anybody, he describes M. Delcommune in great detail—his 'complexion', his 'feature' (*sic*), his 'manners', his 'voice', his 'size', his 'build', and his 'eyes'. M. Delcommune, in each of these particulars, was 'commonplace'. He was a 'common trader'. He had no 'genius for organising, for initiative, or for order; no learning, no intelligence'. He 'inspired neither love nor fear, nor even respect'. Yet there was something that he inspired; it was 'uneasiness'.

Uneasiness! Kings turned pale with anticipation, it is said, when the glance of Voltaire fell upon them. Yet it were better to be a king under the eye of Voltaire, than the Manager of a commercial undertaking under the eye of Conrad.

The commonplace but vaguely disconcerting M. Delcommune did not know this; at the same time he, for his part, may well have entertained a certain feeling of uneasiness, even of antipathy, in the presence of his young visitor, who was neither commonplace nor a common employee. At any rate, Conrad failed to commend himself to his 'Manager' and, as they were going to be brought together in the same boat, it was the more unfortunate. M. Delcommune was going in the *Roi des Belges* to Stanley Falls, the ultimate station of the Company, where the agent's low state of health made it necessary for him to be relieved.

The little steamboat left Kinchassa on the following day, 2nd August 1890, and arrived, in quick time, near Stanley Falls on 1st September.

Conrad writes in *Heart of Darkness*:

'Going up that river was like travelling back to the earliest beginnings of the world, when vegetation rioted on the earth and the big trees were kings. An empty stream, a great silence, an impenetrable forest. The air

was warm, thick, heavy, sluggish. There was no joy in
the brilliance of sunshine. The long stretches of the
waterway ran on, deserted, into the gloom of over-
shadowed distances. On silvery banks hippos and
alligators sunned themselves side by side. The broaden-
ing waters flowed through a mob of wooded islands; you
lost your way on that river as you would in a desert, and
butted all day long against shoals, trying to find the
channel, till you thought yourself bewitched. . . . I had to
keep guessing at the channel; I had to discern, mostly
by inspiration, the signs of hidden banks; I watched for
sunken stones; I was learning to clap my teeth smartly
before my heart flew out, when I shaved by a fluke
some infernal sly old snag that would have ripped the
life out of the tin-pot steamboat and drowned all the
pilgrims. . . .'

He was sick at heart; he felt isolated among his fellow
travellers in a deep solitude, plunged into the 'heart of an
immense darkness'. At night, on deck:

'The subdued thundering mutter of the Stanley Falls
hung in the heavy night air of the last navigable reach
of the Upper Congo. . . . I said to myself with awe, "this
is the very spot of my boyish boast".
'A great melancholy descended on me. Yes, this was
the very spot. But there was no shadowy friend to stand
by my side in the night of the enormous wilderness, no
great haunting memory, but only the unholy recollection
of a prosaic newspaper "stunt" and the distasteful knowledge of the vilest scramble for loot that ever disfigured
the history of human conscience and geographical ex-
ploration. What an end to the idealised realities of a
boy's daydreams!'

Conrad's mental *malaise* was soon attended and aug-
mented by physical ill-being; he was dogged by the twin-
tropical demons of fever and dysentery. If, indeed, he
had 'no great haunting memory' to elevate and sustain his
feelings in the very heart of the African continent, the

recollections that came to him years afterwards were 'haunting' indeed; they engendered in his mnemonic imagination a veritable nightmare that, fervidly taking form in rapid composition, became the masterpiece, *Heart of Darkness.*

It is the story of an appalling transformation in a man's soul, and it is as horrific—and as symbolic—as *Dr. Jekyll and Mr Hyde,* but it is not, as is Stevenson's nightmare story, an extravaganza, for it is true in a realistic way and, in the general circumstances, at least, is faithful to Conrad's own experience.

To what extent the central character, Kurtz, corresponds to his original, the agent of the Falls, is obscure. All that Jean-Aubry was able to ascertain about the agent is that his name was Georges Antoine Klein, that he was a man of French nationality, and that he had 'arrived at the Congo at the end of 1888 and was entrusted with the direction of the Company's establishment at Stanley Falls at the beginning of 1890. He died on the 21st September 1890 on board the *Roi des Belges,* and was buried at Bolobo by the crew.'

'It is impossible to assert without definite proof,' Jean-Aubry continues, 'that the resemblance between Kurtz and Klein is *complete,* but there can be little doubt in the mind of anybody who knows Conrad's psychological methods that these two beings, the one real and the other imaginary, had much more in common than a mere similarity of names'. The 'similarity of names' consists in the fact that Kurz (without the t) means short, and Klein, small.

Heart of Darkness may be summarised as follows:

It is the story of a man whose *soul* went mad, and is told by Marlow, the narrator of *Youth* and of most of *Lord Jim,* at evening on the Thames—which is the scene, too, of the narration of *Falk.*

Marlow, seated cross-legged, with 'sunken cheeks, a yellow complexion, a straight back, an ascetic aspect, and, with his arms dropped, the palms of (his) hands outwards', resembles an 'idol'; and his bearers (Conrad cannot dispense with an element of farce even in the staging of his

OSWALDS,

BISHOPSBOURNE,

KENT.

Jan. 29th. 1924.

My dear Sir.

Since you put it on those grounds I will answer you seriously by asking first what is it that you expect me to tell you?
Story telling, at any rate for me, is a vehicle for artistic
expression. The preferences of a man who has written a considerable number of pages of what he ventures to think, personal prose are not to be thrown out to the public; for this
reason amongst others, that the public would not understand
them. A man may like one of his works specially on account
of some peculiar associations of the time. He may like it
because in his conscience he believes that there he has come
the nearest to his artistic intention, or has conveyed his
meaning with the greatest clearness, or has achieved the
greatest emotional sincerity, or simply has been able to
attain what he thinks is best in plasticity or colouring or
atmosphere. And how can those things be made understandable
to a public which often fails to perceive the whole point of
a composition? I don't blame the public for that in the
least; but I do say that a man is entitled to keep those things
to himself, not only because they are nearest his heart but
also because in the nature of things they could not be made
clear without elaborate explanation, which the public neither
wants nor would be interested in.

And then, let me put the point before you that this is
a private matter. It is eminently and legitimately so, for
why should a man, who looks upon his work as a whole,
be asked to, publicly, pick out one part of it and thus in a
certain sense reduce all the rest to a second rank in the
eyes of the world; or expose himself to the comment that the
author does not know what he has done? It is
like asking for a certificate of imbecility.

A letter from Joseph Conrad to the author (hitherto unpublished).

For you, yourself, I will say, what you will not, perhaps, be
surprised to hear, that there are pages and short passages in all
my work of which I think with particular affection and satisfaction
and perhaps with some pride.   But even to your obvious and
intelligent sympathy I will refrain from pointing them out
specifically, and I can only hope that you will not be angry
with me.for that reserve which is not a matter of prudence
but of a deeper feeling.

Believe me very sincerely
yours J. Conrad.

stories) seem to sink into a kind of intermittent trance, while he goes on and on, apparently for hours on end.

He was a seaman, this subtle story-teller, but he was a 'wanderer too, while most seamen lead, if one may so express it', writes Conrad, 'a sedentary life. Their minds are of the stay-at-home order, and their home is always with them—the ship.' Marlow remarks suddenly:

'And this also has been one of the dark places of the earth'. Then, as the prelude to his story, he conjures up the antique shade of the commander of a trireme,* ordered to the north from the Mediterranean:

'I imagine him here—the very end of the world, a sea the colour of lead, a sky the colour of smoke. . . . Sandbanks, marshes, forests, savages. . . . Here and there a military camp lost in a wilderness . . . cold, fog, tempests, disease, exile, and death.' And commenting, later on, upon the deserted state of the African country through which he had passed, he takes another imaginative flight:

'Well, if a lot of mysterious niggers armed with all kinds of fearful weapons suddenly took to travelling on the road between Deal and Gravesend, catching the yokels right and left to carry heavy loads for them, I fancy every farm and cottage thereabouts would get empty very soon.'

xv

The scene of Marlow's narrative is set at the outset with the 'monotonous grim coast, edged with colossal and almost black jungle', visible day after day on his voyage to the Company's station where he is to take up the command of a river steamboat. It is also suggested by the names of the places that they passed—'names like Gran' Bassam, Little Popo, names that seemed to belong to some sordid farce acted in front of a sinister backcloth'.

He sees a French man-of-war anchored off the coast, shelling the bush in an aimless kind of way: the French,

---

* Conrad was aware of, and troubled by, this offence against verisimilitude.

it appeared, had 'one of their wars going on thereabouts'. She doesn't seem to do much harm, however—except to her crew, who were 'dying of fever at the rate of three a day'. Marlow, in describing her, conveys the suggestion of a kind of dangerous mechanical toy:

'Her ensign dropped limp like a rag; the muzzles of the long eight-inch guns stuck out all over the low hull; the greasy, slimy swell swung her up lazily and let her down, swaying her thin masts. In the empty immensity of earth, sky, and water, there she was, incomprehensible, firing into a continent. Pop would go one of the eight-inch guns; a small flame would dart and vanish, a little white smoke would disappear, a tiny projectile would give a feeble screech—and nothing happened. Nothing could happen. There was a touch of insanity in the proceedings, a sense of lugubrious drollery in the sight. . . .'

'Lugubrious drollery' is good. It sounds the note of Marlow's outlook here, and of his creator's satirical style, which appears as humour with a lugubrious dark background; so that, whether in the first person or the third, it always seems to be the utterance of a repressed and exasperated man, trying to be entertaining.

However, after calling at 'some more places with farcical names' and a 'still and earthy atmosphere as of an over-heated catacomb', Marlow arrives at the Company's station. There he comes upon a 'boiler wallowing in the grass', an 'undersized railway truck lying on its back', with one wheel off, and other discarded gear—a kind of disordered nursery, as it were, of some low, destructive intelligence.

The French man-of-war was in working order; it fired real bursting shells. But here that sort of thing could be done in another way. Suddenly, a 'heavy and dull detonation shook the ground'. They were blasting a cliff, which was 'not in the way or anything'.

They are 'black men'; to whom the 'outraged law, like the bursting shells', had come, an 'insoluble mystery from over the sea'. Six of them, 'balancing small baskets full of earth on their heads', advance in a chain-gang:

'All their meagre breasts panted together, the violently dilated nostrils quivered, the eyes stared stonily up-hill. They passed me within six inches, without a glance, with that complete, deathlike indifference of unhappy savages'. Another—one of the 'reclaimed'—follows in uniform, carrying a rifle.

Marlow had 'seen the devil of violence, and the devil of greed, and the devil of hot desire'; but here, apparently, is a 'flabby, pretending, weak-eyed devil of a rapacious and pitiless folly'. He turns aside from the dismal sight in the sun-glare but, coming under some shady trees, discovers that he has 'stepped into the gloomy circle of some Inferno':

'Black shapes crouched, lay, sat between the trees, leaning against the trunks, clinging to the earth, half coming out, half effaced within the dim light, in all the attitudes of pain, abandonment, and despair. Another mine on the cliff went off, followed by a slight shudder of the soil under my feet. The work was going on. The work! And this was the place where some of the helpers had withdrawn to die.

'They were dying slowly—it was very clear. They were not enemies, they were not criminals, they were nothing earthly now—nothing but black shadows of disease and starvation, lying confusedly in the greenish gloom. Brought from all the recesses of the coast in all the legality of time contracts, lost in uncongenial surroundings, fed on unfamiliar food, they sickened, became inefficient, and were then allowed to crawl away and rest. These moribund shapes were free as air—and nearly as thin. I began to distinguish the gleam of eyes under the trees. Then, glancing down, I saw a face near my hand. The black bones reclined at full length with one shoulder against the tree, and slowly the eyelids rose and the sunken eyes looked up at me, enormous and vacant, a kind of blind, white flicker in the depths of the orbs, which died out slowly.'

Marlow 'didn't want any more loitering in the shade'. While the steamboat which he is to command is being tinkered up—for, like nearly everything else in the station, it has broken down—he avoids his fellow employees: 'these men strolling aimlessly about in the sunshine of the yard', who 'wandered here and there with their absurd long staves in their hands, like a lot of faithless pilgrims bewitched inside a rotten fence. The word "ivory" rang in the air, was whispered, was sighed. You would think they were praying to it. A taint of imbecile rapacity blew through it all. . . .'

Another word that was 'in the air' was *Mr Kurtz*, which was 'whispered, was sighed', with mysterious and furtive expressions of admiration.

'An exceptional man', says the Manager, 'of the greatest importance to the Company. The quantity of ivory he collects is extraordinary. He is, so to speak, *getting too big for his boots*—and yet those boots may soon be in a position to crush any of them.'

Mr Kurtz is rumoured to be ill and his station, far up the river in the interior, to be in jeopardy. He must be relieved. The Manager is 'very, very uneasy'; the rivets necessary for the repairing of the steamboat are a very long time in coming.

Mr Kurtz turns out to be an 'exceptional man' indeed!

He is a man of versatile talents, personal charm, and idealistic temperament, who has become submerged in 'abysmal lusts'; a 'man who betook himself into the wilderness—but not to fast and pray, not to dismiss the devil, the Satan of egotism that stood always before him, and drew him by the power of the wilderness, by the 'awakening of forgotten and brutal instincts, by the memory of gratified and monstrous passions', causing him to 'preside at certain midnight dances ending with unspeakable rites, which—as far as I reluctantly gathered from what I heard at various times' (says his chronicler), 'were offered up to him . . . to Mr Kurtz himself.'

The soul of this man was beautiful, a 'house swept and garnished'. He was hollow and eloquent, like the bald and attenuated Belial that he had become.'And the lofty frontal bone of Mr Kurtz!' cries Marlow. 'They say that the hair goes on growing sometimes, but this—ah—specimen, was impressively bald. The wilderness had patted him on the head, and, behold, it was like a ball—an ivory ball; it had caressed him, and—lo—he had withered; it had taken him, loved him, embraced him, got into his veins, consumed his flesh, and sealed his soul to its own by the inconceivable ceremonies of some devilish initiation.'

He was no fool. 'I take it, no fool ever made a bargain for his soul with the devil,' says Marlow : 'the fool is too much of a fool, or the devil too much of a devil—I don't know which.' He was more than a match for the jealous machinations of his fellow employees in the 'Continental concern' that exploited black men and ivory in that African desolation. 'His intelligence was perfectly clear—concentrated upon himself with horrible intensity, yet clear. . . . But his soul was mad.'

When governed and directed upward (it is written of the mystic 'Solar Force'), this Flame becomes the instrument which the soul uses to build up its deathless spiritual body; but unless governed by the God within, and with selfless purpose, it will intensify the lower passions and make the man a destructive force, working contrary to the law of Nature.

The ruined Kurtz does, indeed, become a 'destructive force', knowing 'no restraint, no faith, and no fear'.[28]

If Conrad had conceived his lost and guilty idealist as a personality in whom pride, or ambition, predominated over sensuality, will over instinct, he might have created a Miltonic character.

Kurtz is a physical as well as a spiritual wreck. On an occasion when he is carried out from the river steamboat on a stretcher, and, with a weird cry from the forest, streams of naked savages, with their primitive arms, fill the vacant clearing before the house, and the stretcher stops, and everything is still, Marlow, watching from the steamboat, sees him gradually sit up, the 'thin arm extended commandingly, the lower jaw moving, the eyes of that

---

[28] Cp. Conrad's description of Napoleon as a 'personality without law or faith'.

apparition shining darkly far in its bony head that nodded with grotesque jerks. . . . He looked at least seven feet long. His covering had fallen off, and his body emerged from it pitiful, and appalling as from a winding-sheet . . . the cage of his ribs all astir, the bones of his arm waving. It was as though an animated image of death carved out of old ivory had been shaking its hand with menaces at a motionless crowd of men made of dark and glittering bronze.'

Later on, Marlow sees him in a 'dark blue space, sparkling with dew and starlight', as he is crawling away in the grass. He has followed him during the night to the edge of the forest, where fires loomed between the trees and there came the murmur of many voices; and a 'black figure stood up, strode on long black legs, waving long black arms, across the glow. It had horns—antelope horns, I think—on its head. Some sorcerer, some witch-man, no doubt: it looked fiend-like enough.' And there, on the verge of something worse than a precipice, Marlow 'struggles with a soul' that, 'knowing no restraint, no faith, and no fear' is yet, in an 'inconceivable mystery, struggling blindly with itself'.

Marlow is successful, and Kurtz returns to die on board the steamboat:

'One evening coming in with a candle', says Marlow, 'I was startled to hear him say a little tremulously, "I am lying here in the dark waiting for death." The light was within a foot of his eyes. I forced myself to murmur, "Oh nonsense!" and stood over him as if transfixed.

'Anything approaching the change that came over his features I have never seen before, and hope never to see again. . . . I saw on that ivory face the expression of sombre pride, of ruthless power, of craven terror—of an intense and hopeless despair. . . . He cried in a whisper at some image, at some vision—he cried out twice, a cry that was no more than a breath: "The horror! The horror!"'

The close of the story achieves the effect that Conrad intended; it produces in the imagination, as it were, the echo of a sinister, deep sound; itself, perhaps, the echo in

Conrad's own imagination of the distant, savage, wild drumming heard at moonrise noted in his diary.

After asserting that *Heart of Darkness* is 'experience pushed a little (and only very little) beyond the actual facts of the case', he explains that the modification was necessary for the 'purpose of bringing it home to the minds and bosoms of the reader'. 'That sombre theme had to be given a sinister resonance, a tonality of its own, a continued vibration that, I hoped, would hang in the air and dwell on the ear after the last note had been struck.'[29]

The nature and degree of this modification obviously bear upon the question how far the dreadful Kurtz corresponds to Klein, the agent at Stanley Falls. Jean-Aubry may well say, therefore, that it is 'impossible to assert without definite proof, that the resemblance between Kurtz and Klein is *complete*'.

      ❀   ❀   ❀   ❀

Conrad at Stanley Falls was sick in mind and body, as has been related. But his Captain, Captain Koch, fell ill —so ill as to be incapacitated—and he was instructed by Camille Delcommune to navigate the steamboat on her return journey to Kinchassa. This duty, despite the low state of his health—with recurrent attacks of fever and dysentery—he successfully performed, so well had he profited already by the practical instruction he had received in fresh-water navigation. But the journey was bitterly unpleasant; for the social atmosphere in the 'tin sardine-box', as he called the little steamboat, was frigid;

---

[29] In the course of correspondence with Conrad, the writer remarked that his novels—especially *The Rescue*—seemed to begin kinetically at the close: the final sentence had the effect of prolonging and expanding the significance of the story as by the striking and vibration of an imaginative bell; a tonal effect, carrying over and potentially unfolding the plot—or, rather, the *dénouement*—as in an internal element. The letter from Conrad reproduced by page 225 of the present volume was in reply to the particular letter in which this observation (in some such words) was included; but Conrad refers to it only by implication. The date of the correspondence preceded the above 'Author's Note'.

his fellow-employees became the more repellent the longer he was cooped up with them.

But his fate reserved him to more woe. The *Roi des Belges* reached Kinchassa on 24th September, after about eighteen days' passage, and soon afterwards another expedition arrived. It came in the *Florida*, the steamboat which Conrad had originally been appointed to command; and just as Mr Burns, it will be remembered, had expected to be put in command of the *Otago* after navigating her safely to port, so Conrad expected to be put in command of the *Florida*. But the head of the expedition was Alexandre Delcommune, the brother of the 'Manager'; who, in Jean-Aubry's opinion, set him against Conrad— who did not receive the appointment.

Alexandre Delcommune is described in *Heart of Darkness*:

> 'In exterior he resembled a butcher in a poor neighbourhood, and his eyes had a look of sleepy cunning. He carried his fat paunch with ostentation on his short legs, and during the time his gang infested the station, spoke to no one but his nephew.[30] You could see these two roaming about all day long with their heads close together in an everlasting confab.'

There was some vague prospect of Conrad's eventually commanding a Company's steamboat, although. M. Delcommune informed him that he could hope for neither promotion nor an increase in salary however long he remained in the Congo. As for any promises made to him in Europe, M. Delcommune pointed out, they would not be honoured unless they were in the contract.

Conrad was indeed in the bad books of M. Delcommune. He had already written to Uncle Tadeusz in his consciousness of 'injured merit' and now, smarting under the spurns of the common, common-place Belgian official, he wrote to Mme. Poradowska, communicating that unconscionable person's observations. She, in her turn, transmitted them to Thys, who had made the unhonoured promises.

---

[30] Actually his *uncle*.

Conrad had also asked her to convey his desire to be transferred to one of the commercial Companies' sea-going ships, and this she did.

For any good that came of her letter, however, Mme. Poradowska was wasting her time, and Conrad his patience, which was now almost exhausted. Finally it ran out. One night, a big native canoe, commissioned for the purpose, went blundering down the river; the stream was turbulent, and the canoe had only half of her complement of paddlers. She held on or sheered the bank, at times almost swamped, shedding various articles of luggage, and, at a specially awkward turn of the Congo between Kinchassa and Leopoldville, nearly foundering. Conrad, her passenger, narrowly escaped drowning, 'too weak to care whether he did or not'.

He arrived at Boma, with the copybook MS. of *Almayer's Folly* safe in his pocket. He was shaking the dust of 'Darkest Africa' from off his feet, and he was going home; but 'before the departure of the steamer which was to take me home', he declares in *A Personal Record*, 'I had the time to wish myself dead over and over again with perfect sincerity'.

xvi

Conrad reached Europe in mid-January, no whit better in health, suffering from persistent fever, and seized with his first attack of gout; fever and gout were to affect him intermittently for the rest of his life.

After a journey to Glasgow in search of another command, he collapsed. He had been met on his arrival in London by Krieger, and now, through the intermediary of that faithful friend, he was removed to the German hospital. There, with his legs and hands exceedingly swollen, and compelled to lie on his back, he remained for six weeks, in mind and spirits no less prostrated. He contrived to write to his uncle, however, informing him of his illness, while at the same time making light of it.

The German doctor—Dr Ludwig—who attended him, eventually arranged for his removal to a hydropathic establishment at Champel, near Geneva; where, in residence at a *pension*, he stayed for three or four weeks.

His health, both physical and mental, improved rapidly and, one day, soon after his arrival there, his thoughts turned energetically to the copybook of a hundred pages that he had carried about with him for two years, and he began to write the eighth chapter of *Almayer's Folly*.

He was now thirty-four years old, and he had been nearly twenty years at sea, living an active, exciting and, for the most part, careless life; it had been the life, in general, of what is currently called an 'extrovert'; but he was now a changed—or, rather, changing—man. His experiences in Africa lay heavy on his soul, and the long period of recumbent discomfort he had undergone in the German hospital—an ordeal made horrible by nightmares and fantasies in which his heritage of Polish gloom and sordid, sultry extravaganzas in Africa, intermingled—had harassed his spirit and, as it were, ploughed and opened his mind for reflection. He had begun to see himself and his life, as in a mirror, with hectic introspection. So, at least, it would appear in the light of subsequent developments. A crisis had occurred; a transformation succinctly described in a remark that Edward Garnett told Jean-Aubry Conrad had made to him several years after his return from Africa: 'Before the Congo I was just a mere animal'.

Such crises, such transformations, are patent in the lives of great writers no less than in the lives of men of religious genius. Something terrible must have happened to Shakespeare in the interval before the production of his great tragedies; while the soul of Milton underwent a catastrophe before the production of *Paradise Lost*. Jean-Aubry holds that Conrad's illness prepared the way for that state of 'energetic despair' (excellent phrase!) which was to vitalise his creative work.

That his avocation as a sailor was threatened, the invalid himself was probably aware, and there is some

reason to think that he was already considering the possibility of becoming an author (probably encouraged by
Mme. Poradowska). At any rate, he was contemplating
changing his course in some way. Thus, his uncle writes
on 30th July 1891, which was about a month before
Conrad left Champel, 'Your weakness comes from the
Nalecz Korzeniowski. Your grandfather and uncle were
always entertaining projects which had no validity except
in their imaginations. . . . All three of them were
ambitious. . . . Alas, in making plans, you too allow yourself to be carried away by your imagination.'

While he was still at Champel Conrad had the offer of
serving in a ship on the Niger but, apart from the disability of his ill-health, the loathing he had conceived
for Africa caused him to reject it.

He returned to London at the end of June, and all that
is known about his life then is that he paid several visits
during the summer and autumn to Mme Poradowska in
Brussels (however he could afford the expense); visits
which may well have had literary no less than social
inducements.

But he understood that if he could not go to sea—at any
rate, at that time—some form of activity was necessary to
him to regain his mental stability; there was also the
necessity of earning his living. Consequently, he accepted
employment, obtained for him by his friends, Adolf
Krieger and G. F. W. Hope, as Manager of a warehouse
on the banks of the Thames. To this he refers in *A Personal
Record*:

'That work, undertaken to accustom myself again to the
activities of a healthy existence, soon came to an end. The
earth had nothing to hold me with for very long.' At this
time, also, he wrote the greater part of the ninth chapter
of *Almayer's Folly*. Yet the curse of dejection came upon
him again, a lugubrious state so eloquently described in
the old dreary phrase, 'when the clouds return after the
rain'. The condition of his mind is illustrated by the
following extract from a letter from Uncle Tadeusz:

'My dear boy,

'I begin as I always do, but I ought to address you as "my dear pessimist"; for judging from your letters that description would fit you best. I cannot say I am pleased by your state of mind, or that I am without apprehension about your future. Of course I am thankful for your frankness in not hiding from me what you really feel. I know human nature too well and I love you too much not to read between the lines of your letters. . . .

'I may be mistaken but I think this tendency to pessimism was already in you as long ago as the days when you were at Marseilles, but it was then part of your youth. I am sure that with your melancholy temperament you ought to avoid all meditations which lead to pessimistic conclusions.'

This period of desuetude and vacillation, to such a spirit as Conrad's, was a psychological wilderness, a pilgrim's progress through the slough of despond, and it lasted for nearly two years; then his strength and will came back to him, and he took an opportunity that occurred to resume his sea-calling. He received and eagerly accepted the berth of Mate in the *Torrens*, a full-rigged ship of about 1,300 tons; a ship of note in those days of sail.

She left London on 25th November 1891, bound for Adelaide; where she arrived on 28th February 1892. The voyage completely restored Conrad's health and spirits; a circumstance that much rejoiced his affectionate and epistolary uncle. The *Torrens* returned to London on the 11th August; to sail again, with Conrad as Mate, on 28th October.

This second voyage is notable because, in the course of it, *Almayer's Folly*—as much as had been written of it—obtained its first reader. He—a young Cambridge graduate travelling for the sake of his health (he did not live long after)—was one of those quiet, intelligent, sympathetic souls who are a blessing to their fellow mortals. And, as according to the adage, no fool should be permitted to see an unfinished work, so Jacques—Conrad's first reader— was the only passenger among the sixty aboard the *Torrens* to whom Conrad could have shown his unfinished MS.

Many eulogies of Conrad as a writer were to follow, and of these Jacques' critique was in the nature of an adumbration. Also, it seems curiously to bridge the divided stages of Conrad's life—the nautical and the literary, the probationary and the effective or creative. Yet it remains on the anterior side, among the materials, the experiences, the recollections, within the field of the 'mirror'. The episode, as was only natural, vastly impressed Conrad; who records it—on the principle of 'emotion recollected in tranquillity'—in *A Personal Record*:

' "Would it bore you very much reading a MS. in a handwriting like mine?" I asked him one evening on a sudden impulse at the end of a longish conversation whose subject was Gibbon's History. Jacques . . . was sitting in my cabin one stormy dog-watch below, after bringing me a book to read from his own travelling store.

' "Not at all," he answered with his courteous intonation and a faint smile. As I pulled a drawer open his suddenly aroused curiosity gave him a watchful expression. I wonder what he expected to see. A poem, maybe. . . . In his attractive reserved manner, and in a veiled, sympathetic voice, he asked:

' "What is this?" "It is a sort of tale," I answered with an effort. "It is not even finished yet. Nevertheless, I would like to know what you think of it." He put the MS. in the breast pocket of his jacket. . . . "I will read it tomorrow," he remarked. . . .

'Next day . . . Jacques entered my cabin. He had a thick, woollen muffler round his throat and the MS. was in his hand. He tendered it to me with a steady look but without a word. I took it in silence. He sat down on the couch and still said nothing. I opened and shut a drawer

under my desk. . . . I turned my back squarely on the
desk. And even then Jacques never offered a word.
"Well, what do you say?" I asked at last. "Is it worth
finishing?" . . .

' "Distinctly," he answered in his sedate, veiled voice
and then coughed a little.

' "Were you interested?" I inquired further, almost
in a whisper.

' "Very much!" . . .

' "Now let me ask you one more thing: is the story
quite clear to you as it stands?"

'He raised his dark, gentle eyes to my face and
seemed surprised.

' "Yes! Perfectly."

'This was all I was to hear from his lips concerning
the merits of *Almayer's Folly.*'

The *Torrens* reached Adelaide on 19th March 1893. The
homeward voyage, which began a little later, was no less
notable, and far more important, in Conrad's affairs than
the outward voyage had been. It was the means of
effecting another bridge, so to express it, between
Conrad's two very different worlds; for one of the passengers was the young John Galsworthy, who eventually
became Conrad's greatest, most-esteemed, most-admired
and admiring friend. He, with another young Oxford man,
was returning after an abortive attempt (their allotted
time having given out) to visit Robert Louis Stevenson in
Samoa; a kind of exotic pilgrimage of the 'nineties comparable with the achievement of visiting Napoleon at St
Helena, in earlier days.

The three young men had long talks with Conrad on the
poop in the evening watch; during which he told them
tales of 'ships and storms, of Polish revolution, of his youthful Carlist gun-running adventures, of the Malay seas, and
the Congo; and of men and men'. Conrad was 'tanned,
with a peaked brown beard, almost black hair, and dark
brown eyes over which the lids were deeply folded. He
was thin, not tall, his arms very long, his shoulders broad,

his head set rather forward'. He spoke with a 'strong foreign accent'. He was a 'good seaman, watchful of the weather; quick in handling the ship; considerate with the apprentices'—especially with a 'long, unhappy Belgian youth among them, who took unhandily to the sea and dreaded going aloft. Conrad compassionately spared him all he could.[31] With the crew he was popular; they were individuals to him, not a mere gang; and long after he would talk of this or that among them, especially of old Andy the sailmaker: "I liked that old fellow, you know." He was respectful, if faintly ironic, with his whiskered, stout old Captain' (Captain Cope). 'Fascination was Conrad's great characteristic—the fascination of vivid expressiveness and zest, of his deeply affectionate heart, and his far-ranging, subtle mind. He was extraordinarily perceptive and receptive.'[32]

Conrad was indeed 'extraordinarily perceptive and receptive', and he doubtless divined in Galsworthy the eminently humane qualities that distinguished his character and were to distinguish his work. Yet the hallmark of humanity in a character like Galsworthy's would have been visible to less percipient eyes. It is no wonder that the bond between the two men was forged from the very beginning. What is remarkable is that, in all these pleasant conversations, in so congenial an atmosphere, neither of the two potential novelists apparently became aware of the other's literary aspirations. 'On that ship he told of life,' says Galsworthy, 'not literature.' Yet, with Jacques, Conrad had talked of literature. This curiously brings out the social superiority of Jacques, that pathetic passenger who was on his way to Australia, and also to that 'bourne from which no traveller returns'. It is not implied, of course, that Galsworthy was lacking in good manners, or manner, in *savoir faire*, or in the art of charming away the uneasiness of a fellow, if consciously inferior,

---

[31] Jean-Aubry quotes letters to Conrad from one-time apprentices, vehemently expressing appreciation of kindly treatment.

[32] *Reminiscences of Conrad.*

creature—he was assuredly proficient in that agreeable art; only, Jacques was more sympathetic. Perhaps, because he was dying, and was aware of the fact, he had lost the sense of inhibitions—those well-dug-in defences of an island race which it is the function of *savoir faire* to conceal. Perhaps, all the barriers were down. Conrad, disarmed by such ingenuous defencelessness, and with a 'sudden impulse' (as has been related), showed Jacques his MS., betrayed his 'secret sharer', and divulged the ambition he had been hesitant to acknowledge even to himself. He did not so much as hint at such secluded matters to Galsworthy.

xvii

Conrad arrived in London, after an unduly slow passage, on 26th July 1893, to find a letter from his uncle desiring him to come to Poland as soon as might be.

He set out early in August, the journey nearly costing him the loss of his familiar MS., which he left forgotten in a waiting-room at Berlin. He gives a long, delightful account of this journey in *A Personal Record*. At length:

> 'I saw again the sun setting on the plains', he writes, 'as I saw it in the travels of my childhood. It set, clear and red, dipping into the snow in full view as if it were setting on the sea. It was twenty-three years since I had seen the sun set over that land; and we drove on in the darkness which fell swiftly upon the livid expanse of snow till, out of the waste of a white earth joining a bestarred sky, surged up black shapes, the clumps of trees about a village of the Ukrainian plain. A cottage or two glided by, a slow interminable wall and then, glimmering and winking through a screen of fir-trees, the lights of the master's house.
>
> 'That very evening the wandering MS. of *Almayer's Folly* was unpacked and unostentatiously laid on the writing-table in my room, the guest-room which had been, I was informed in an affectedly careless tone, awaiting me for some fifteen years or so. It attracted no

attention from the affectionate presence hovering round
the son of the favourite sister.

' "You won't have many hours to yourself while you
are staying with me, brother," he said—this form of
address borrowed from the speech of our peasants being
the usual expression of the highest good humour in a
moment of affectionate elation. "I shall be always
coming in for a chat." . . . The tinkle of the traveller's
bells . . . had faded away quickly, and the tumult of
barking dogs in the village had calmed down at last.
My uncle, lounging in the corner of a small couch,
smoked his long Turkish *chibouk* in silence.

' "This is an extremely nice writing-table you have got
for my room," I remarked.

' "It is really your property," he said, keeping his eyes
on me, with an interested and wistful expression as he
had done ever since I had entered the house. "Forty
years ago your mother used to write at this very
table".'

He went on to talk of his past and of those whom he had
known and loved, especially the 'favourite sister', whom
his nephew's presence brought intimately to his thoughts.

After staying about two months at Kazimierowka,
Conrad returned to London in October, 1893.

In the same month he parted from the *Torrens*, taking
a long look at the ship he was to see no more. Then, like
a man driven by a great grief—like Apollo, like Captain
Beard of the *Palestine*—he plunged into occupation and
preoccupation, until, at last, he became as a 'haunted man
who looks for nothing but words wherein to capture his
visions'. But Captain Freud, the benefactor of shipless
sailors, desired from him a favour; he could not find a
ship's officer who could speak French fluently, for a
steamer on which such an officer was wanted: Conrad
was the only man. Captain Freud tendered the offer of
the berth—or, rather, the suggestion that it should be
accepted—apologetically. It was only the berth of a second
officer and the steamer was a very ordinary sort of steamer.

Conrad accepted reluctantly, out of the kindness of his heart and his esteem for Captain Freud.

The affair proved to be a fiasco. The steamer, the *Adowa*, lying at Rouen, had been chartered to convey French emigrants to Canada. However, no emigrants appeared; only a director or two belonging to the Company, and some idle citizens with their wives and children, visited the ship, while Conrad 'in his smartest uniform', says Jean-Aubry, 'did the honours'. She stayed there for thirty days, and duly returned to London. The Company had to write off the undertaking as a loss. Conrad, however, in his cabin at Rouen, completed the ninth chapter of *Almayer's Folly*.

The *Adowa*, although thus farcical, was Conrad's last ship. His career of twenty years in the Merchant Service, as he once remarked to Jean-Aubry, 'began at one French port and closed at another'. It began at Marseilles, the 'nurse of all navigators', as he himself calls it, and ended at Rouen, the town of the old Vikings. It originated in the reading of books, and it produced the writing of books.

Conrad avers that he never had the slightest notion of the new life that was in store for him, nor any premonition at all when he stepped off the gangway of the *Adowa*, that he had 'stepped out of' his 'sea life altogether'. He had started his sea life under the compulsion of his will, or heart's desire; inspired by an ideal. Will and desire, thus inspired, become identical. Conrad himself (although he emphatically denied any belief in the 'supernatural') postulated the 'inexorable fate', or the 'unknown powers that shape our destinies'. And there again we conceive an identity; for since love, or a 'form of love', was the efficient agent in Conrad's career, and nothing could be more powerful, those 'unknown powers' must themselves have been instigated by that supreme incentive.

And circumstances, in Conrad's destiny, conjoined; conditions conformed—inevitably so; for desire, which is will, and not will-o'-the-wisp, and love, which is not infatuation, are universally imperative.

Conrad's literary life, which was about to begin, may also have been, in effect, a 'form of love', on the principle enunciated in the following passage from the *Apology Against a Pamphlet*—the author, John Milton, like Conrad, a 'man of destiny':

'. . . true eloquence I find to be none, but the serious and hearty love of truth: And that whose mind soever is fully possesst with a fervent desire to know good things, and with the dearest charity to infuse the knowledge of them into others, when such a man would speak, his words (by what I can expresse) like so many nimble and airy servitors trip about him at command, and in well order'd files, as he would wish, fall aptly into their own places.'

BIBLIOGRAPHICAL LIST
OF CONRAD'S WORKS

T н i s bibliographical list is reproduced from *Joseph Conrad's Mind and Method*, by R. L. Mégroz (Faber & Faber, 1931), by kind permission of the author.

Almayer's Folly and Tales of Unrest. (One vol. Uniform and Concord Editions, 1923.)

Almayer's Folly. A Story of An Eastern River. T. Fisher Unwin, London, 1895.

Tales of Unrest. T. Fisher Unwin, London, 1895.
> Contents :—'Karain : A Memory.' 'The Idiots.' 'An Outpost of Progress.' 'The Return.' 'The Lagoon.'

An Outcast of the Islands. (1923.)

An Outcast of the Islands. T. Fisher Unwin, 1896.

The Nigger of the Narcissus and Typhoon and Other Stories. (1923.)

The Nigger of the Narcissus. A Tale of the Sea. William Heinemann, 1898. (In Henley's *New Review*, five monthly issues, August-December, 1897.)

> *Note.*—The 1898 edition was the first published one, but seven copies of the book, subtitled 'A Tale of the Forecastle', were printed by Heinemann for copyright purposes in 1897 and technically 'published'. The first American edition, by Dodd, Mead Co., was published in 1897, and entitled 'The Children of the Sea. A Tale of the Forecastle'.

Typhoon and Other Stories. (1923.)

> *Typhoon* (First separate edition), G. P. Putnam's Sons, London and New York, 1902.

> *Typhoon and Other Stories,* William Heinemann, London, 1903.

Contents: —'Typhoon.' 'Amy Foster.' 'Falk: A Reminiscence.' 'To-Morrow.'

Note.—'Falk, Amy Foster, To-morrow. Three Stories', appeared as a separate book, McClure, Phillips & Co., New York, 1903.

Lord Jim. A Tale. (1923.)

Lord Jim. A Tale. William Blackwood & Sons, Edinburgh and London, 1900.

Note.—The story was serialised in *Blackwood's Magazine.* The first American edition, by Doubleday & McClure Co., 1900, was subtitled 'A Romance'.

The Inheritors. An Extravagant Story. By J. Conrad and F. M. Hueffer. (1923.)

The Inheritors. An Extravagant Story. By Joseph Conrad and Ford M. Hueffer, McClure, Phillips & Co., New York, 1901, and William Heinnemann, London, 1901.

Youth : A Narrative and Two Other Stories. (1923.)

Youth: A Narrative and Two Other Stories. William Blackwood & Sons, Edinburgh and London, 1902.

Contents: —'Youth: A Narrative.' 'Heart of Darkness.' 'The End of the Tether.'

Note.—All three stories were first published in *Blackwood's Magazine,* from 1900 to 1902.

Youth and Gaspar Ruiz. J. M. Dent & Sons, London, 1920.

Romance. By J. Conrad and F. M. Hueffer. (1923.)

Romance. A Novel by Joseph Conrad and Ford Madox Hueffer. Smith, Elder & Co., London, 1903.

Nostromo. A Tale of the Seaboard. (1923.)

Nostromo. A Tale of the Seaboard. Harper & Brothers, London & New York, 1904.

The Mirror of the Sea : Memories and Impressions. And A Personal Record : Some Reminiscences. (1923.)

The Mirror of the Sea: Memories and Impressions. Methuen, London, 1906.

A Personal Record. Harper & Brothers, New York, 1912.

Note.—First English edition under this title, Thomas Nelson & Sons, 1916, but the original publication of the book was 'Some Reminiscences', Eveleigh Nash, London, 1912. Under this title it was

first printed in the *English Review,* under Mr. Ford
Madox Hueffer's editorship, monthly from December,
1908, to June, 1909.

The Secret Agent. A Simple Tale. (1923.)

The Secret Agent. A Simple Tale. Methuen & Cr
London, 1907.

A Set of Six. (1923.)

A Set of Six. Methuen & Co., London,, 1908.

> Contents:—A Romantic Tale: 'Gaspar Ruiz.' An
> Ironic Tale: 'The Informer.' An Indignant Tale: 'The
> Brute.' A Desperate Tale: 'An Anarchist.' A Military
> Tale: 'The Duel.' A Pathetic Tale: 'Il Conde.'

> *Note.*—'The Duel' was published separately as *The
> Point of Honor: A Military Tale,* by The McClure
> Co., New York, 1908.

Under Western Eyes. (1923.)

Under Western Eyes. Methuen & Co., London, 1911.

'Twixt Land and Sea. Tales. (1923.)

'Twixt Land and Sea. Tales. J. M. Dent & Sons, 1912.

> Contents:—'A Smile of Fortune': A Harbour
> Story. 'The Secret Sharer': An Episode from the
> Coast. 'Freya of the Seven Isles': A Story of Shallow
> Waters.

Chance. A Tale in Two Parts. (1923.)

Chance. A Tale in Two Parts. Methuen & Co., London,
1913.

The Shadow Line: A Confession; and Within the Tides.
Tales. (1923.)

The Shadow Line: A Confession. J. M. Dent & Sons,
London, 1917.

Within the Tides. Tales. J. M. Dent & Sons, London,
1915.

> Contents:—'The Planter of Malata.' 'The Partner.'
> 'The Inn of the Two Witches.' 'Because of the
> Dollars.'

Victory. An Island Tale. (1923.)

Victory. An Island Tale. Methuen & Co., London, 1915.

One Day More. A Play in One Act. The Beaumont Press,
London, 1919.

Note.—Privately printed in 1917 by Clement Shorter. (The play is Conrad's dramatic version of the story 'To-Morrow' included in the *Nigger* and *Typhoon* volume.)

The Arrow of Gold. A Story Between Two Notes. (1923.)

The Arrow of Gold. A Story Between Two Notes. Doubleday, Page & Co., New York, 1919, and T. Fisher Unwin, London, 1919.

The Rescue. A Romance of the Shallows. (1923.)

The Rescue. A Romance of the Shallows. Doubleday, Page & Co., New York, 1920. J. M. Dent & Sons, London, 1920.

Note.—Serialised in *Land and Water*, weekly, 30 January to 31 July, 1919.

The Works of Joseph Conrad. Wm. Heinemann, London, 1921. (20 volumes.)

The Nature of a Crime, by Joseph Conrad and F. M. Hueffer. J. M. Dent & Sons, London, 1924. (Includes Prefaces by Conrad and Hueffer, and an Appendix: 'A Note on *Romance*', by Hueffer.)

Notes on Life and Letters. J. M. Dent & Sons, London, 1921. (Also a private first issue of 33 copies by same publishers.)

Contents:

Part 1, Letters: Books; Henry James; Alphonse Daudet; Guy de Maupassant; Anatole France; Turgenev; Stephen Crane, A Note without Dates; Tales of the Sea; An Observer in Malaya; A Happy Wanderer; The Life Beyond; The Ascending Effort; The Censor of Plays.

Part 2, Life: Autocracy and War; The Crime of Partition; A Note on the Polish Problem; Poland Revisited; First News; Well Done; Tradition; Confidence; Flight; Some Reflections on the Loss of the *Titanic*; Certain Aspects of the Admirable Inquiry; Protection of Ocean Liners; A Friendly Place.

Note.—All but three of the above were published first in periodicals. The De Maupassant essay was written as a Preface to *Yvette and Other Stories* by

Guy de Maupassant. Translated by 'A. G.', Duckworth & Co., London, 1904. 'A. G.' was Mrs John Galsworthy. Like many of the pieces in *Life and Letters*, it was privately printed as a pamphlet. The Turgenev essay appeared first as Foreword to '*Turgenev*. A Study by Edward Garnett', W. Collins, Sons & Co., London, 1917.

The Rover. (1923.)

The Rover. Doubleday, Page & Co., New York, 1923, and T. Fisher Unwin, London, 1923. (Before the publication of these first editions, Doubleday made a large-paper issue of 377 copies.)

Suspense. (1927.)

Suspense. A Napoleonic Novel. Doubleday, Page & Co., New York, 1925, and J. M. Dent & Sons, 1925. (The English edition has the first printing of an Introduction by Richard Curle. Doubleday issued a large-paper edition of 377 copies just before the first regular edition.)

Tales of Hearsay and Last Essays. (1928.)

Tales of Hearsay. T. Fisher Unwin, London, 1925. (Preface by R. B. Cunninghame Graham.)

Contents :—'The Warrior's Soul.' 'Prince Roman. 'The Tale.' 'The Black Mate.'

Note.—'The Warrior's Soul' was privately printed for the author in 1920. It first appeared in *Land and Water*, 29 March, 1917. 'Prince Roman' was privately printed for the author, in 1920, and so was 'The Black Mate', in 1922. 'The Tale' first appeared in the *Strand Magazine*, London, October, 1917, and was privately printed for Clement Shorter in 1919.

Last Essays. J. M. Dent & Sons, London, 1926.

Joseph Conrad's Diary of his Journey up the Valley of the Congo in 1890. Privately printed, London, 1926. With Introduction and Notes by Richard Curle. (Included in *Last Essays*.)

The Collected Works of Joseph Conrad are now available in 21 volumes. J. M. Dent & Sons. London, 1955.

INDEX

J